ROB CADE.

METEOROLOGY FOR PILOTS

Meteorology for Pilots

K. M. Wickson
Fellow of the
Royal Meteorological Society

Airlife
England

Copyright © 1992 K. M. Wickson

First published in the UK in 1992
by Airlife Publishing Ltd

British Library Cataloguing in Publication Data
A catalogue record of this book is available from the British Library

ISBN 1 85310 316 0

Printed by Livesey Ltd, Shrewsbury, England.

Airlife Publishing Ltd

101 Longden Road, Shrewsbury SY3 9EB

LIST OF CONTENTS

Operating Procedures. Runway Visual Range.
Aircraft Meteorological Observations and Reports.
Appendix: UK AIP Met Documents.
Criteria for Special Reports, Trend, TAF
Amendment and Route/Area Forecast Amendment.
OPMET Details. Actual and Forecast Weather
Records. Turbulence, Icing and Windshear
Reporting Criteria. Met Charts Symbology. Met
Abbreviations.

LIST OF FIGURES   Drawings by J. E. Hitchcock

LIST OF CENTRE PAGES PHOTOGRAPHS

Plate No.

Preface

This book has been compiled to prepare the *ab initio* and 'improver' student pilot for all the British Civil Aviation Authority examinations in Meteorology. The coverage is also sufficiently extensive to meet the proposed and expected syllabus requirements for a new European Airline Pilot's licence.

Acknowledgements

The assistance of Maurice Crewe and the staff and facilities of the National Meteorological Library, Bracknell, is gratefully acknowledged. The permission of the Civil Aviation Authority to publish the main extracts from the June 1990 edition of CAP32 and through the National Air Traffic Services permission to reproduce diagrams is much appreciated.

Thanks are also due to the United States Marine Corps and the McDonnell Douglas Aircraft Corporation for permission to include photographs of exceptional hail damage to an AV-8B Harrier aircraft. Additionally to Captain Julie S. Simmonds and Captain David M. A. Wells for their cloud photographs, also to Phil Garner for permission to publish his photograph of a funnel cloud.

Introduction

This book deals with the basis of the oldest scientific studies. The establishment.of modern disciplines, such as physics, are a direct result of early atmospheric and weather experience. None the less, meteorology is a live and growing subject. It was, after all, only in the 1920s that the high speed transport of air by means of jet streams at high level was discovered. It is only since the 1950s that the important part played by carbon dioxide in heating the atmosphere has been widely appreciated. Other new phenomena are bound to surface in the years ahead and some of these will doubtless bear directly on aviation. There is still much new knowledge to be acquired, and the pilot with a good meteorological background will appreciate and benefit from these new discoveries.

The envelope of air surrounding the earth is constantly moving. There is a predominant main air circulation which starts with surface heating along the equator. This air is lifted and then moves at around 50 000 ft in two streams, one to overhead the North Pole and one to overhead the South Pole. This air descends at the poles and then makes its way, circuitously on the surface, back to the equator. The circulation of the air could be just as straightforward as this statement supposes, provided the surface temperatures decreased everywhere uniformly from the equator and the earth did not rotate. The actual variation in surface temperature does not vary solely with latitude, it varies due to land/sea disposition and the fact that some land surfaces accept and retain heat from the sun more readily than others. These variations lead to changes in pressure and air, acting like a fluid, will react to these myriad pressure changes and also to the earth's rotation. To give detailed weather predictions is thus a difficult task. This difficulty is enhanced when considering not just surface conditions but also those in the lower atmosphere where large scale horizontal and vertical movements in the air occur. Understanding of the meteorological factors and the reactions of one factor upon another is necessary for effective forecasting and weather appreciation.

Meteorology is, therefore, a study of conditions in the atmosphere and of the interactions with the underlying surfaces. The subject embraces climatology which is the examination of long term average and extreme conditions in different parts of the world. For aviation the study of meteorology provides knowledge and awareness of the atmosphere, which is, after all, the medium within which the pilot works. This awareness is probably best exemplified by the fact that all pilots habitually on awakening, go to the bedroom window and look at the sky to see what the day may bring in the way of weather. Secondly, a proper study of the subject will provide the basis which can enable a pilot to properly appreciate the weather forecast given to him for a flight — and indeed to forecast for himself. Technical aircraft safety is now approaching the highest standards, whilst safety affected by particular weather conditions remains a large problem. Clearly a proper study of meteorology can only assist the pilot in providing safe passages.

Chapter 1
The Atmosphere

The atmosphere can be considered as an ocean of air which rotates with the earth and is supported by the earth's surface at the base and extends to the fringes of space at the top. There are three warm regions of the atmosphere which are heated by solar radiation reacting on the atmospheric particles, and there are two relatively cold atmospheric regions. These five layers are shown diagramatically at Figure 1.1. It should be noted that boundary heights for these regions can vary considerably.

The Exosphere
This is the uppermost atmospheric layer where gas density is very low and some air particles can escape from the earth's gravitation. This warm region is at heights greater than 700 km.

The Ionosphere
This is the warm region below the exosphere and extends to within about 80 km of the earth's surface. It is a region where much of the air becomes ionised, that is, positively charged by the action of ultra-violet and X-ray solar radiation. There are separate layers within the ionosphere with different heights and degrees of ionisation. These separate layers; D, E, F1 and F2 have a profound effect on the transmission of certain radio waves and can be used to increase considerably the range of navigational aids and communications for aircraft.

The Mesosphere
This is a cold layer which can extend from about 50 km to 80 km above the earth's surface and is immediately below the ionosphere. The main characteristic is a steep temperature lapse rate, so it is a region becoming colder with increase of height.

The Stratosphere
This is the third warm region of the atmosphere which extends from about 11 km to 50 km. The heat is provided by a layer of ozone which traps ultra-violet radiation from the sun and then re-transmits this as infra-red heat. The depth of the ozone layer varies with

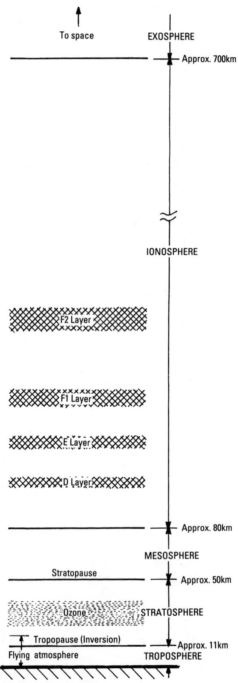

Figure 1.1. Five Layers of the Atmosphere

latitude and in recent years there has been evidence of gaps or holes in the layer, particularly above the South Pole. Depletion of the ozone is said to be partly due to the release of man-made gases, such as the chlorofluorocarbons (CFCs). However, it is worth making the point that there is little transfer of air from one hemisphere to another. Most CFCs are released in the higher populated northern hemisphere. Hence unanswered questions remain on this subject. Broadly speaking, temperatures are constant for a particular latitude within the lower stratosphere with higher temperatures over the poles. Temperature values are of the order − 30°C to −70°C. From about 65 000 ft (19.8 km) upwards temperature increases and near the 50 km level the ozone effects are such that temperatures approach 0°C at all latitudes.

The Troposphere

This is the lowest layer of the atmosphere which extends from the earth's surface to an average height of 11 km. In this region the temperature reduces with increase of height at an average rate of 2°C per 1000 ft.

The Aviation Portion of the Atmosphere

Flying takes place in the lower regions of the atmosphere. These are the troposphere and the lower stratosphere. Together these will be referred to as the atmosphere. Nearly all weather and nearly all flying takes places in the troposphere. A little weather and some flying takes place in the lower stratosphere. Most present day jet transport aircraft cruise at levels close to the boundary line between the troposphere and the stratosphere, which is called the tropopause. The composition of the air in the aviation atmosphere is gases which include nitrogen, oxygen, argon, carbon dioxide and water vapour, together with solid particles such as dust, sand and carbon (smoke). There are also traces of other gases such as helium, hydrogen and neon. The height of the tropopause and hence the depth of the troposphere varies. A simplified average situation in the flying atmosphere is at Figure 1.2.

The density of gases and solid particles which we call the air, will be greatest near the earth's surface because of the greater weight of air above. This value will of course decrease with increase of height. In fact, over 90 per cent of the mass of air is contained in the aviation atmosphere. This reduction in density must also affect the amount of water vapour present in the air and it can be expected that this amount will decrease with increase of height so that the air in the lower stratosphere is almost dry. The water vapour can

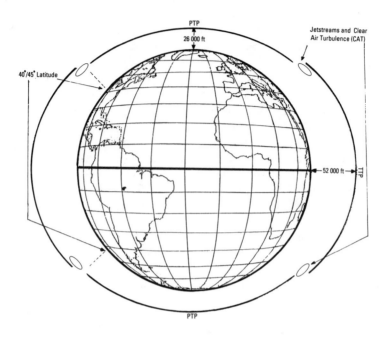

Figure 1.2. Simplified Average Tropopause Heights in the Flying Atmosphere

condense out as water droplets to form cloud, fog or mist. It can also form dew or frost on the ground and indirectly, precipitation (rain, drizzle, snow or hail). The solid particles and other impurities in the atmosphere provide the nuclei around which condensation of water vapour occurs. (This is the reason why rain-water is dirty). The solids can also restrict visibility as smoke haze, dust haze or sand storms. The water vapour, together with carbon dioxide, plays an important part in the heating of the atmosphere. (Other gases such as nitrous oxide also play a small part).

The most important single property of the troposphere is its variability. It is continuously variable both horizontally and vertically in pressure, temperature, density and humidity. Another important property is that the air is a very poor conductor of heat. Indeed, experiments show that the difference in temperature between air lying on a heated road surface and the air one foot above the road surface can be as much as 10°C. This can only happen because of a lack of heat conductivity between the very shallow layer of air on the surface with the air above. A third property is 'fluidity'. Air acts like a fluid. It will therefore always try to flow from high pressure to low air pressure.

The Tropopause

This boundary line between the troposphere and the stratosphere becomes apparent when the temperature no longer reduces with increase of height.

Figure 1.2 shows the average height of the tropopause as 26000 ft over the poles (8 km) and 52000 ft over the equator (16 km). Further, that breaks occur at around 45° North and South latitude, so that effectively there is a Tropical Tropopause (TTP) and two Polar Tropopauses (PTP). The reason for the difference in height and the breaks in the tropopause is the greater transport of warm air from the surface in the tropical regions to the higher levels, than is the case at the higher latitudes. In fact, this shows itself as different types of air as far as mean temperature below a level is concerned. This in turn can cause strong winds called 'jet streams' and associated with them, clear air turbulence (CAT) can be experienced. The height of the tropopause varies with latitude, season, day to day and throughout the 24 hours i.e. diurnally. The actual height is important to a pilot because it will normally represent the height beyond which clouds will not occur, and it will be an indicator of the height of jet streams and the associated CAT. Additionally an increase of temperature can occur at the tropopause (an inversion) which can affect aircraft performance. There are often more than one tropical and one polar tropopause in a hemisphere. A moving airmass will bring its own particular tropopause with it and thus large scale air movements, particularly from north and south, will give sudden tropopause height changes. These will also effect the general position of jet streams and CAT as shown in Figure 1.2.

Standard Atmospheres

It has already been stated that the atmosphere is continuously variable, horizontally and vertically in pressure, temperature, density and humidity. It is therefore not possible to relate *directly*, the performance of an aircraft to the real atmosphere. For example, on a very cold day the air will have a high density and aircraft engines and airframes will be more efficient than on a warm day. It is also necessary for instruments like the altimeter to have a definitive relationship between a pressure change and height. Again this is not possible with an atmosphere which is not constant. To overcome these problems and indeed to enable a comparison to be made between the performance of one aircraft and another, hypothetical atmospheres have been devised. The more widely used of these is the International Standard Atmosphere (ISA) which

5

as its name implies, has been agreed to by the aviation nations of the world. The ISA gives a set value for Mean Sea Level pressure and temperature and density all over the world, standard temperature lapse rates for the atmosphere and a constant tropopause height. The values are roughly equivalent to the mean values in temperate latitudes. In detail the parameters are:

MSL Pressure ·	1013.25 mb
MSL Temperature	+15°C
Temperature Lapse Rate	1.98°C per 1000 ft up to a tropopause height of 36090 ft (11 kilometres) where temperature becomes −56.5°C and is then constant up to a height of 65617 ft (20 km). Thereafter the temperature is assumed to rise at a rate of 0.3°C per 1000 ft up to a height of 104987 ft (32 km).
MSL Density	1225 gm per cubic metre, reducing with height in accord with ISA temperature and pressure values.

A detailed breakdown of ISA values up to 65000 ft level, with kilometre values in brackets, is as follows:

Height ft (km)	Temp °C	Pressure mb	Relative Density %	
65000 (19.8)	−56.5	56.9	7.4	
60000 (18.3)	−56.5	72.3	9.5	
55000 (16.8)	−56.5	91.8	12.0	
50000 (15.2)	−56.5	116.6	15.3	
45000 (13.7)	−56.5	148.2	19.5	
40000 (12.2)	−56.5	188.2	24.7	
38662 (11.8)	−56.5	200.0	26.3	
36090 (11.0)	−56.5	228.2	29.7	Tropopause

Height ft (km)	Temp °C	Pressure mb	Relative Density %
30065	−44.4	300.0	36.8
(9.2)			
18289	−21.2	500.0	56.4
(5.6)			
10000	− 4.8	696.8	73.8
(3.0)			
9882	− 4.6	700.0	74.1
(3.0)			
4781	5.5	850.0	87.3
(1.5)	15.0	1013.25	100.0 MSL (1225 gm/m³)

A cross section diagram of the ISA is at Figure 1.3.

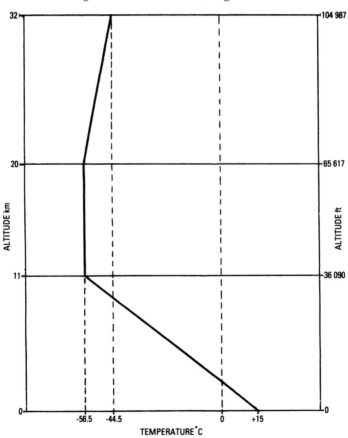

Mean Sea Level 1013.25 millibars. Mean Sea Level Density 1225 gm/m³

Figure 1.3. Cross Section Diagram of the ISA

The ISA, as previously indicated, is used to provide a basis for the calibration of instruments like the altimeter. The altimeter, in particular, must be calibrated to a common worldwide standard. This is necessary so that all altimeters, no matter in which country they are made, read the same value at the same height. It is only in this fashion that proper and safe separation between aircraft can be assured by the allocation of heights to fly.

The use of a standard atmosphere for the provision of aircraft performance data, is done initially by determining aircraft performance in the standard atmosphere. Thereafter, to relate these values to the real atmosphere, performance data is published against an argument of the difference in temperature/height between the standard atmosphere and the real or forecast ambient conditions for a flight.

Other standard atmospheres include the Jet Standard Atmosphere. This supposes a temperature at MSL of +15°C, a lapse rate of 2°C per 1000 ft add infinitum; so there is no tropopause. This atmosphere is commonly used by engine manufacturers.

Chapter 2
Weather Reporting

Introduction

Pilots rely on forecasts for knowledge of the expected weather for a flight. These are given in the form of charts, actual airfield weather reports, forecasts for en-route conditions, and forecasts for terminal and possible diversion airfields. Detailed information on these facilities is given in Chapter 19. Forecasts are necessarily an extension from weather reports. For the long range flights which are a daily feature of civil aviation, these forecasts must cross the boundaries of a number of countries. The requirements for synchronous weather reporting worldwide is therefore clearly established. Furthermore, the system of reporting and the discipline involved needs to be standardised. This is achieved through the World Meteorological Organisation (WMO) and the International Civil Aviation Organisation (ICAO).

Weather Information

The sources of information include:

Surface Reports

These are made from land stations across the world, which include many airfields. The reports are made half-hourly from major airfield reporting stations and hourly or three-hourly from other land stations. Surface reports are also given by the captains of ocean weather ships and by other mercantile captains. The hourly reports are usually made in the following sequence:

Temperatures (dry and wet bulb), Amount of cloud, Type of cloud, Cloud base, Present weather, Visibility, Wind direction and speed, Pressure tendency and Pressure. The last item, pressure, is usually timed to be recorded at the actual report time.

Upper Air Data

The main information is provided by a worldwide network of reporting stations which release radiosonde equipment suspended from hydrogen-filled balloons. The radiosonde carries sensors to continually measure pressure, temperature and humidity throughout ascent from the surface to heights in excess of 100 000 ft (30 km). Further details of radiosondes is at Chapter 15.

There are also reports from aircraft captains which augment and supplement the radiosonde information. This is particularly pertinent for upper wind data where the very accurate present day navigation equipment is reflected in the accuracy of wind finding. There is also some support in particular areas of the world where meteorological flights are carried out. These sometimes employ sondes which are dropped from high level. The sondes transmit radio reports to the dropping aircraft, on conditions at the levels through which the sonde descends.

Radio and Satellite
Ground radar stations are used to indicate areas of precipitation and their movement. These systems can also show the development of showers and thunderstorms. Satellites can provide visual real-time reporting of clouds and fronts. They prove particularly useful for areas where ground station reporting is sparse. Further detailed information on the use of satellites is at Chapter 20.

Communications
There is worldwide intercommunication of weather reports. This involves teleprinter and fascimile systems from reporting stations to their national centres. This is followed by international exchange between these centres. The teleprinter reports of land stations are given in coded form called SYNOP messages. These are a series of five-figure groups representing location and time followed by all the weather reported factors. The SYNOP message is rarely seen by pilots in its teleprinter form. However, the decoded information is displayed on surface weather charts. These are often referred to as Synoptic charts and can be available for pilots to study.

The Synoptic Chart
Synoptic charts can be compiled for any reporting hour; they are more usually produced for the Major Synoptic hours: 0600; 1200; 1800 and 0000 and for the Minor Synoptic hours: 0300; 0900; 1500 and 2100. Small circles representing the location of the reports are printed on Synoptic charts. Figures and symbols are disposed around the station circles to represent the reported weather. In this fashion it is possible by study to readily appreciate a complete situation for a region. Further, these charts can be used as a basis for pilot forecasting as detailed in Chapter 17. An example of a station circle weather report is at Figure 2.1. Full details of the

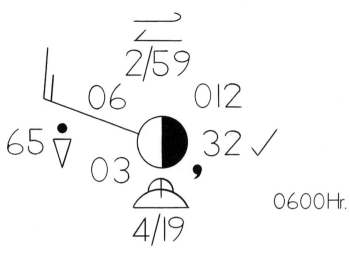

Figure 2.1. Example of a Station Circle Display

meanings of station circle figures and symbology is given at Appendix 'A'. Changes are made to these details from time to time and therefore care is required to ensure that the information at Appendix 'A' is current. The decode of the weather portrayed at the station circle above, from the 1 o'clock position is as follows:

012	—	QFF 1001.2 mb.
32 √	—	During the past 3 hours the pressure has fallen slightly and then risen. The net rise is 3.2 mb.
﹐	—	There has been drizzle during the past 6 hours.
⚏ 4/19	—	Low cloud is 4/8 of CB without anvil, base 1900 ft.
03	—	Dewpoint temperature +3°C.
65	—	Visibility 15 kilometres.
⚇	—	Present weather is slight rain showers.
⚲	—	Surface W/V 290/15.
06	—	Surface air temperature is +6°C.
⌐ 2/59	—	Medium level cloud is 2/8 of thin AS base 9000 ft.
⌐	—	High cloud is CI not increasing in amount.

11

Chapter 3
Pressure

A knowledge of atmospheric pressure is of great assistance to forecasting because air acts like a fluid and therefore, high pressures in a locality will result in a tendency for the air to move outwards towards comparatively low pressure areas. Atmospheric pressure can be defined as the weight of air in the column above unit area of the earth's surface. This weight is considerable and is approximately 10 tons of air reaching up to space above a square metre of the earth's surface. Pressure is usually expressed in hectopascals or millibars; these have the same value. A millibar equals 10 Newtons per square metre. Pressure can also be expressed as the height of the column of mercury in a barometer. Average Mean Seal Level (MSL) values for this height in relation to millibars are:

750 millimetres = 29.5 inches = 1000 millibars

Pressure Measurement
The meaning of pressure can be displayed by examining a simple

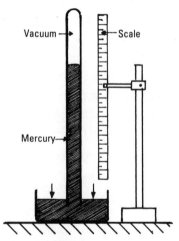

Figure 3.1. A Simple Mercury Barometer

mercury barometer as shown as Figure 3.1. Pressure acting on the surface of the mercury in the bottom tank will force it up the glass tube, so the height of the mercury is a measure of the atmospheric pressure acting on the mercury surface. There are also precision aneroid, i.e. capsule type barometers, used for measuring pressure at an observing station, although frequently an accurate mercury barometer is employed.

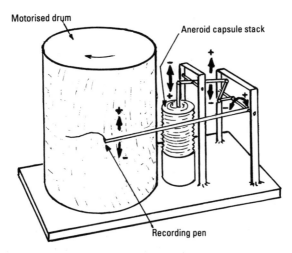

Figure 3.2. An Aneroid Barograph

The aneroid barograph, displayed at Figure 3.2, is an instrument for measuring the rate of change of pressure. It employs an expanding and contracting capsule similar to that used in aircraft altimeters. A recording device is used so that hourly pressure changes over a 7 day period can be examined on recorded graph paper. It is used particularly for assessing pressure tendency, i.e. the change of pressure over the past 3 hours.

Corrected Pressure Values

The pressure at aerodrome or reporting station level starts from the value obtained from either the precision aneroid, or the mercury barometer. This value is corrected for the difference in height between the position of the instrument and the official level for the station. For an aerodrome this is the highest usable point in the landing area. This pressure value is then given the code QFE. If a number of QFE values are obtained for different stations at the same observation time, then it is certain that the lowest pressures will apply to the stations having the greatest elevation. This must be the case because the depth of the column of air up to space is reduced by the elevation of the reporting station. An example of this is shown at Figure 3.3.

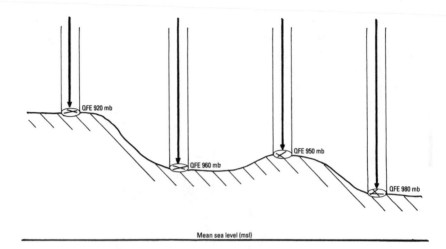

Figure 3.3. QFE Values for stations at Different Elevations

Whilst the QFE can be used with aircraft altimeters it clearly cannot be used for weather prognosis in its present form. If the QFE values can be changed to correct for the differences in elevation, and provided this is done accurately, then these new pressure values will have meteorological meaning.

QFE values can be corrected to MSL. This is done by supposing that a column of air exists below the reporting airfield location, right down to MSL. The weight of air in this column is assessed by reference to the airfield level temperature and the airfield elevation. The new pressure value so found is given the code QFF. Correcting the QFE values at Figure 3.3 to QFF values could produce a pressure situation as displayed at Figure 3.4. It can now

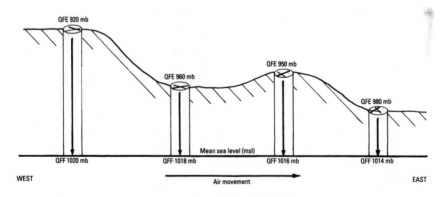

Figure 3.4. Correction of QFE values at Figure 3.3 to MSL

be seen that pressure is high to the West and low to the East, and this is a relatively important meteorological observation.

The atmospheric pressures in SYNOP weather reports are QFF values. The normal expected range of QFF values is 950 mb to 1050 mb anywhere in the world. This fact is used in decoding the figure codes for the station circle pressure value. Three figures are given, the last one being tenths of a mb. e.g. 814 – 81.4 mb. The figure before 81.4 must be a nine giving 981.4 mb. The other alternative is to prefix the three figures with a ten. This would give a value of 1081.4 mb and as this is outside the expected QFF range it is discarded.

There can be occasions when QFFs will be outside the expected range. For example, the lowest QFF recorded was 877 mb at Guam, the Pacific island, in 1967. However, when there are such unusual occurences, previous reports will indicate that they will occur and no anomalies should ensue.

Variations in Pressure

Horizontally. Pressure will vary from day to day and place to place and changes can occur hourly. These are caused by movement of the air and by changes in temperature.

Vertically. Pressure will reduce with increase of height because the depth of the column of air above will be reduced. The rate of reduction with height will vary horizontally (for the reasons given above), and vertically because the air becomes less dense with increase of height. Hence near MSL an increase of height of about 30 ft (9 m) will produce a decrease of pressure of 1 mb; at 20000 ft (6 km) an increase of 50 ft (15.5 m) would be necessary to produce a similar pressure reduction of 1 mb.

Diurnally. There is a change in pressure throughout the 24 hours (i.e. diurnally) caused by a natural oscillation of the atmosphere, with a twelve-hour period. The result of this is two peak pressure values around 1000 hr and 2200 hr and two low pressure values around 1600 hr and 0400 hr. In temperate latitudes (35°-65°) the effect is small, about 1 mb between peak and low and the effects are frequently masked by pressure changes for other reasons. In tropical and sub-tropical latitudes (0°-35°C) the effect is larger, about 3 mb beween peak and low and it is more discernible because in these latitudes pressure changes far less than elsewhere on the earth. Normally, therefore, the diurnal variation of pressure is an expected daily occurence. When it does not occur, it is usually a sign of a sudden weather change, often in fact a sign of a nearby tropical revolving storm. Diurnal variation of pressure is shown diagramatically at Figure 3.5.

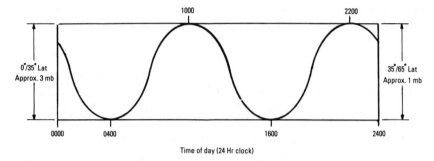

Figure 3.5. Typical Graph of the Diurnal Variation of Pressure

Chapter 4
Density

Density of the atmosphere is defined as the mass of air per unit volume, and it is usually expressed in gm per cubic metre of air. There is inevitably an interplay between pressure and density because if density is high then the weight of air at a place, the pressure, should also be high. Density is also affected by temperature. The connection between density, pressure and temperature is well explained by the fundamental gas equation for dry air:

$$\rho = \frac{P}{RT}$$

Where ρ is the density, P is the pressure, T is absolute temperature and R is a constant.

The equation simply says: For a fixed temperature, the density will increase as the pressure increases. This appears straightforward, for imagine if the atmosphere was full of feathers, then the greatest density of feathers would be where the greatest pressure applied i.e. MSL. The equation also says: If the pressure is constant, the density will decrease as the temperature increases. An increase of temperature infers expansion, and if the air expands, there will be less weight per unit volume.

Variation in Density at the Surface
It can be expected that with low pressure and high temperatures in the equatorial regions, density will be low. An average value is about 1200 gm per cubic metre at sea level. Similarly with high pressure and low temperature at the poles, density will be considerably higher. Density is particularly high, around 1500 gm per cubic metre, in Siberia in winter when pressure is consistently high and temperatures very low.

The Effect of Water Vapour
The gas equation quoted above was for dry air. Water vapour which is always present in varying quantities in the atmosphere, weighs less than dry air at the same pressure and temperature. Therefore, moist air will be less dense than completely dry air. The

reduction in total density is relatively small, less than 1 per cent. It can be ignored for aviation purposes except at low level in the tropics where the amount of water vapour present can exceed 40 gm per kg of dry air.

Variation of Density with Height

With increase of height the pressure will fall and therefore, density will reduce. However, with increase of height the temperature will fall and therefore, density should increase. The average pressure fall near MSL is 10 mb in 300 ft, which would produce a reduction in density of about 1 per cent. An increase of height of 300 ft would produce an average temperature reduction of under 1°C and a lowering of temperature by 1°C would only produce a density increase of some 0.3 per cent. Hence the pressure effect is much greater than the effect of a fall in temperature and therefore, with increase of height the density reduces. A study of the Standard Atmosphere table in Chapter 1 will show that on average the rate of reduction of density decreases rapidly with increase of height. For example, the table shows that at 20 000 ft (6 km) the density is almost half the surface value, at 40 000 ft (12 km) it is about a quarter, and at 60 000 ft (18 km) about one tenth of surface value.

Now consider the two columns of air at Figure 4.1 and which of

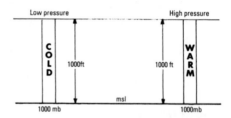

Figure 4.1. Decrease of Pressure with height at Different Temperatures

these will have the lower pressure with increase of height. It must be the cold column. This is because the air is more dense and thus a greater subtraction of weight, or pressure, with increase of height applies here, than where the air is warm and less dense. Hence pressure reduces more rapidly with increase of height in cold air than in warm air. As a consequence pressure tends to be higher above warm air. This is an important fact which bears on future topics.

Referring now to the true atmosphere as distinct from ISA, which takes no account of temperature and density changes at different latitudes, the actual upper level density picture is modified. At the surface over the poles pressure is high and temperature is low, in comparison with the tropics. Therefore density is higher at the surface over the poles. With increase of height this effect is rapidly diminished because pressure reduces more quickly with height in cold air than in warm. As a result, at about 26 000 ft (8 km) density is more or less constant at all latitudes. Above this level there is a gradual reversal so that at 50 000 ft (15 km) density is greater over the tropics than it is over the poles. This is because the warm air above the tropics produces higher pressure and thus higher densities. These density variations are shown by diagram at Figure 4.2. A study of Figure 4.2 will show than an aircraft could fly in

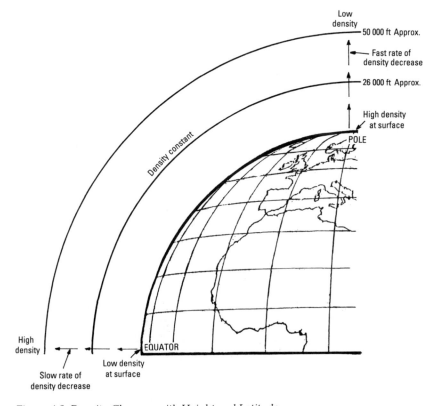

Figure 4.2. Density Changes with Height and Latitude

higher density air, and thus with better performance at differing heights dependent on latitude. This is a fact which is hidden when considering purely ISA conditions.

Density and Flight

Low air density can considerably reduce the performance of

engines and airframes. In the former case because of the reduction in the mass of air entering the engine. For airframes, the amount of lift from a wing is directly proportional to the density. For these reasons, for both take-off and landing, when density is very low, the pilot must either use a longer take-off and landing run or, alternatively, reduce the aircraft weight (either fuel or payload). Cruising at height in a jet aircraft the lower density gives reduced thrust. However, the aircraft's drag is also reduced because of the lower density, and the lower thrust produced by the engine means it will have a lower fuel consumption. As a consequence fuel consumption can be expected to reduce as height increases.

For helicopters the engine effects are as for fixed wing aircraft. The equivalent to lift from a wing is lift from the rotor blades. In low density conditions the rotor blades have to be set at a higher angle of attack, and this makes the retreating blade more liable to stall. A lower density can also significantly reduce the hovering ceiling. Lastly, in extreme cases of low density, vertical take-off or landing may not be possible, necessitating a 'running' take-off and landing.

Low density conditions are most likely to occur where:

- airfield elevation is 'High' (hence low pressure);
- temperature is 'High'; and
- humidity is 'High'.

Each of these will produce low density. An airfield with a high elevation near the equator in the rainy season will therefore suffer from all low density effects.

A good example of the above is Nairobi airport at latitude 01°19'S which has an elevation of some 5500 ft (1.7 km). It is a frequent occurrence that aircraft have to operate with a reduced payload when taking-off in the early afternoon. Another, somewhat less of a low density regime, concerns Bahrain in the Arabian Gulf. In summer, in the afternoon temperatures are high and humidity is high. Despite the fact that the airfield is virtually at sea level, when a Concorde service operated from Bahrain its passenger load had to be reduced for take-offs during summer. It is for this reason that the Concorde service to Bahrain was terminated. Singapore at latitude 01°21'N is widely used as a refuelling stop for aircraft flying to Japan and Australasia. These stops are usually scheduled for night time or the early morning hours when temperatures are cooler and thus density is greater.

Density Altitude
Performance of an aircraft, and particularly for helicopters, is often

argued against the term Density Altitude. This is the height in the ISA which has a density corresponding to the actual ambient density at a specific location. Alternatively it can be considered as the pressure altitude corrected for temperature. Hence if reference is made to a high Density Altitude it means that the air density as such, must be low.

Chapter 5
Altimetry

Introduction

Altimetry is concerned with altimeters and how they perform in an aircraft. Altimeters operate by measuring atmospheric pressure and it is therefore sensible that this instrument and its performance should be considered here. The subject deserves separate treatment, in a chapter of its own, because height errors can be very dangerous unless they are properly understood. The altimeter is an inaccurate instrument and must therefore be used with care.

An altimeter measures the difference in pressure between a particular pressure surface and the pressure at the aircraft level. It then converts the pressure difference to a height, on the basis of the ISA and displays it on a dial. So, effectively, the dial is calibrated in accord with the ISA. The height registered is the height above a particular pressure surface. The drawing at Figure 5.1 shows the

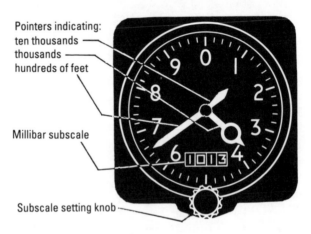

Figure 5.1. An Altimeter

face of the altimeter. It can be seen that there is a separate subscale at the lower centre. The particular pressure surface above which height will be measured, can be fed into the altimeter by means of this scale by the pilot. The height so measured could only be accurate if the real atmosphere on the day was exactly the same as the ISA. This is highly unlikely. An illustration of the extent of the error can be gauged by the fact that an ambient temperature 10°C warmer than ISA can give an under-reading by the altimeter of some 4 per cent. Hence whilst errors at aerodrome level due to this cause are nil, and are small within 1000 ft (300 m) of the runway, at 30000 ft (9.2 km) and higher, errors of 2000 ft (600 m) in height reading are not particularly unusual.

Circuit Flying

The setting on the sub-scale will determine at what height zero will appear on the altimeter face. For circuit flying the sub-scale is normally set to QFE. As stated before, this is the aerodrome level pressure measured for the highest point in the landing area. Therefore with QFE set the altimeter will register height above the airfield landing area. Suppose that an aircraft with QFE set on the sub-scale has landed and at that time the altimeter reading was zero feet — as it should be. If the aircraft is now left for a few hours it is likely on return, that the altimeter will no longer read zero. This is because normal atmospheric pressure can change very quickly and unless the QFE is measured frequently by Air Traffic Control and is passed to the pilot so that he can reset the sub-scale, the altimeter will give an inaccurate reading. It is therefore necessary, when a pilot is engaged in circuit flying, to regularly reset the QFE value on the basis of the latest QFE information from Air Traffic Control.

En-route Flying

If a pilot intends to fly from one airfield to another he will consult a map and refer to the height information in order to determine a height to fly. The height information is given as height above MSL and therefore, ideally, the pilot would wish to have zero height indication on his altimeter at MSL. To do this it is necessary to set a sub-scale pressure value equal to MSL pressure. MSL pressure at an airfield is apparently an impossibility. However, a close approximation can be found by starting with QFE and then correcting this pressure in accord with the elevation of the airfield and ISA conditions. This is sensible as the altimeter is calibrated in accord with ISA. This approximation to MSL pressure is termed the airfield QNH. (*Note*: this is not the same as QFF, where actual airfield temperature is used to provide a correction to MSL).

Suppose a pilot takes off from airfield A with QNH of 1010 mb set on the sub-scale of the altimeter, to fly to airfield B where QNH is higher. The situation may be as displayed at Figure 5.2. In this example the pilot selects a height to fly of 2000' and will maintain

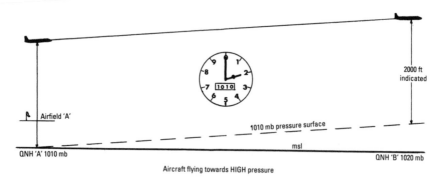

Figure 5.2. Altimeter Errors for an Aircraft Flying towards High Pressure

this indication on the altimeter during the flight to B. In fact the aircraft will be flying at 2000 ft above the pressure surface of 1010 mb. Because the pressure surface slopes upwards, at B the aircraft is flying higher above the ground than indicated. In the reverse situation where an aircraft is flying towards a lower pressure, the altimeter will read high, i.e. it will indicate a greater height than in fact the aircraft is flying with respect to the ground. This is shown at Figure 5.3.

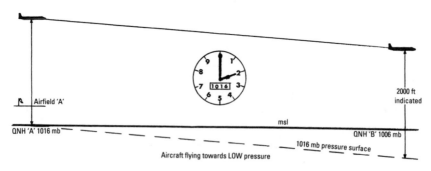

Figure 5.3. Altimeter Errors for an Aircraft Flying towards Low Pressure

Clearly in this case, if no adjustment is made to the QNH sub-scale setting, then the aircraft could strike high ground. Therefore, flying towards low pressure can be dangerous. A pilot can ascertain whether he is flying towards low pressure by application of Buys Ballot's Law (see Chapter 6), together with knowledge of drift. The 'Starboard Drift Law' states: if an aircraft in the northern hemisphere experiences starboard drift then it is flying towards low pressure. In the southern hemisphere port drift would indicate

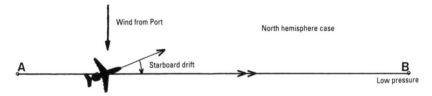

Figure 5.4. Starboard Drift Law

that the aircraft was flying towards low pressure. The northern hemisphere case is displayed at Figure 5.4.

A method by which the dangers of flight towards low pressure can be overcome is by use of Regional QNH. This is used only in the United Kingdom. The regional QNH is the lowest forecast QNH in a specified region. This is forecast by the meteorological office for 2 hours ahead, and is valid for a 1 hour period only. If a pilot sets the regional QNH on the sub-scale of the altimeter then as far as the instrument is concerned the aircraft will always be flying towards a higher pressure. Therefore, the altimeter will always register a height less than the true height above ground, this should ensure safe clearance over the terrain anywhere within the specified region.

En-route Flying in Controlled Airspace

The main altimeter setting system for en-route flying, worldwide, is the use of the Standard Altimeter Setting. This is 1013 mb. This setting has to be used for all flying in controlled airspace. The main principle behind use of the standard setting is that whilst altimeters at height are basically inaccurate, as long as all aircraft use the same setting, then aircraft flying in the same airspace, at the same height will have the same altimeter height reading. This

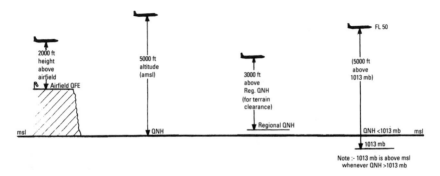

Figure 5.5. Aircraft Flying with Different Altimeter Settings

presupposes of course that as stated previously, all altimeters are calibrated in accord with the ISA. By use of the standard setting, it is possible for ground controllers to allocate heights for aircraft to fly with full confidence that separation between aircraft will be as the controller intends. A diagram showing aircraft with different settings on the sub-scale is at Figure 5.5.

The height displayed on the altimeter when the standard setting of 1013 mb is set on the sub-scale is called the 'Pressure Altitude'. The pressure altitude in hundreds of feet at specified intervals is named 'Flight Level' e.g. A pressure altitude of 23 500 ft is also a Flight Level of 235.

For some airfields with a very high elevation such as Senaa in the Yemen, height 7000 ft AMSL and small airfields in the Andes of South America with elevations around 9000 ft, it is physically impossible to set QFE on the sub-scale because the engraved scale does not always register below 800 mb. (Some American altimeters will not register below 950 mb). QNE has been devised to assist the pilot in landing at these high level airfields. QNE is not a pressure setting, it is the height shown on the altimeter when the sub-scale is set to 1013 mb and the aircraft is on the ground at the end of the runway in use. It is also therefore, the pressure altitude when the aircraft is on the end of the runway. Use of QNE will enable the pilot to adjust his approach to land so that on the runway the QNE value is shown as the height.

'D' Value and Pressure Variations

The errors of the altimeter caused by ISA calibration have been discussed. These errors can be corrected by use of a navigation computer. In practice it is rarely necessary to know the accurate height when a pilot is flying at high level. There is however one particular case when accurate height is necessary, and this is for aerial photographic survey work. For this type of flying a Difference value, called the D value has to be known. This is the amount which has to be applied to the indicated pressure altitude to give the true height above MSL.

Whilst knowledge of the location of low pressure areas can be obtained from a synoptic chart, or by application of Buys Ballot's Law, small local pressure variations can cause situations at low level where incorrect readings may affect survey accuracy. These can occur due to small lee depressions which form on the downwind side of hills and to small pressure reductions on crossing a coast on a warm sunny day. These pressure falls may only be 2 or 3 mb but the 100 ft or so of error could be significant and particularly so for low flying helicopters.

Pilots also need to be aware that the small pressure reductions referred to above can be accompanied by downdrafts of air which can add to the height problems. Both of these factors become particularly significant and large in the vicinity of thunderstorms.

Chapter 6
World and Synoptic Pressures

World Pressures

In Chapter 3 it was shown that pressure is the weight of the total column of air up to space, high temperature gives low density and thus low pressure, and vice versa. Further, increase of height in warm air can provide a relatively high pressure at the upper levels because the rate of reduction of pressure with height is greater in cold air. Relating these facts to an imperfect globe which rotates and inclines towards and away from the sun would be massively complicated. However, looking at the earth as a simple static globe in an unrefined atmospheric environment, as at Figures 6.1 and 6.2, can lead to an appreciation of certain world pressure facts:

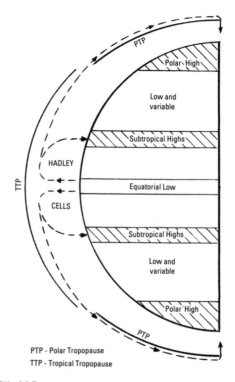

PTP - Polar Tropopause
TTP - Tropical Tropopause

Figure 6.1. Basic World Pressures

28

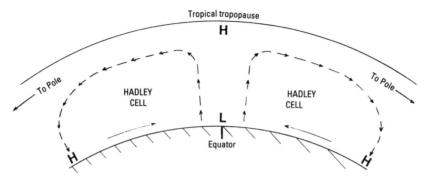

Figure 6.2. Hadley Cells

a) Pressures are high at the Poles.
b) Pressure is low at the equator.
c) Above the equator around 50 000 ft pressure will be high compared with the same level at the poles.
d) Warm air at the surface equator will be less dense and will therefore rise.
e) Lifted equatorial air will be replaced by surface air from a higher latitude either side of the equator — from the subtropics (say 30°).
f) The movement of surface tropical air will cause air at height above the tropics to descend — keeping the air at these latitudes at a relatively high pressure.

The cells of rising air over the equator and descending air to the tropics are called Hadley cells after the London doctor who first postulated these motions in 1786. Between the polar and subtropical high pressure regions pressures will be low and variable. This area embraces the temperate latitudes. Figure 6.1 gives a fair picture of general MSL pressure distribution over the earth. There are however two large scale anomalies in the northern hemisphere. These concern the large continents of Asia and North America. In winter due to surface cooling, these become regions of high pressure: This applies particularly to Siberia and Canada. The same continents in summer become centres of low pressure caused by surface heating. Surface world pressures are examined in more detail in Chapter 18.

Synoptic Pressures

Isobars

QFF values for the large number of station reports on a synoptic chart can be examined to determine where pressures are high and low. For this purpose it is necessary to draw isobars. These are lines joining places where the pressure is the same at the same level. By convention isobars are always drawn for even whole number values of pressure; e.g. 1000 mb, 1002 mb, 1004 mb etc., or for a large scale chart 1000 mb, 1004 mb, 1008 mb. When isobars are drawn, it quickly becomes apparent that they form particular patterns. If a series of charts are examined then different standard patterns can be recognised as configurations for high and low pressure, leading to particular types of weather. These standard patterns include those for: an Anticyclone, a Depression, a Ridge of High, a Trough of Low, a Col and a Secondary Low. Clearly, recognition of these pressure systems, together with knowledge of their weather associations can aid forecasting.

The Anticyclone
This is a region of high pressure where roughly circular enclosed

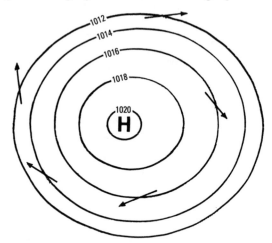

Figure 6.3. Plan View of an Anticyclone

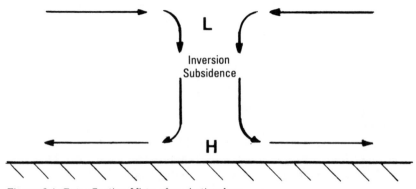

Figure 6.4. Cross Section View of an Anticyclone

isobars have the highest pressure value in the centre. The air in an anticyclone will be moving away from the centre at the surface to fill up any neighbouring low pressure areas. This will cause air from above to descend in order to replace the diverging air. This descent of air is referred to as subsidence. It is, therefore, a region of diverging and descending air. The anticyclone is shown in plan and in cross-section at Figures 6.3 and 6.4 respectively.

There are cold and warm anticyclones. The cold anticyclones are those caused by low temperatures and thus high density. They are winter permanent and include the Siberian high and the North American high. There are also temporary cold high pressure areas and these occur as ridges of high pressure between low pressure systems which can then develop into full anticyclones. In summer these tend to collapse quickly.

The warm anticyclones are caused by an excess of air at height and are the subtropical anticyclones formed with the Hadley cells. They are permanent but move seasonally. Temporary warm areas occur as extensions from the warm anticyclones. An example is the extension from the subtropical anticyclone over the Azores islands in the Atlantic, which covers the Mediterranean sea in summer.

The highs over the poles are of the cold type. They are also of the warm type as there is an excess of air at height from the lifted and transported air originating at the equator.

Anticyclonic Weather

Generally good with light surface winds blowing clockwise across the isobars away from the centre in the northern hemisphere and anticlockwise in the southern hemisphere. Weather is clear and stable except at the edges where some low cloud and light precipitation can occur. In the centre with clear skies fog can form in winter and haze in summer. There is often a temperature inversion (an increase of temperature with increase of height) caused by the subsidence. The rate of subsidence is quite small, around 3000 ft per day. The subsidence restricts any lifting in the centre and therefore cloud developments.

The Depression

This is a region of low pressure where roughly circular enclosed isobars have the lowest pressure value in the centre. Depressions are also known as cyclones. It is a region of converging and rising air as a result of inflow from high pressure areas. The depression is shown in plan and cross-section at Figures 6.5 and 6.6 respectively.

The rising air in the centre of the depression will cause relatively

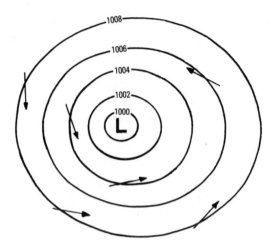

Figure 6.5. Plan View of a Depression

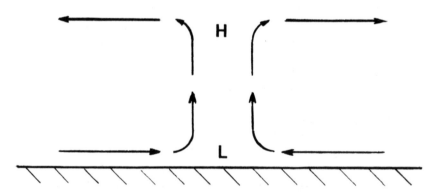

Figure 6.6. Cross Section View of a Depression

high pressure at heights above the surface compared with nearby pressures at the same level. Outflow at these upper levels above the depression centre will then cause any initial small surface low pressure system to develop and deepen, thus becoming more active. The lifting process will cause cloud to form and thus bad weather is associated with depressions and much cloud and precipitation can be expected. Surface winds blow anticlockwise in the northern hemisphere and across the isobars towards the centre of low. In the southern hemisphere the surface winds blow clockwise. There are three basic types of depression: Polar Front, Thermal and Orographic. These will be examined in detail in later chapters.

Ridge of High

This is an extension of the isobars from an anticyclone in the form of a 'U'. A plan view is shown at Figure 6.7. Weather and wind direction are as for anticyclones. Sometimes the ridge can develop into a full anticyclone; this is more likely to happen with winter low

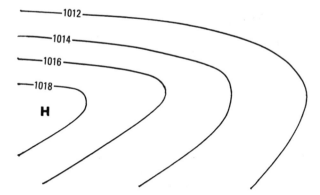

Figure 6.7. Ridge of High Pressure

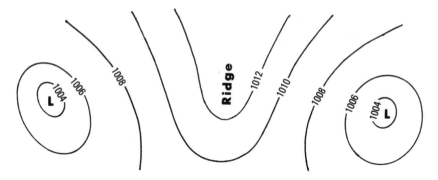

Figure 6.8. A Ridge between two Lows

temperatures. A ridge frequently occurs between two polar front depressions. It then often provides a period of good weather for 24 hr or 48 hr between the two lows. In these conditions as indicated at Figure 6.8, the ridge can provide a very welcome break in a lengthy period of bad weather.

Trough of Low

This is an extension of the isobars from a depression in the form of a 'V'. The trough gives generally bad weather. A plan view of a trough is at Figure 6.9.

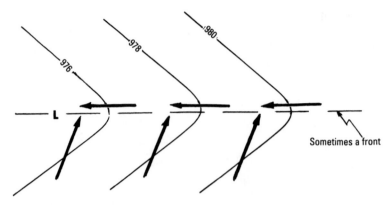

Figure 6.9. Trough of Low Pressure

Frequently a front lies along the centre line of the trough. A front is the boundary between two masses of air at different temperatures. Under these conditions the weather will be in accord with the type of front — cold front weather or warm front weather. If there is no front present then the strong convergence of the air either side of the trough centre line meeting from different directions can cause the air to lift sharply. The weather can then include towering clouds, thunderstorms and heavy showers.

Col

This is a region of almost stationary air between two anticyclones and two depressions. It is a region where surface winds are very

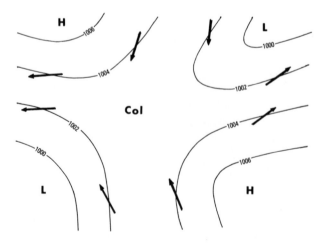

Figure 6.10. An area of Col

light and variable in direction. A plan view is shown at Figure 6.10.

It is perhaps of interest to note that whilst anticyclonic winds blow clockwise and depression winds blow anticlockwise in the northern hemisphere, where the two pressure systems are adjacent and here Figure 6.10 refers, in fact the winds are blowing in the same direction. The very light winds result in air being in contact with the ground for a considerable time. Thus during the day in summer the air in contact with the warm ground can become heated, less dense and rise causing towering clouds and thunderstorms. Similarly during the night in winter the air in contact with the cold ground can become cooled and this often results in the formation of fog.

Secondary Low
This is a small vigorous area of low pressure which forms on the fringe of a main depression. It can give very active bad weather with gales. A plan view is at Figure 6.11. In essence, the secondary

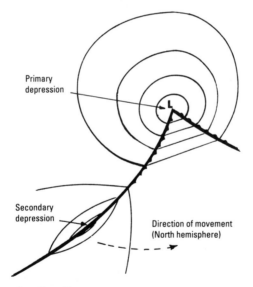

Figure 6.11. Secondary Low Pressure

is a younger depression and this accounts for its greater activity, i.e. more cloud, more precipitation and gales. It will tend to move anticlockwise around the main area of low pressure in the northern hemisphere and can in time take over as the main depression. On occasions the secondary can become absorbed fairly rapidly by the primary depression and then quickly loses its identity.

There is a fairly common secondary depression situation which arises when there is a main depression to the north of Ireland and a front with cold air behind it approaching the northwest coast of France. The lifting of the air against the French coast causes a secondary depression to form and this can often result in thunderstorm weather with the secondary brought anticlockwise into

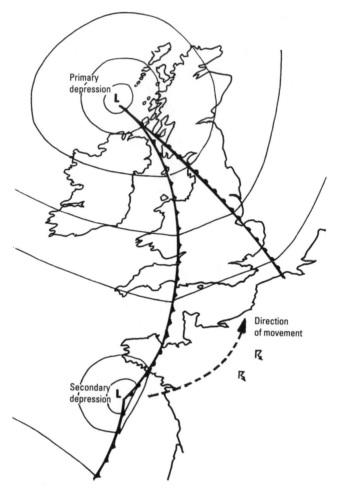

Figure 6.12. Secondary Low over Northwest France

southeast England. The situation is shown at Figure 6.12. This is typical of secondaries which form across a coast or mountain range, where the orographic uplift causes divergence at height and surface pressure to fall.

Pressure System Movement

Anticyclones tend to be slow moving and can be more or less static over a region for some period of weeks. Depressions tend to move rapidly and also to fill up or disappear in about 2 weeks. Depressions have a propensity for movement towards a region where pressure is falling most rapidly. Cols rarely last longer than a few days before being absorbed in some other pressure system. Clearly then, pressure systems do not move entirely in accord with the winds which blow within them; they predominently move under the influence of neighbouring systems and the relative pressures with those systems. There is, however, a firm connection between pressure and wind direction. This is explained in the law of Buys Ballot, a Dutch meteorologist: 'If an observer stands with his back to the wind in the northern hemisphere the region of lower pressure is on his left. In the southern hemisphere it is on his right.' Examination of the wind arrows in the previous Figures will show that Buys Ballot's Law holds good.

Pressure tendency, the change in pressure during the past 3 hours, can be found from the trace of an Aneroid Barograph. Lines joining places experiencing the same pressure tendency value are called 'isallobars'. These isallobars are used to assist in the forecast movements of pressure systems.

Pressure Gradient

It will be seen from a comparison of the isobar spacing for anticyclones and depressions that isobars are closer together for the depression than they are for the anticyclone. This must indicate a greater pressure change over a unit distance and recalling again the fluid characteristic of air, it follows that the movement of air, the wind, should blow stronger with a depression than it does in an anticyclone. In fact this is generally the case. The change in presure in unit distance is called the Pressure Gradient. This value must be greater when isobars are closer together. Pressure Gradients are referred to as 'steep' or 'slack' as displayed in Figure 6.13.

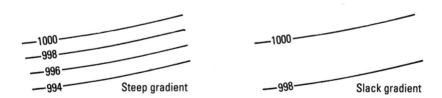

Figure 6.13. Steep and Slack Pressure Gradients

Chapter 7
Temperature

Introduction
It can be said that temperature is the controlling factor in meteorology. Changes of temperature lead to density changes which cause vertical air movements. The density changes also cause variations in pressure leading to horizontal air movements and winds.

It is the temperature of the air on the earth's surface itself which provides the greatest impact on weather, initiating air movement and cloud development. However, these temperatures on the surface vary markedly at any one location and time. Furthermore, they could not provide a sensible basis for temperature comparison at different reporting locations. For these reasons advantage is taken of the poor conductivity of air, to isolate the temperature on the surface, from the air temperature some 4 ft (1.25 metres) above. It is at this level that air temperature is measured.

Scales of Measurement
There are three scales for the measurement of temperature. Fahrenheit, a 180 degree scale where the freezing point of water is 32°F and the boiling point is 212°F. Use of this scale for practical expression of temperature is now very much reduced. The Absolute or Kelvin scale is widely used scientifically and provides a freezing point of 273°K and a boiling point of 373°K. For meteorological purposes, temperatures are measured in degrees Celsius, after the Swedish astronomer of that name, who devised the Centigrade scale. The scale specifies 0°C as the freezing point of ice and 100°C as the boiling point of water. To convert Fahrenheit to Celsius and vice versa:

$$(°F - 32) \times \frac{5}{9} = °C \qquad (°C \times \frac{9}{5}) + 32 = °F$$

To convert °K to Celsius and vice versa is simply a question of applying minus or plus 273° respectively.

Temperatures for meteorological reports are read to the nearest 0.1°C and are reported to the nearest whole number, with the 0.5°C value always applied to the nearest whole odd number. For example air temperature and dewpoint temperature may both be reported as +13°C. However the air temperature may have been read as 12.5°C and the dewpoint as 13.5°C. Hence a report of equal air and dewpoint temperatures does not necessarily mean that the air is saturated.

Temperatures on the Earth's Surface

These temperatures include those on the surface itself together with temperatures of the surface air 4 ft above the ground. It is again emphasised that these temperatures are not the same because air is a poor conductor of heat. Nevertheless there is an interconnection because they are both subject to solar radiation effects. The temperatures measured and reported, are the surface temperatures obtained using mercury thermometers housed in a louvred screen, usually of the Stevenson variety as shown in Figure 7.1.

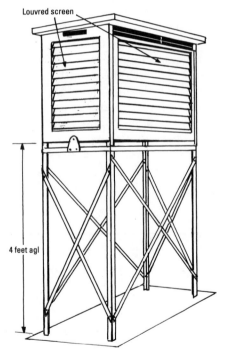

Figure 7.1. The Stevenson Screen

The screen provides a shaded environment, yet still allows the ambient air to circulate around the thermometers. The screen, and thus the air temperature measurement, is at 4 ft (1.25 m) above the ground. This is standard worldwide practice. The temperatures are largely governed by the degree of solar radiation and the type of earth's surface where temperatures are being considered. Other factors include cloud cover, surface wind speed, and where the air has recently originated. Another important factor is the radiation from the earth, terrestrial radiation, which reduces surface temperatures.

Solar Radiation
The radiation from the sun covers a very wide band of wavelengths encompassing gamma and X-rays, ultra-violet through the small visible spectrum to infra-red and radio waves. Much of the radiation at wavelengths either side of the visible spectrum is reflected back to space form, or absorbed by, the upper layers of the atmosphere proper. The ultra-violet radiation in particular, is absorbed by the ozone layer in the stratosphere. The majority of the solar radiation which reaches the earth is therefore in the visible spectrum at wavelengths of less than 2 microns (1 micron = a millionth of a metre) and the bulk of this radiation is at wavelengths less than 1 micron. Nearly all the radiation passes through the atmosphere as if it was transparent apart from reflection back to space from cloud tops. The amount of solar radiation incident on unit area of the earth's surface is termed 'insolation'. Some of the insolation heats the earth's surface and raises the temperature. Heat which is used to alter temperature is referred to as sensible heat. Part of the radiation is reflected back to space from sea and snow-covered surfaces, particularly when the sun's elevation is low.

Latent Heat
It has been estimated that approximately one-third of the total insolation is used to provide the evaporation of water and the melting of ice. The heat from the sun in this case is used to alter the state of water or ice, not to raise the temperature. This is therefore called latent or hidden heat because no change in temperature is involved. Latent heat can be transposed to sensible heat when water vapour changes to water droplets, or when water droplets freeze.

Angular Elevation of the Sun
As the angular elevation of the sun varies, so will the temperature of the surface. The angular elevation is dependent on the latitude, the season of the year and the time of day.

Latitude

The earth is small in diameter compared with the sun and the two are some 93 million miles apart: Therefore the sun's rays are effectively parallel at the earth's surface. The angle of the sun's rays within 20° of the equator is always close to 90° at noon. With increase of latitude this angle is progressively reduced, with the result that the ground area being radiated is increased, so the degree of insolation reduces with increase of latitude. This effect is displayed at Figure 7.2.

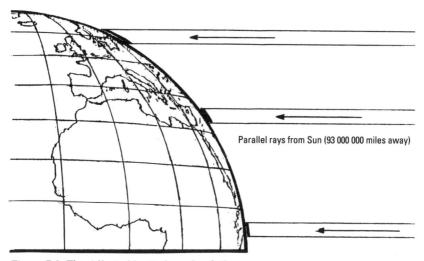

Parallel rays from Sun (93 000 000 miles away)

Figure 7.2. The Affect of Latitude on Insolation

Season of the Year

The season will modify the latitude effect on the elevation of the sun. The northern hemisphere of the earth inclines towards the sun in summer. The inclination is greatest on 22 June (the summer solstice) when the earth is receiving the most direct radiation at noon at latitude 23½ degrees north. The northern hemisphere inclines away from the sun in winter so that by 22 December the 90° elevation is received at noon at 23½ degrees south (the winter solstice). At the equinoxes (21 March and 22 September) the sun is providing the 90° direct radiation at noon on the equator. The general effect of these changes, together with latitude effects can be seen at Figure 7.3. This shows mean temperatures by latitude for January and July.

Diurnal Variation and Temperature Effects

The insolation changes through the 24 hours of a day will result in rhythmic temperature changes at the surface. From sunrise as the angular elevation of the sun increases, the ground and the surface air temperatures will also increase. The maximum insolation is received at noon, but temperatures continue to rise up to about 1500 hours. During any 24 hours the earth is giving off radiation termed terrestrial radiation. From sunrise to about 1500 hours the heat lost by terrestrial radiation is less than the heat gained by the insolation. After this time the heat loss caused by terrestrial

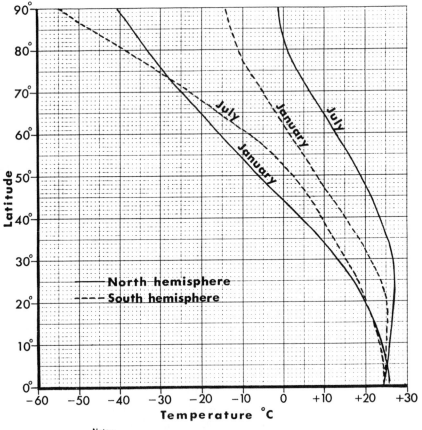

Note :-
1. The range of temperatures is small within 10° of the equator and then increases with latitude.
2. The north hemisphere is warmer in summer and colder in winter - reflecting the larger ratio of land to sea.
3. Temperatures are extra cold over the land mass of Antarctica in July.
4. There can be large variations longitudinally.

Figure 7.3. Graphs of Mean Temperatures by Latitude

radiation is greater, and the result is that the temperatures start to fall. They will continue to fall until sunrise the next day. The warmest time of day is thus about 1500 hours and the coldest temperature is at sunrise (nominally, say around 0500 hours) and at both of these times the incoming solar radiation and the outgoing terrestrial radiation are roughly in balance. A graph of the diurnal variation (DV) of surface air temperature for a cloudless calm day is at Figure 7.4.

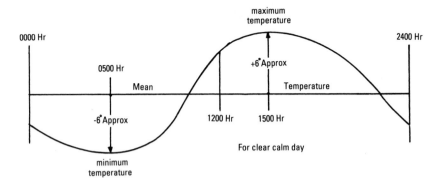

Figure 7.4. Diurnal Variation of Surface Air Temperature

An average value of the DV in temperate latitudes is ±6°C about the mean, but the value will vary considerably. Over desert areas ±20°C about the mean is not unusual. On the other hand a low figure could be expected near coasts due to the moderating sea influence on temperature.

The Effect of Cloud Cover on DV of Temperature
Cloud will reflect some of the incident solar radiation thereby reducing the expected daytime temperatures. At night some of the terrestrial radiation will be re-radiated back to the earth's surface from the cloud thereby giving higher night temperatures. This is sometimes called the blanket effect. Hence overall, cloud will cause a reduction in the value of DV.

The Effect of Wind on DV of Temperature
Wind will cause turbulence, and naturally this turbulence will increase with wind speed. This will cause the warm air on the

surface by day to be mixed with the cooler air above. Additionally it will reduce the amount of time that any air is in contact with the warm land surface. For both these reasons the day temperatures will be lower than normal. At night, under clear sky circumstances, air temperatures will increase with increase of height, below, say 2000 ft. As the earth rapidly cools off, there will be a low level inversion. The turbulent mixing of the cold air on the surface with the warm air above will cause the night temperatures to be higher than normal. Additionally the amount of time air is in contact with the cold ground will be reduced, again causing night temperatures to be higher than normal. The overall effect is therefore similar to the effect of cloud — a reduction in the value of diurnal variation.

Nature of the Surface
Different surfaces on the earth have different capabilities in transposing insolation into sensible heat. For example stone and sand will show a rise in temperature far more quickly than grass or wet soil. A major difference in the transposition capacity applies between water and land. The thermal capacity of water, the amount of heat necessary to raise the temperature by 1°C, is much greater than that for land. Insolation will only heat the first few inches of a land surface during the day, whilst the heat received by a water surface will be spread through a much greater depth — a number of feet, and horizontally. Further, a proportion of the incident solar radiation at a water surface (or even a damp surface) will be used in the evaporation process, to provide latent heat. For the reasons given above the DV of temperature over a sea surface, is therefore quite small, about 1°C.

In similar circumstances the land will gain and give up its heat more readily than water. Therefore, in essence it is true to say that the land heats and cools quickly whilst sea surfaces take a long time to heat and a long time to cool. The meteorological implications of this statement are far-reaching, for it is the basic reason for land and sea breezes. Further, in worldwide terms, the rapid cooling of the continents in winter leads to high density and high pressure and thus a general movement of air from the continents to the oceans. This is reversed in summer when rapid continental heating leads to low pressure over the land and a general air movement from the oceans to the continents.

The comparative effect of differing surfaces in descending ability to accept insolation and transpose it to sensible heat, is shown by the following table:

a) Bare Rock or Stone
b) Dry Sand
c) Concrete
d) Tarmacadam
e) Dry Soil
f) Grassland
g) Wet Soil
h) Woods
i) Rivers
j) Deep Lakes
k) Oceans
l) Snow Surfaces

Snow surfaces are particularly poor for providing temperature increases as they normally occur at the higher latitudes where the sun's angle of elevation is low at all times and up to 80 per cent of the solar radiation can be reflected away. Further, snow does not prevent terrestrial radiation, and therefore, the air above snow surfaces tends to become progressively colder. A good example of this is Verkhoyansk in Siberia, where the surface air temperature at the end of winter can be below −70°C.

Location Effect
Air in a valley will attain a higher temperature by day than air on an exposed hill. The air in the valley is sheltered from the wind and will therefore be in contact with the warm ground for a lengthy period and can thus become warmed more quickly. At night however with a cold ground, a location on a hill should be warmer. In this exposed position the air is in contact with the cold ground for relatively short time periods compared with the valley situation. Additionally, air on the sides of a hill at night will be cooler, denser and heavier than the free air alongside and it will therefore sink to the valley floor, again lowering the temperature. It is partly for these reasons that mist and fog tend to form firstly in valleys.

Origin of the Air
The air tends to hold its basic characteristics of temperature and humidity over reasonably long periods of time. These characteristics being absorbed from the initial earth surface of origin of the air. A good example of this applies in England when there is an easterly wind in winter. The origin of this air is Siberia and thus the easterly wind brings very low temperatures. Similarly air from a lower latitude will normally bring higher temperatures and the reverse

45

will apply where the origin is from a higher latitude. The origin of the air affects both surface temperatures and temperatures in the atmosphere.

Temperatures in the Atmosphere

It has already been stated that the incoming solar radiation passes through the atmosphere almost as if it was transparent. Hence the heating of the troposphere must be from below. One of the main processes by which the heating occurs is terrestrial radiation. This has a comparatively long wavelength of around 10 microns whilst the solar radiation is centred on a wavelength of 1 micron. Water vapour, carbon dioxide and some other gases can absorb these 10 micron wavelength radiations, become heated and then transmit this heat in all directions to the surrounding air, thus raising the temperature. This is analogous to the way a greenhouse is heated. The glass allows the very short wave solar radiation to pass through unimpeded, but resists the passage of longer wavelength radiation from the floor and objects within the greenhouse. Hence the temperature inside increases. For this reason this basic method by which the troposphere is heated is sometimes referred to as the 'Greenhouse Effect'.

The amount of water vapour in the atmosphere and the presence of carbon dioxide et al. reduces with increase of height. Therefore the amount of atmospheric heating caused by absorption of terrestrial radiation also reduces. This is a reason for the lapse rate, the reduction of temperature with height, in the atmosphere. It is also a reason why temperature in the air above desert areas can be comparatively low.

An amount of atmospheric heating is afforded by conduction, the transfer of heat by contact between the earth and the air lying on it. This initially only affects the one or two feet (less than one metre) of air on the earth's surface. Heat is then transferred vertically by this warmed air becoming less dense and therefore lifting, causing what are called thermal upcurrents or 'thermals'. This lifting process is usually referred to as convection.

Another main atmospheric heating process concerns the release of latent heat. It will be recalled that when evaporation takes place, latent heat is used in the change from liquid water and it was seen that a large proportion of insolation was used in the process. When air from the ground is lifted it will cool and the water vapour can change back to water droplets forming cloud. When this condensation occurs, the latent heat previously absorbed in the evaporation process is released, thereby raising the temperature of the surrounding air. The latent heat is thus transposed to sensible heat.

Whilst the foregoing paragraphs refer to heat being transferred vertically, it is also transferred horizontally by turbulence at all levels, and also by wind. The horizontal movement of air causing temperature change is called advection. Few of the troposphere heating processes effect the stratosphere, mainly because there is little or no water vapour present and the density of absorbing gases is low. The heating provided here is by means of ozone absorbing ultra-violet radiation.

Terrestrial Radiation at Night

Terrestrial radiation is continuous throughout the 24 hours of a day. However, more radiation occurs during daylight hours because of the higher temperatures. At night the terrestrial radiation lowers the temperature of the ground itself and also of the one or two feet of air lying on the ground. The temperature above this level will normally be higher, particularly during a clear night when there are no clouds to obstruct the terrestrial radiation.

Inversion and Isothermal Layer

If there is an increase of temperature with increase of height in the atmosphere this is called a temperature inversion. Temperature inversions can occur at night as mentioned in the previous paragraph. They can also occur in anticyclones, where the air which is made to descend (i.e. subsidence) is subject to compression due to the higher pressures at the lower levels. There is usually an inversion at the tropopause, also with fronts and above certain cloud types.

If there is a layer in the atmosphere where the temperature is constant with increase of height, this is called an isothermal layer. The stratosphere is an isothermal layer in a wide sense. A graph of temperature against height in the atmosphere, displaying inversions and isothermal layers together with the normal lapse rates is at Figure 7.5.

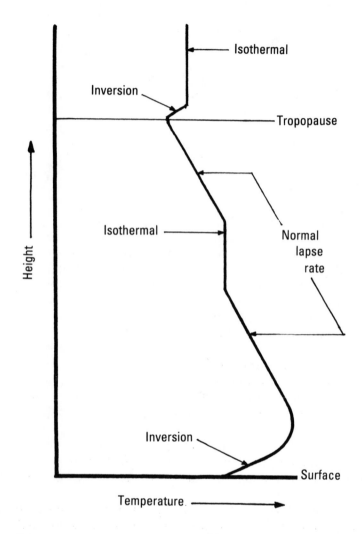

Figure 7.5. Temperature/Height diagram for Inversions and Isothermal Layers

Chapter 8
Humidity

Introduction

The term humidity refers to the amount of water vapour in the air. However, if someone enquires about 'the humidity' this is usually given as a percentage figure — say 80 per cent and means the relative humidity which will be considered later.

Water vapour is completely transparent and so knowledge of the amount actually in the air cannot be seen and has to be measured. Water vapour can change to water droplets, liquid water and to ice. When and how this occurs and the processes involved are germane to the formation of cloud and fog and to precipitation.

Water Vapour in the Air

The amount of water vapour in unit volume of air is called the Absolute Humidity and is given as grammes per cubic metre. The maximum amount of water vapour will be dependent on the temperature of the volume of air. If the temperature is high the air can hold more water vapour than air with a low temperature. When a volume of air holds the maximum amount of water vapour possible at its particular temperature, the air is said to be saturated.

Another method of expressing humidity is the Humidity Mixing Ratio. This is the weight of water vapour per mass of dry air and is expressed as grammes of water vapour per kilogramme of dry air. In effect it is the absolute humidity in terms of weight instead of volume.

The Humidity Mixing Ratio is usually given for air that is saturated. It is therefore a useful tool to show how the maximum amount of water vapour the air can hold varies at different temperatures. This is shown by graph at Figure 8.1. A study of the graph will show that at a temperature of +30°C the maximum amount of water vapour the air can hold is 28 gm per kg of dry air. Whilst at a temperature of −30°C the maximum falls to only half a gm per kg of dry air. It will thus be clear that there is a very large disparity in the ability of air to hold water vapour and this is controlled by temperature. Very simply warm air can hold very much more vapour than cold air.

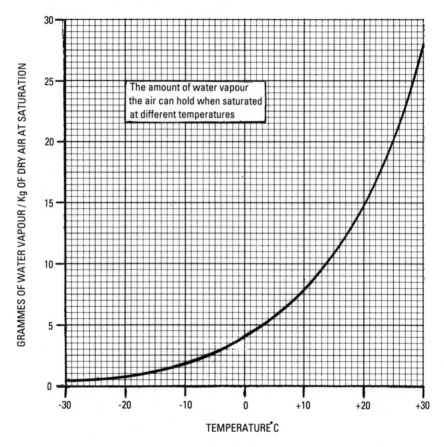

Figure 8.1. Graph of the Humidity Mixing Ratio for Saturated air at Different Temperatures

Evaporation and Condensation

Water vapour is released into the atmosphere by evaporation, i.e. by the change from liquid water to the gaseous state. Evaporation can occur at any temperature and is in fact single molecules being released from a water surface. The rate at which this occurs is much greater in warm air than in cold. Hence the use of hair dryers which are a method of warming the air allowing more rapid evaporation and hence drying of the hair itself. Nevertheless, evaporation can occur at any temperature and even from the surface of ice. Even on a cold day it is sometimes astonishing how quickly puddles on the ground can disappear by evaporation.

Evaporation stops if the air is saturated. Hence in the case of the puddles just mentioned, if the air is saturated over the puddles then evaporation stops, even on a warm day. Conversely on a cold day with a very dry wind blowing, evaporation will clear the puddles quite quickly.

Consider the graph at Figure 8.1 and suppose that the temperature is +30°C and there is 15 gm of water vapour per kg of dry air. If this air was cooled to +20°C, then it would become saturated. Hence air can become saturated by being cooled. Saturation can also occur by water vapour being added to the air.

If saturated air is cooled, then the air will give up its water vapour as water droplets. The droplets form around condensation nuclei, which can be minute particles of dust, salt, carbon etc. (These nuclei are usually hygroscopic — they have an affinity to water). A good example of the basic processes happens in a bedroom, at night, when the occupants are breathing out water vapour which gradually saturates the air in the room. The air up against the cold window glass is cooled so that the water vapour condenses out as water droplets. This is seen as condensation on the windows. To recapitulate: if air is cooled saturation can occur and if cooled further, condensation will take place.

Dewpoint
The dewpoint is the temperature to which a volume of air must be cooled at constant pressure for saturation to occur. Mention is made of constant pressure because when air is lifted, the pressure changes. This can cause dewpoint temperature changes bringing a further complication into the use of dewpoint measured at the surface.

Consider again the example where the temperature is +30°C and there is 15 gm of water vapour per kg of dry air. If this air is cooled to +20°C saturation will occur; therefore +20°C is the dewpoint temperature. Another example: air temperature +15°C with 5 gm of water vapour per kg of dry air. From the graph the dewpoint temperature is +3.3°C.

Sublimation
Water vapour can change to ice without becoming liquid. This can happen if the air is saturated and is cooled below the freezing point. This can cause frost to form on the ground. It also has application to airframe icing and to the formation of hail. A change in the reverse sense — ice to water vapour — is also called sublimation.

Saturation Vapour Pressure

In some circumstances it is convenient to refer to humidity by vapour pressure. Water vapour in the air exerts a pressure. This is referred to as a partial pressure because water vapour is a partial constituent of the air. This pressure will be a maximum when the air is saturated with water vapour. For a given vapour pressure there is only one temperature at which air will start to become saturated. This is uniquely determined by the dewpoint temperature. Further, all parcels of air having the same vapour pressure also have the same dewpoint.

When a parcel of air rises, it expands. This expansion will cause the pressure in the parcel of air to reduce. The partial pressure of the water vapour will also reduce and this reduces the dewpoint. The value of the adiabatic lapse rate of dewpoint is about ½°C per 1000 ft for unsaturated air. When the air is saturated, further lifting and cooling causes condensation. This reduces the water vapour content and thus the vapour pressure. It follows that the dewpoint will fall at a greater rate than the previous ½°C per 1000 ft.

The actual value of the saturated vapour pressure does vary with the surface over which the air is resting. It is markedly lower over an ice surface (this may be ice crystals in a cloud) than over a water surface. One result of this is sublimation. If unsaturated air is cooled below 0°C, although the vapour pressure will fall, it can reach the saturated vapour pressure level for ice before it reaches the level for a water surface. In these circumstances the water vapour in the air can change immediately to ice. The result is sublimation.

Latent Heat

For reasons of continuity the basics of latent heat are repeated here. When evaporation takes place heat is required for the process to occur. This heat does not raise the temperature of the water vapour, it is heat which is hidden. This same heat is given out when water vapour changes back to liquid water or when sublimation occurs and the water vapour changes immediately to ice. The release of the latent heat raises the temperature of the surrounding air i.e. it becomes sensible heat.

Latent heat is thus hidden heat which is absorbed or released without change of temperature when water changes state. The effects can be shown diagrammatically as follows:

Ice $\longrightarrow$ Water $\longrightarrow$ Vapour $\longrightarrow$ Latent Heat absorbed

Vapour $\longrightarrow$ Water $\longrightarrow$ Ice $\longrightarrow$ Latent Heat released

Relative Humiity
The term relative humidity (RH) is widely used to express the percentage degree of saturation of the air. Precisely it is the amount of water vapour present in a volume of air divided by the maximum amount of water vapour the air could hold at the same temperature expressed as a percentage.

Referring to Figure 8.1 and the basic situation referred to previously — temperature +30°C: 15 gm of water vapour per kg of dry air. This would provide an RH of $\frac{15\,gm}{28\,gm} = 54$ per cent.

Thus from the basic figures the graph has provided a dewpoint of +20°C and an RH of 54 per cent.

Using basic figures of temperature +20°C and 12½ gm of water vapour per kg of dry air. The RH = $\frac{12\frac{1}{2}\,gm}{15\quad gm} = 83$ per cent.

The dewpoint in this case will be approximately +17°C.

Summary
If air is cooled to the dewpoint temperature it is then saturated and the relative humidity is 100 per cent. Cooling below dewpoint temperature will cause condensation and thus dew, cloud or fog can result. As condensation takes place latent heat is released which will raise the temperature of the surroundings.

Diurnal Variation of Relative Humidity
During the day the temperature rises. As this occurs, the maximum amount of water vapour that the air could hold increases. Thus the value of relative humidity must reduce, provided the absolute amount of water in the air stays constant. The lowest RH will be at

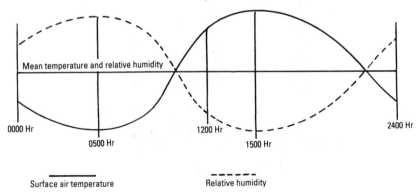

Figure 8.2. Graph of the Diurnal Variation of Relative Humidity

around 1500 hours when the temperature is highest. Similarly if the absolute humidity stays constant, after 1500 hours the temperature will reduce and thus the maximum amount of water vapour the air can hold will also reduce. Thus the relative humidity will increase. The highest RH will be at around sunrise when the temperature is lowest.

The graph of the diurnal variation of RH can be looked on as a mirror image of the graph of the diurnal variation of temperature, as shown at Figure 8.2.

Measurement of Humidity
Materials which expand and contract markedly with change of humidity such as human hair and the inside of a sheep's intestine (also known as gold beater's skin) are used as hygrometers. The most common hygrometer employs a normal mercury thermometer and another where the bulb of the instrument is kept continuously wet by means of a wet cloth around the thermometer bulb as displayed in Figure 8.3.

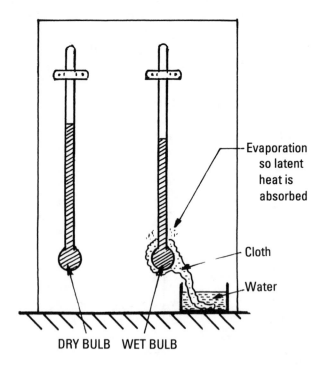

DRY BULB   WET BULB

Figure 8.3. A Wet and Dry Bulb Hygrometer

A comparison of the dry and wet bulb readings can be used as a measure of humidity. If the surrounding air is saturated, there will be no evaporation from the wet bulb and the two thermometers will have the same value. If the air is not saturated then evaporation will take place from the wet bulb. As this occurs latent heat will be absorbed from the wet bulb with the result that the wet bulb reading will be lower than the reading on the dry bulb thermometer.

The two readings can be entered in a book of tables from which absolute humidity, dewpoint and relative humidity can be extracted. It should be noted that the wet bulb temperature is the lowest temperature to which the air can be cooled by evaporation, it should not be confused with dewpoint temperature. However, if the air is saturated, then the dry bulb temperature, the wet bulb temperature and the dewpoint must be the same.

Dry Air
For the purposes of meteorology, air which is *not* saturated is termed dry air. Hence air with an RH of 99.9 per cent is termed 'dry air'.

Chapter 9
Vertical Motions of the Air

Introduction
Vertical motions include the effects of:

a) Adiabatics
b) Stability
c) Turbulence near the surface
d) Turbulence in clouds

Vertical movements concerned with clear air turbulence, mountain waves, rotors, wake turbulence and microbursts are dealt with in Chapter 16 — Aviation Hazards.

Stability and Instability
Adiabatics
When air is allowed to expand the molecules have more space in which to move; they therefore slow down thus causing a fall in temperature. Similarly if air is compressed the molecular movement space is restricted, causing them to increase their movement leading to an increase of temperature. These temperature changes thus involve no exchange of heat with the surroundings but occur within the molecular structure of the air itself. These temperature changes are called adiabatic.

Examples of adiabatic temperature changes in everyday life include the diesel engine. Here there is no ignition system *per se.* Firing of the fuel/air mixture is attained by compression of the mixture in the cylinders thus raising the temperature sufficiently for combustion to result. Another example is pumping up a bicycle tyre which causes the bottom of the pump itself to become heated due to compression of the air as pumping action takes place. When the bicycle tyre valve is undone the air rushes out from the inner tube and expands as it meets the lower pressure outside. The result is a drop in temperature of the air from the tyre.

If a volume of air is made to rise it will move to a region of lower pressure. The air will therefore expand — the volume becoming greater — and the lifted air will immediately cool adiabatically. It will be recalled that air is a poor conductor of heat and therefore any lowering of temperature in the lifted air due to the colder environment above would take some time. Hence the only reason that lifted air cools in a sensible time span can only be due to adiabatic expansion.

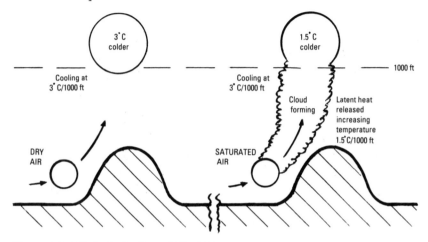

Figure 9.1. Adiabatic Cooling of Lifted Air

The rate at which lifted air cools adiabatically is constant and has a value of 3°C per 1000 ft (1°C per 100 metres). Consider now two equal volumes of air being lifted to the same level. One of these volumes is dry whilst the other is saturated. This is displayed at Figure 9.1. The saturated air cools in a similar fashion to the dry air 3°C per 1000 ft. However, if saturated air is lifted and cooled condensation will take place, the water vapour condensing out as droplets forming cloud. As this occurs latent heat is released and this will reduce the rate of cooling. In temperate latitudes near the surface the average value of this heating is 1½°C per 1000 ft. Therefore if saturated air is cooled at 3°C per 1000 ft and is also heated at 1½C per 1000 ft the result is a lapse rate of 1½C per 1000 ft (½°C per 100 metres).

The adiabatic lapse rate for dry air is therefore 3°C per 1000 ft. Whilst the average lapse rate for saturated air is 1½°C per 1000 ft. The difference being due to the release of latent heat in the case of saturated air.

The Variable Saturated Adiabatic Lapse Rate

The Saturated Adiabatic Lapse Rate (SALR) averages 1½°C per 1000 ft and this applies when the surface air temperature is about

+10°C. It will be recalled that the amount of water vapour actually in the air at saturation depends on the temperature. The amount increases as the temperature at saturation increases (the graph at Figure 8.1 refers).

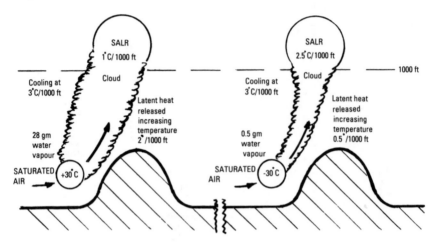

Figure 9.2. Variation of SALR with Temperature

Consider the two 1 kg parcels of air at Figure 9.2. One is saturated at −30°C and the other is saturated at +30°C. Both parcels will be cooled at 3°C per 1000 ft and both will be heated by the release of latent heat as the saturated air is lifted and condensation occurs. In the case of the lifted air at +30°C there will be some 28 gm of water vapour in the air per kg of dry air in accordance with the graph at Figure 8.1. When this condenses out there will be a large release of temperature from this source of say, 2°C per 1000 ft and the resulting SALR would be about 1°C per 1000 ft.

The colder parcel of air at −30°C will contain about ½ gm of water vapour per kg of dry air, again Figure 8.1 refers. When this condenses out due to the lifting and adiabatic cooling, there will again be a release of latent heat. However, this will be considerably less than the heating in the warmer air as there is less water vapour present. Supposing the heating is of the order of say ½°C per 1000 ft, the resulting SALR would be about 2½°C per 1000 ft. This small amount of water vapour condensing out at the low temperature can be illustrated by the clouds which form under these conditions. At heights where temperatures are low, the clouds which form are very thin because there is little water vapour in the air although saturated, to condense out and form the cloud. At

58

these heights close to the tropopause, the heating effect due to condensation is very small and in fact SALR and DALR (Dry Adiabatic Lapse Rate) are both 3°C per 1000 ft. The same can apply at the surface at high latitudes where again temperatures can be very low.

Descending Air

The case of air being lifted and the subsequent lapse rates is important because it has a direct bearing on cloud formation. Air can be made to descend as well as to rise. This occurs in clouds and also with anticyclones. In this latter case the air diverges from the centre of the anticyclone at the surface causing subsidence of the air above. The result is adiabatic warming of the descending air as it is forced to a lower level where the pressure is greater. As previously mentioned this compression of the air can cause a temperature inversion.

Stability

If a volume of air is blown against a building and lifted, when that air has moved away from the buildings and is in the lee, one of two things will happen. Either the air will tend to sink back to the ground, or alternatively, it will continue to rise. These two conditions are representative of atmospheric conditions which are termed stable or unstable respectively.

The atmosphere is said to be stable, if when air is lifted and the lifting force is removed the rising air tends to return to its original

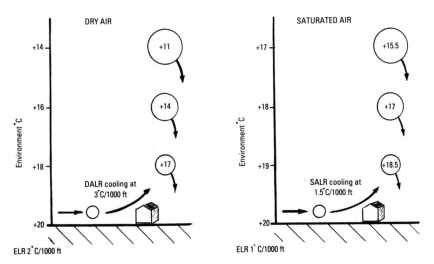

Figure 9.3. Stability of Lifted Air

level. This situation must appertain if the lifted volume of air as it rises, becomes colder than the atmosphere at the same level. The volume would then be denser and heavier than the surrounding air, which we can term the environmental air, and will therefore try to sink.

The lapse rate in the surrounding air within which a volume of air is being lifted is termed the environmental lapse rate. This is important as it largely controls whether the atmosphere is stable or unstable. The average environmental lapse rate (ELR) is of course 2°C per 1000 ft (⅔°C per 100 metres). However, it is variable. During the day when the earth is well heated, the lapse rate in the very low levels can be around 3°C per 1000 ft. Equally, at night there is often a low level inversion if there is a clear night sky. Figure 9.3 shows that if the ELR is less than 3°C per 1000 ft for dry air or less than 1½°C per 1000 ft for saturated air, the atmosphere is stable.

Instability

The atmosphere is said to be unstable if when air is lifted and the lifting force is removed, the rising air continues to ascend. This situation must apply if the lifted volume of air is progressively warmer than the surrounding air within which it is rising, because then it is less dense and lighter. This is displayed at Figure 9.4 which shows that if the ELR is greater than 3°C per 1000 ft for dry air, or greater than 1½°C per 1000 ft for saturated air the atmosphere is unstable.

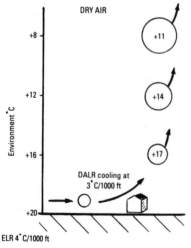

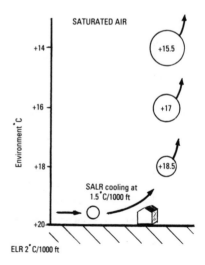

Figure 9.4. Instability of Lifted Air

Conditional Instability

When the ELR is between 1.5°C and 3°C per 1000 ft the atmosphere is said to be conditionally unstable. Under these conditions the atmosphere is stable if dry and unstable if saturated. Figure 9.5 refers. This is the most likely situation as the average ELR is 2°C per 1000 ft. Further, it would be most unusual for an ELR to reach a value of 4°C as supposed at Figure 9.4. An ELR of less than 2°C per 1000 ft is quite common and so is full stability.

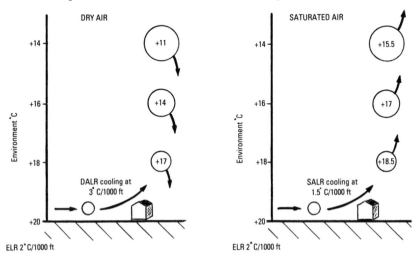

Figure 9.5. Conditional Instability of Lifted Air

Stability in Practice

The state of the lower atmosphere with respect to stability will affect the degree of uplift of rising air and this in turn will enhance or reduce the effect of turbulence as explained below. Further, the formation of cloud is directly affected by the state of stability and controls the basic type of cloud which forms. For all practical purposes: an ELR of less than 1½°C per 1000 ft equals stability. An ELR of less than 3°C per 1000 ft when the air is dry equals stability. An ELR of less than 3°C per 1000 ft but greater than 1½°C per 1000 ft when the air is saturated equalls instability. These factors are considered further in the next chapter.

Turbulence

Turbulence Near the Surface

Turbulence in the lower few thousands of feet next to the earth's surface is mainly caused by thermal turbulence and mechanical turbulence.

61

Thermal Turbulence

When insolation takes place the heated earth will also heat the air in contact by conduction. This heated air being less dense will rise causing convection currents. These currents will interfere with the normal flow of wind over the surface of the earth and thus turbulence will occur. This turbulence will be enhanced when the insolation at the surface varies as this will also vary the strength of the convection currents. Clearly these effects are most marked on a warm sunny day in summer around 1500 hours when insolation is greatest.

Mechanical Turbulence

A surface wind blowing against physical obstructions such as hills, mountains, coastlines, trees or buildings can be forced up and down thereby causing turbulence. The more rugged the terrain and the stronger the wind the more marked the turbulence. A good example of severe mechanical turbulence occurs around the rock of Gibraltar. The effects are such that the Gibraltar runway is unusable with the wind blowing around the rock from certain directions. When this happens the airfield at Gibraltar is closed to all traffic.

Friction Layer

The depth of the turbulent or friction layer where thermal and mechanical turbulence occurs has an average value of 2000 ft from the earth's surface. This depth will be increased:

a) If the surface wind is strong;
b) if the surface is rugged, variable and easily accepts insolation;
c) in summer around 1500 hours, and lastly
d) if the atmosphere is unstable because then, the lifted air, once disturbed from the surface will continue to rise.

Additionally, all these factors will tend to enhance the vigour of the turbulence.

The turbulence in the friction layer can thus affect a pilot's ability to maintain a required approach path and touch down. This is shown diagrammatically at Figure 9.6.

Turbulence in Clouds

All clouds are formed by air being lifted. Some of this air will inevitably tend to descend due to gravity and also because the water droplets and ice crystals in the cloud will try to fall. Each droplet or crystal will bring air with it as it descends. These up and down currents cause turbulence in varying degrees, dependent on cloud size and formation. The one factor which will be all important for the degree of turbulence in the cloud is stability.

Clouds formed in unstable conditions will have increased uplift and this will increase turbulence. In stable conditions which will tend to restrict the uplift and depth of the cloud, only light turbulence should apply.

Turbulence Description
The Turbulence is described as 'Light', 'Moderate' or 'Severe'. The full meaning of these terms is given at Chapter 19.

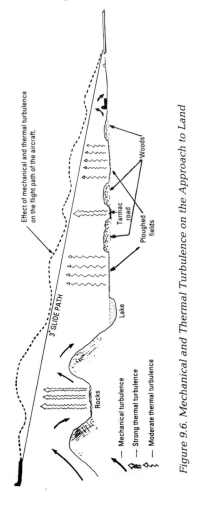

Figure 9.6. Mechanical and Thermal Turbulence on the Approach to Land

Chapter 10
Clouds and Precipitation

Clouds

Introduction

Clouds are the meteorological signposts in the sky. They can tell the pilot if flight is going to be turbulent, if there will be difficulties regarding visibility and the type of precipitation that may occur. Even more importantly they can give warning of dangers and assist in foretelling the weather for some hours ahead.

Clouds are simply collections of water droplets or ice crystals, or a combination of both in particular formations. They appear white when the sun is able to reflect from the water or ice and grey or dark grey when hidden from sunlight. Hence many clouds will look dark from underneath, but sparkling white from above. The average life of a cloud is some 15 to 20 minutes. By the end of this time, the contents have evaporated, or alternatively there has been precipitation. The exception to this general statement concerns Cumulonimbus (CB) and thunderstorms in particular where the time period from development to dissipation averages two to three hours.

The two main methods of classifying clouds is by the height bands within which they form and secondly by the formation occuring in either stable or unstable conditions. These two conditions lead to clouds being specified as Layer or Heap respectively. All clouds form by air being lifted and cooled adiabatically to below dewpoint temperature. The water vapour then condenses out as droplets or directly as ice crystals by sublimation. Some of the water droplets can exist at temperatures well below zero and become supercooled. These droplets are important in the formation of ice on an airframe.

Cloud Types

The cloud types by name and abbreviation are shown below with reference to the height bands within which they are normally found in the temperate latitudes. It will be noted that the medium level clouds are given a top height of 23000 ft whilst the bottom height for the high level clouds is 16500 ft. The reason for this apparent overlap is that in summer the former can extend above 16500 ft, and in winter the lower level of the band within which the high clouds are found descends from 23000 ft to 16500 ft. Photographs of the different cloud types together with cloud details are in the centre pages.

Layer Clouds — Formed in Stable Conditions:

Cirrus	— CI	High level clouds
Cirrocumulus	— CC	16500 ft to 45000 ft.
Cirrostratus	— CS	

Altostratus	— AS	Medium level clouds
Altocumulus	— AC	6500 ft to 23000 ft.

Nimbostratus	— NS	Low level clouds
Stratocumulus	— SC	surface to 6500 ft.
Stratus	— ST	

Heap Clouds — Formed in Unstable Conditions:

Cumulus	— CU	Surface to some 25000 ft.
Cumulonimbus	— CB	Surface to Tropopause.
Altocumulus Castellanus	— ACc	65000 ft to 23000 ft.

Whilst NS is listed as a low cloud, it can extend into the medium level and act like a heap cloud if there is very strong lifting. Altocumulus can develop into a heap cloud when a stable atmosphere suddenly changes to instability.

The layer clouds concern stable conditions in which lifted air will necessarily be restricted in the height of ascent. For this reason they will spread out and be large horizontally whilst vertically they will be small. The heap clouds form in unstable conditions where lifting is not restricted, in fact it is enhanced by the instability. Hence the clouds which form are small horizontally but large in the vertical.

Cloud Amounts, Base and Tops
Cloud amounts are reported and forecast as the number of eighths or oktas of the sky which is cloud covered. Thus 8/8 indicates that the sky is completely cloud covered. Other terms used include:

SKC	=	Sky clear
SCT	=	Scattered — 1/8 to 4/8
BKN	=	Broken — 5/8 to 7/8
OVC	=	Overcast — 8/8

For CB cloud only:
ISOL — Isolated — Individual CB.
OCNL — Occasional — well separated CB.
FRQ — Frequent — CB with little or no separation.
EMBD — Embedded — CB contained in layers of other cloud
(usually NS)

Knowledge of cloud base is very important, particularly to a pilot on the descent to an airfield through cloud. Cloud base is given as the height of the base of the cloud above a particular level. It is also sometimes referred to as the condensation level. For aerodrome reports and forecasts the base is the height above the official aerodrome level. For large international aerodromes reports should refer to the approach area, or for airfields equipped with ILS (Instrument Landing System) reference should be to the site of the Middle Marker beacon. Bases can be estimated by competent observers (this includes ATC personnel). They can also be measured by balloon, by aircraft observation and by cloud base recorder equipment.

Clearly the height of the cloud base must be dependent on how high the air has to be lifted for saturation and condensation to occur. Therefore the closer the values of air temperature and dewpoint, the lower the cloud base will be at an airfield location. As the air temperature rises so should the cloud base, for the air has to be lifted further to be cooled below dewpoint. Therefore, other things being equal, cloud bases should be highest around 1500 hours.

Cloud tops, i.e. the height or heights of the top of cloud will be controlled by the amount of lifting of the air and also by its water vapour content. For if air is lifted to say 4000 ft and all the water vapour has been condensed out then no further cloud will form. In practice it more frequently occurs that the amount of lifting is the first control and the second concerns how dry the air is into which the lifted air is ascending. If condensation takes place into very dry air the water droplets quickly evaporate and the cloud will stop at that level. This situation can often apply with heap clouds. For obvious reasons it is difficult to determine the height of cloud tops from the ground. Pilots are therefore frequently asked to report the height of cloud tops on climb-out.

Cloud Formation
When air is lifted to the condensation level the water vapour condenses out on to hygroscopic nuclei. These are small particles of

dust, salt, or carbon which readily absorb water vapour and can even cause saturation when the RH is less than 100 per cent. The methods by which air is lifted to form cloud are sometimes termed cloud triggers. The analogy being that the atmosphere is like a gun always ready to fire and produce cloud — the trigger being the lifting agent. These lifting agents or triggers involve:

a) Turbulence.
b) Convection.
c) Orographic lifting.
d) Frontal lifting.
e) Convergence.

Turbulence Cloud

Turbulence can provide low level layer cloud — ST or SC — which in turn can give precipitation in the form of drizzle or light rain or snow. The conditions necessary for this cloud to form are:

a) Stable air.
b) Turbulence to steepen the lapse rate.
c) A condensation level within the turbulent layer.

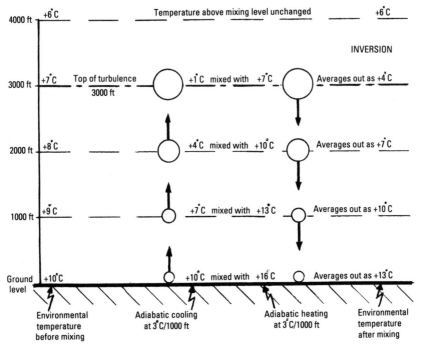

10.1. A Modified Temperature Regime in a Turbulent Layer

67

Consider Figure 10.1 which shows a stable ELR at 1°C per 1000 ft and turbulence from the surface up to 3000 ft. Suppose that the turbulence initially lifts a parcel of air from the surface to the top of the turbulent layer. If this air is dry it will cool from the surface temperature, adiabatically, at 3°C per 1000 ft. The temperature structure in this lifted air is shown in the diagram. Similarly, initial turbulence will cause a parcel of air at the top of the layer to be dragged down to the surface. This parcel will heat adiabatically from the 3000 ft temperature, at 3°C per 1000 ft. Again the temperature structure of this descending air is shown in the diagram. Subsequently all the air will be turbulently mixed below 3000 ft and two particular factors emerge. The surface temperature is raised by the turbulence, secondly the lapse rate has now increased to 3°C per 1000 ft. Note that the temperature above the 3000 ft turbulent layer is now warmer than the air below, i.e. a temperature inversion has been formed.

If we now introduce a dewpoint value into the situation of say + 7°C it will be seen from Figure 10.2 that the air will be saturated at 2000 ft and the cloud base should be just above this level. The cloud top will be coincident with the top of the turbulent layer —

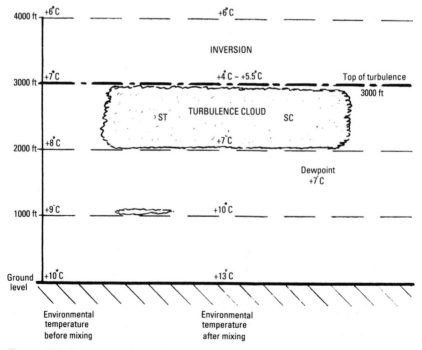

Figure 10.2. Formation of Turbulence Cloud

the atmosphere being stable, no more lifting will occur. Within the cloud the SALR will be some 1½°C per 1000 ft, even so, this will still produce an inversion above the cloud. For this reason the cloud will have a flat top. Figure 10.1 shows initial lifting and a small volume of air at +7°C. This can produce some broken cloud below the subsequent main cloud base. This is often observed in practice. The temperature height diagram at Figure 10.3 shows the ELR

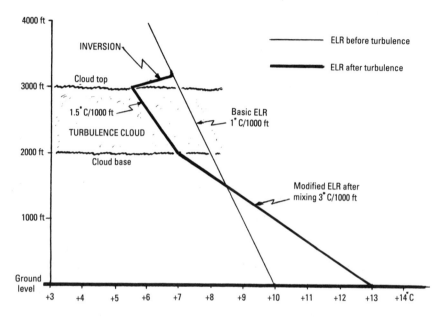

Figure 10.3. Temperature/Height Diagram for Turbulence Cloud Formation

before turbulence, the ELR after turbulence, cloud base and cloud top and the relevant temperature profiles.

Mechanical turbulence will usually require a windspeed greater than 10 kn although once the cloud has formed the cloud may persist with a lower windspeed. Clearly there will be turbulent conditions inside and under the cloud. Above the cloud in the inversion, conditions will be very smooth. The cloud will be continually forming during turbulent ascent and evaporating in descent. When these processes occur as a layer of air rising and falling and particularly with thermal turbulence, the cloud type is more likely to be stratocumulus than stratus. Although the precipitation type is drizzle or light, frequently there will be no precipitation but very dull overcast conditions. These clouds often form on the edges of anticyclones where the air is stable but some turbulence is evident. Stratus will often result from fog overland, which has been lifted due to an increasing windspeed. A typical scenario being: fog at night which thickens soon after dawn due to initial thermal turbulence and then with a strengthening wind the fog being lifted to form stratus with a rising cloud base as the day progresses: sometimes followed by evaporation and clearance.

Convection

Air heated by conduction over a land surface rises and if cooled below dewpoint produces cloud. If this occurs in a stable friction layer then stratocumulus is likely to form as a turbulence cloud. If the lifting is from discrete warm spots such as roads, runways etc. then the parcels of lifted air can progress above the friction layer producing individual clouds of the cumulus type. Where the cloud is restricted to a few thousand feet by lack of sufficient lift, stability or dryness of the air, the cloud is termed fair weather cumulus. These are isolated clouds, of insufficient size to give precipitation and are usually produced in an otherwise clear sky hence the term fair weather. These clouds move quickly with the winds allowing other clouds to form over the same areas. They soon cease in the evening as the surface temperature falls. When fair weather CU is seen in the early morning after sunrise it will often result in large CU or CB later in the day as the surface temperature rises, increasing the strength of lifting. If the fair weather CU appears later in the day then it will simply confirm the good weather during the day and quickly disappear in the early evening. This situation can often be seen in the Mediterranean coastal regions in summer. If similar lifting occurs in an unstable or conditionally unstable environment then the cumulus clouds can have considerable depth and may develop into cumulonimbus and produce heavy showers. This latter case is more likely in the late afternoon in summer when the surface land temperatures are high. Again, these clouds will tend to die out in the early evening.

A simple temperature/height diagram for convection cloud is at Figure 10.4. This is self explanatory. The more detailed diagram at Figure 10.5 shows the surface temperature at dawn of $+10°C$ and the early morning inversion just above the surface. Thereafter an average lapse rate in the environment of $2°C$ per 1000 ft is assumed. If it is supposed that the dewpoint temperature is $+6°C$ then it is possible to trace what happens as the air temperature rises. If the surface heating after dawn raises the surface temperature to $+13°C$ the air will rise, cooling at the DALR of $3°C$ per 1000 ft. As a result, the lifted air at 1000 ft will have a temperature

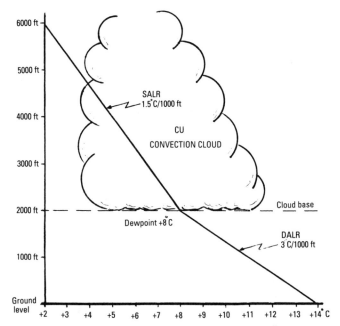

Figure 10.4. Simple Temperature/Height Diagram for Convection Cloud Formation

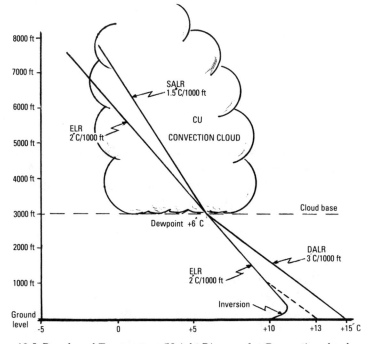

Figure 10.5. Developed Temperature/Height Diagram for Convection cloud

71

of +10°C, the same temperature as the environment. Therefore this dry air will not rise any further. Suppose now that the surface air temperature is raised later in the day to +15°C, this air will rise and also cool at 3°C per 1000 ft. It will not be at the same temperature as the environment until a height of 3000 ft when the temperature will be +6°C. It will then be at dewpoint temperature and be saturated. Thenceforth lifting will produce cloud and cooling will be at the SALR of around 1½°C per 1000 ft. The temperature of +15°C in this instance is called the Critical Temperature, i.e. the surface temperature to which the air must be heated for cloud to form. As the surface temperature increases above the critical value the cloud base must rise. This is a normal expectation and convection cloud bases will normally rise as a day progresses. The cloud will then evaporate as the temperature and lift reduces in the early evening.

Advection
When surface air temperature is modified by movement from one surface, to another it is called advection. The particular case of cold air moving over a progressively warmer sea surface can cause advection and instability. The mechanics are the same as for convection cloud and can result in the development of large CU and CB with shower activity. Such a situation appertains over the UK with a northwesterly airflow. These clouds will continue to form over the sea day and night. Overland however they will tend to clear due to the cold ground at night.

Orographic Lifting
Lifting against hills, mountains and coastlines can result in mechanical turbulence and the development of ST and SC when the conditions are stable. If the lifting is through the surface friction layer then, again in stable conditions AC can form. The AC often occurs in a lenticular form where the air is lifted on the upwind side of the hills, becoming saturated, is lifted further causing cloud to form over the crest. Thereafter the air descends and warms because of the stability, causing rapid evaporation of the cloud droplets. The result of this is a shallow cloud with pointed ends taking the shape of a lens in cross section — hence lenticular cloud. These lenticular clouds are firm evidence that mountain waves are present (see Chapter 16). The accompanying turbulence may or may not be severe. The AC lenticular can sometimes be seen from the surface as a series of lines of cloud. This can be the familiar mackerel sky. From above it can appear as a series of 'streets' of cloud below the

flight level, the streets being parallel to the mountain or hill ranges. If conditions are unstable or conditionally unstable the cloud type will be CU or CB with the clouds forming predominantly on the upwind side and the crest of the high ground. Sometimes there is orographic lifting and the stable atmospheric conditions change to instability. This causes an increase in lifting and the AC cloud can develop separate vertical towers and become AC Castellanus. These castle like protuberances indicate that the atmosphere has suddenly become unstable and are often a forerunner of thunderstorms within the next 24 hours. (Stratocumulus can also be castellanus, but at this level the degree of instability may be confined to a relatively shallow vertical band). Clouds already formed by other triggers can be moved close to high ground. They can then become deeper in the vertical and produce larger and heavier concentrations of water droplets as a result of the effect of the orographic lifting. On the downwind side of high ground there is often a region sometimes referred to as the 'Rain Shadow'. Most of the cloud and subsequent precipitation occurs on the upwind side and above the crest of high ground so that the lee or downwind side is relatively precipitation free — hence rain shadow. Figure 10.6 shows typical orographic cloud formations in stable and unstable conditions.

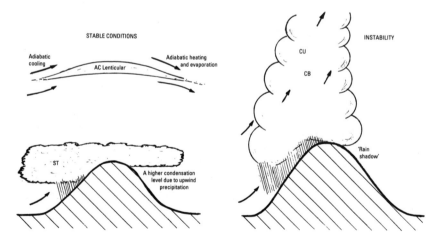

Figure 10.6. Orographic Cloud Formations

Frontal Lifting

The essence of frontal lifting is the meeting of two air masses of different temperature. When this occurs the warmer less dense air will attempt to rise over the colder heavier air. From another viewpoint, the colder denser air will undercut the warmer lighter air. The result is frontal lifting, for the surface where the two air masses meet is termed a front. Whilst fronts themselves are considered in depth in later chapters, there are two fronts of particular significance, a warm front and a cold front. Consider the air masses meeting at Figure 10.7. The lifting which occurs at the

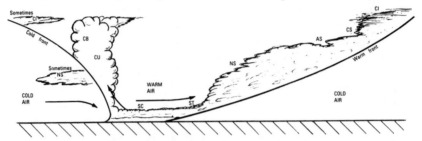

Figure 10.7. Frontal Cloud Formations

warm front concerns stable air and stability type cloud is formed in sequence from the surface. These types most frequently involve ST, NS, AS, CS and CI. The actual slope of the warm frontal surface is quite shallow at low level and then steepens so that the average slope is in the region of 1 in 150 to 1 in 100. It has been established that all lifted dry air cools adiabatically, as the sole reason for cooling, at 3°C per 1000 ft. Hence for all clouds considered so far the lapse rate under the cloud must be 3°C per 1000 ft. However, in this case where air is lifted up a sloping surface and cooling at the DALR, the vertical lapse rate under the cloud will be something less than 3° and will be closer to the average ELR of 2°C per 1000 ft. The slope of the lifting surface at the cold front is very close to vertical at the lower levels. The cloud which forms is CU CB as the lifted air is unstable or made unstable by the lifting. In this case the lapse rate under the cloud is 3°C per 1000 ft for all practical purposes. Even in this situation where instability is the expectation, there can be an odd shallow stability layer in the air and this can sometimes cause some NS and at the higher level, CI to form. There is also a degree of convergence at a front. A study of Figure 10.8

Figure 10.8. Convergence at a Front

shows the surface winds meeting at the front and converging, this will assist the lifting process and the formation of clouds.

Convergence

If there are no frontal surfaces but convergence is present then the subsequent lifting will cause cloud to form. The prime case of convergence cloud occurs at a non-frontal trough of low pressure (see Figures 10.9 and 10.10). Here the convergence of the surface

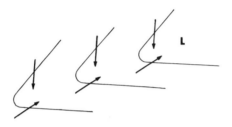

Figure 10.9. Non Frontal Convergence at a Trough of Low

winds will cause lifting and despite the fact that the atmosphere is stable (ELR 2°C per 1000 ft and dry), the lifting will quickly cause saturation and instability. This will result in the development of CU CB along the trough line. If the air was very stable then turbulence cloud could occur, but most frequently the air is subject to strong vertical uplift due to the convergence with the result that the atmosphere can be made unstable by the lifting process, if it is not already in an unstable state.

Convective Instability

Air can be made unstable by lifting as shown at Figure 10.10. Consider Figure 10.11. In this case the means of lifting are orographic, but it could equally apply to the other forms of lifting. The ELR varies between 1°C and 2°C per 1000 ft and the condition is stable. A strong wind is blowing environmental air against a hillside and this lifted air is cooled at the DALR of 3°C per 1000 ft until it becomes saturated i.e. at the dewpoint temperature of +6°C. If the lifting force of the wind is strong enough to lift the now saturated air to above 7000 ft it will be seen that at this level the lifted air is warmer than the environment and now there is instability. In Chapter 9 the possibility of an ELR greater than 3°C per 1000 ft was postulated as a means of atmospheric instability. In practice an ELR of this high value is a rare occurence. Therefore

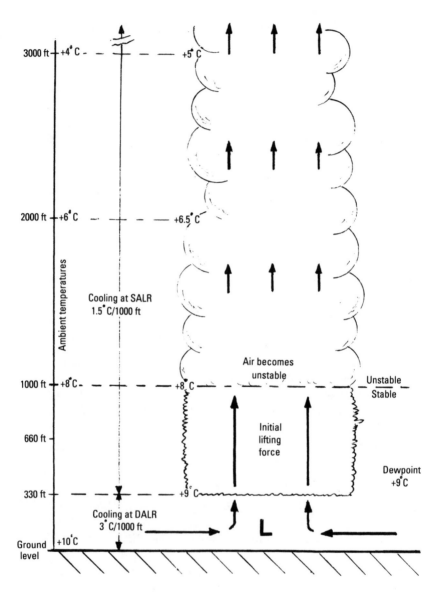

Figure 10.10. Convergence Causing Lifting

instability is almost invariably caused by the lifting of moist air as detailed above. Figures 10.10 and 10.11 show two reasonably extreme cases of convective instability. The extremes, or the facility with which the air is made unstable, being governed by the ELR and the humidity state.

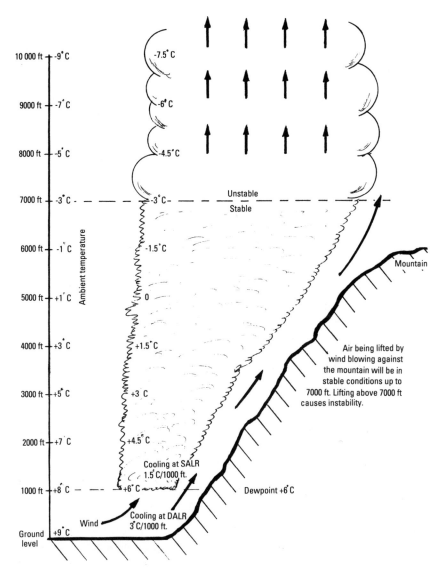

Figure 10.11. Convective Instability

Precipitation

There are three separate types of water formation in clouds: water, ice and supercooled water. The latter are water droplets still in the liquid state at temperatures below, and even well below (down to − 45°C) zero °C. All three types can produce precipitation.

When condensation first occurs at a cloud base the condensed droplets are very small, but they grow quickly in size by collision with other droplets. This process then produces cloud droplets which eventually become rain drops which vary in size between 0.2 mm diameter and 5.5 mm diameter. This larger size is the maximum to which a cloud droplet can grow. Any growth beyond this size results in a loss of surface tension and the droplet will then split into separate parts. An important by-product of this process is a release of static electricity as the splitting occurs. The growth of droplets will be greater in clouds where the upcurrents are strongest so that the droplets have a longer cloud life before precipitating. Hence the larger droplets are to be found in clouds formed in unstable conditions, i.e. CU CB. A full understanding of the causes of precipitation has yet to be totally accepted. There are two particular theories: Bergeron, which supposes that there must be ice crystals in the cloud tops which in falling to the lower levels grow to emerge from the cloud as snowflakes or raindrops dependent on temperature. The Coalescense theory suggests that there will be more large water droplets near a cloud top due to the rising air and the subsequent collisions or coalescence. This higher concentration of water is said to be due to the slower movement upwards of larger droplets allowing a greater chance of collisions.

Eventually the larger droplets will fall from the cloud setting up a chain reaction. Clearly there will not be ice crystals in all clouds. Nonetheless, the two theories do suggest a requirement for a greater droplet size/concentration to apply, compared with a non-precipitating cloud. It is therefore not a particular over simplification to state that where the strength of the upcurrents becomes insufficiently strong to support the weight of water and or ice crystals in the cloud, precipitation will take place. The types of precipitation include:

a) Drizzle — very small rain drops — 0.2 mm diameter. (It provides no noticeable impact on a water surface).

b) Rain — from 0.2 mm to 5.5 mm diameter (impact with a water surface is seen).

c) Snow — ice in the form of crystals in:
   i) formation as grains.
   ii) formation as needles.
   iii) composite crystals making snowflakes.

d) Sleet — a mixture of rain and snow.

e) Hail — ice in the form of pellets or balls. These can grow to some 1 kg in weight and 8 cm across.

Snow can reach the ground still in its frozen state with a surface temperature up to +4°C. Usually the flakes are larger when the temperature is close to freezing point.

Hail starts as an ice crystal and then grows by two processes: collision with supercooled water droplets and sublimation where the water vapour in the cloud changes immediately into ice on to the crystals or growing hail. When sublimation takes place static electricity is released into the cloud. A large number of transits up and down inside the cloud is necessary for hail to form. This can only happen in CB apart from extremely exceptional circumstances. It is therefore considered a fact that hail only forms and falls from CB. Large sized hail is common in tropical storms containing CB but is rare in the temperate zone CB clouds. The table below shows the intensity and type of precipitation expected from the different cloud types.

Layer		Heap	
Stability Clouds		*Instability Clouds*	
CI CS CC	— Nil	CU —	Slight/moderate showers
ST (sometimes SC)	— Drizzle	CB —	Heavy showers can be of hail
AS AC) ST SC)	— Slight continuous		
NS	— Moderate continuous		

Note: There is no precipitation from the CI CS CC because as the small ice crystals fall from high level they will be heated and evaporate completely before reaching lower levels.

Chapter 11
Low Level Winds

Introduction

Wind is the sustained movement of air from one place to another. The term wind velocity refers to both speed and direction. Wind direction is always given as the direction from which the wind is blowing and is given as degrees true in written form. Verbally, from the control tower it is given in degrees magnetic so that direction relative to a runway can be assessed. Terms veer and back are used to indicate direction changes: A veer is a change in a clockwise direction (e.g. 120° to 170°) and a back is a change in an anticlockwise sense (e.g. 300° to 260°).

Windspeed is given in knots (kn or kt). Terms gust, squall and gale are used to indicate speed changes. A gust is a sudden increase in windspeed often with a change in direction; it lasts for a few seconds only and is very local in effect. A squall is similar to a gust except that it lasts for some minutes, can cover a few square miles in area and is particularly associated with the passage of CB clouds. Where CB with or without thunderstorms form in a line at a cold front there can be a squall under each CB and this is referred to as a line squall. A gale is used to describe a mean wind speed of 34 kn or more or a wind which is gusting to 43 kn or more. Gale warnings are important when light aircraft are parked on an airfield. They should then be tethered, or turned into wind or both.

Surface Wind Forces

When a surface wind is reported or given from the control tower, by international agreement it is the wind at 33 ft above ground level (10 metres). This height is now akin to cockpit height for some of the largest passenger aircraft. In some forecasts, particularly for shipping, wind speeds are given by Beaufort scale number. This scale was a means of estimating windspeed by reference to the appearance of the sea and the effect on sailing ships. It has now been adapted for use on land according to the effects on smoke, trees and buildings so that a scale number is given which relates to a particular speed band. The Beaufort Scale is shown at Figure 11.1.

There are 3 principal forces acting on the air at the surface, they are Pressure Gradient Force, Geostrophic Force and Friction. It is

THE BEAUFORT SCALE OF WIND FORCE

Beaufort Number	Descriptive Title	Specification for use on land	Average speeds	
			Km/hr.	Knots
0	Calm	Smoke rises vertically	1	0
1	Light air	Direction shown by smoke but not by wind vanes	4	2
2	Light breeze	Wind felt on face; leaves rustle; ordinary vane moved by wind	9	5
3	Gentle breeze	Leaves and small twigs in constant motion; wind extends light flag	17	9
4	Moderate breeze	Raises dust and loose paper; small branches are moved	25	14
5	Fresh breeze	Small trees in leaf begin to sway; crested wavelets form on inland waters	31	19
6	Strong breeze	Large branches in motion; whistling heard in telegraph wires; umbrellas used with difficulty	40	24
7	Moderate gale	Whole trees in motion; inconvenience felt when walking against the wind	49	30
8	Fresh gale	Breaks twigs off trees; generally impedes progress	60	37
9	Strong gale	Slight structural damage occurs (chimney pots and slates removed)	71	44
10	Whole gale	Seldom experienced inland; trees uprooted; considerable structural damage occurs	84	52
11	Storm	Very rarely experienced; accompanied by widespread damage	97	60
12	Hurricane		Above 105	Above 65

Figure 11.1. The Beaufort Wind Scale

more convenient at this stage to consider the wind just above the friction layer, i.e. above say 2000 ft and to consider the wind within the friction layer subsequently. The Pressure Gradient Force (PGF) is the force caused by the pressure gradient which tries to move air from high pressure to low pressure as shown in Figure 11.2. The

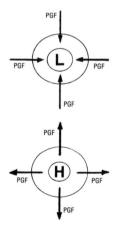

Figure 11.2. Pressure Gradient Force Acting on the air

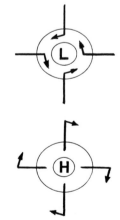

Figure 11.3. The Effect of Geostrophic Force on Moving Air

Geostrophic Force (GF) is the force caused by the rotation of the earth and this rotation will affect air which is moving within the atmosphere. It will turn a volume of moving air to the right in the northern hemisphere as shown in Figure 11.3. In the southern hemisphere moving air will be turned to the left. It can be seen that winds blow clockwise around an anticyclone and anticlockwise around a depression in the northern hemisphere. In the southern hemisphere this is reversed. It will be recalled that Buys Ballot explained this succintly by saying that with your back to the wind in the northern hemisphere low pressure will be on your left and in the southern hemisphere, on your right. The value of PGF is apparent from the value of the pressure gradient and can be assessed from the distance between isobars. The value of PGF is given by the formula:

$$GF = 2 \, \Omega \, \rho \, V \text{ sine latitude}$$

where Ω = The constant angular rotation of the earth, ρ = Density and V = Windspeed. From the formula it can be seen that there is a direct relationship between the three variable factors and geostrophic force. If density, windspeed or latitude increase, so does the value of geostrophic force. The formula also shows that within 5° of the equator (sine 5° = 0.07) the GF is virtually zero and within 15° of the equator (sine 15° = 0.26) it is very small. Further the geostrophic force cannot come into play until the air has moved under the influence of PGF.

Geostrophic Wind
In a relatively constant situation but with windspeed gradually increasing to a particular value, GF would do the same, increasing

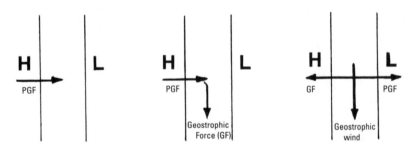

Figure 11.4. PGF, GF and Balanced Air Flow

with windspeed. The two force values can then be the same. Where this occurs, PGF and GF are in balance and the wind is said to be 'geostrophic'. At Figure 11.4 are three north hemisphere diagrams showing PGF, the effect of GF and lastly the balanced flow situation where PGF and GF are equal. The diagrams show that the geostrophic wind blows parallel to the isobars such that with one's back to the wind in the northern hemisphere, low pressure is on the left. Low pressure would be on the right in the southern hemisphere. Speed of the wind is indirectly proportional to the distance between the isobars, as this distance reduces the speed will increase. The other important force concerns friction and the geostrophic wind can only apply above the friction layer.

The windspeed V can be resolved in the geostrophic formula as follows:

$$GF = 2\,\Omega\,\rho\,V \text{ sine latitude}$$

$$\therefore V = \frac{GF}{2\,\Omega\,\rho \text{ sine latitude}}$$

If the wind is geostrophic then PGF = GF hence:

$$V = \frac{PGF}{2\,\Omega\,\rho \text{ sine latitude}}$$

This formula shows that for a particular PGF value (or distance between the isobars) as the latitude reduces, so does sine latitude and therefore V, the windspeed will increase. This applies down to a latitude of 15°, below which the geostrophic formula breaks down and Buys Ballot's law no longer applies. For a small latitude band and a density for a small altitude band, the bottom half of this equation, with Ω standard, could be replaced by a constant. Thus:

$$V \text{ (windspeed)} = \frac{PGF}{K}$$

These facts are used to produce a scale called the Geostrophic Wind Scale. This can be in the form of a scaled ruler that can be used directly on a weather chart and be placed perpendicularly across the isobars. Additionally a geostrophic wind scale is normally printed in the bottom left hand corner of MSL synoptic charts. To use this scale, the shortest distance between adjacent isobars passing through the position at which windspeed is required is taken to the scale with the distance plotted from the small mark to the extreme left, to a speed indicated to the right. Care should be taken in using the scale because it is exponential and speed is read from right to left. Examples of the two types of scale are at Figure 11.5. The value of K will change for different latitude and density bands so accordingly there are different geostrophic wind scales.

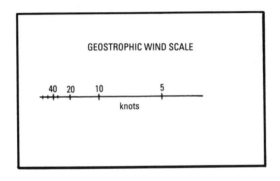

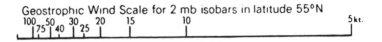

Geostrophic Wind Scale for 2 mb isobars in latitude 55°N

Figure 11.5. Two Types of Geostrophic Wind Scale

The importance of the geostrophic wind is evident because it can apply at all heights and is easily found by reference to the isobars on all weather maps. It only applies however, when no other forces act on the air. Forces other than PGF and GF include friction, the pressure rising or falling so rapidly that GF cannot keep up with the changing PGF (isallobaric effect) and another force which comes into play when isobars are not straight and parallel. In this latter case the air will then follow the curve of the isobars bringing into play a force called centripetal force — the force acting towards the centre of motion when the path is curved. In meteorological terms this is called Cyclostrophic Force — the force acting towards the centre of a pressure system when isobars are curved.

Gradient Wind
This is the wind which blows parallel to curved isobars due to a combination of three forces, pressure gradient force, geostrophic force and cyclostrophic force. The gradient wind therefore differs from the geostrophic wind. The difference however is relatively small. The direction is still parallel to the isobars, albeit curved ones. The surface speed on average differs by some 3 to 4 kn and some forecasters consider this difference to be relatively minor and therefore use the Geostrophic Wind Scale even when isobars are curved. Other forecasters are more meticulous and use the cyclostrophic formula for unit volume of air: $\rho V2/r$ where r is the

84

radius of curvature, to effect a correction to geostrophic wind speed. The actual effect of the cyclostrophic force on the wind speed as compared with the geostrophic speed depends on whether the pressure system concerned is high or low.

If air is moving steadily around a depression then the cyclostrophic force is provided from the pressure gradient force which will reduce windspeed. This is displayed in Figure 11.6A which shows

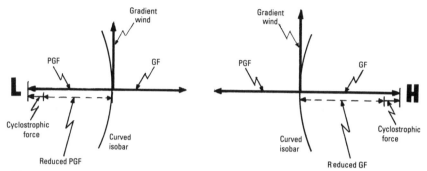

Figure 11.6A. Gradient Wind Around a Depression

Figure 11.6B. Gradient Wind Around an Anticyclone

that the V gradient = V geostrophic minus cyclostrophic effect. The gradient windspeed around a depression is less than the geostrophic speed for the same isobar interval and if the geostrophic wind scale is used it will read too high a value. Referring now to Figure 11.6B where the air is moving steadily around an anticyclone it will be seen that the cyclostrophic force is provided from the geostrophic force to make the air follow a curved path and thus V gradient = V geostrophic + cyclostrophic effect. For the same isobar interval the gradient windspeed around an anticyclone is greater than the geostrophic speed and if the geostrophic wind scale is used it will read too low a value. Clearly the greater the curvature of the isobars the greater the difference between geostrophic and gradient wind speeds.

Cyclostrophic Wind
In low latitudes where geostrophic force is negligible the cyclostrophic force is necessarily provided by the pressure gradient. The resulting wind is termed cyclostrophic and it can apply particularly where there is strong circular air motion in low latitudes, for example in tropical revolving storms and in tornadoes.

Wind in the Friction Layer
Compared with the windspeed above the friction layer, the wind at

lower levels must be reduced in speed by friction, with the greatest reduction near the surface itself. Any reduction in speed must reduce the value of GF. (GF = 2 Ω ρ V sine latitude). The result of this is a change in wind direction as PGF is now the stronger of the two forces and will therefore pull the airflow across the isobars towards the centre of low pressure. Figures 11.7A and B show the

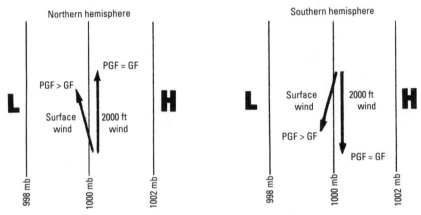

Figure 11.7A. The Change from Geostrophic to Surface wind – Northern Hemisphere

Figure 11.7B. The Change from Geostrophic to Surface Wind – Southern Hemisphere

effect of this on wind direction in the northern and southern hemispheres respectively. Further that the surface wind will be backed from geostrophic in the northern hemisphere and veered from geostrophic in the southern hemisphere. The amount of wind change will obviously depend on the amount of friction. Over the sea average figures for the northern hemisphere are backed by 15° from geostrophic and speed reduced to 2/3rds of geostrophic speed. Over a land surface the depth of the friction layer and the amount of friction depend on a number of factors including the type of terrain. Average northern hemisphere figures are: backed by 25° from geostrophic and speed reduced by 1/2. These average figures necessarily are subject to a wider spread than those over a sea surface. In the southern hemisphere figures are the same but the direction change is a veer from geostrophic.

Diurnal Variation of the Surface Wind
The degree of frictional turbulence will vary markedly throughout the 24 hours of a day and this has a direct effect on the surface wind. It will veer and increase by day reaching a maximum strength around 1500 hours. It backs and decreases thereafter with

a minimum strength around dawn. The basic cause of these changes is thermal turbulence which mixes the air at the surface with air moving more freely above in the friction layer. Any increase in thermal turbulence causing an increase in windspeed will also result in mechanical turbulence increasing as well. The effects are therefore most marked on clear sunny days and particularly if there is instability to increase the depth of turbulence. Sometimes these conditions are followed by a clear night giving ample scope for surface cooling and the development of a low level inversion. This can separate a calm condition at the surface from a

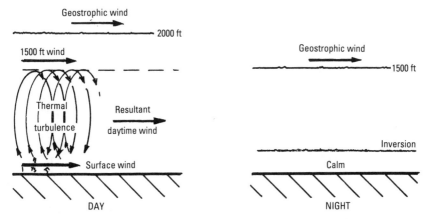

Figure 11.8. Cause and Effect of Diurnal Variation of the Surface W/V

reasonably strong wind above. The diagram at Figure 11.8 shows the type of changes which can occur through the 24 hours of a day and Figure 11.9 shows how these changes can apply with respect to

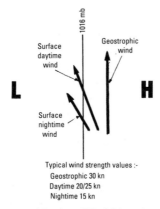

Figure 11.9. Diurnal Variation of Surface Wind Direction
compared with Geostrophic

87

isobar directions and the geostrophic wind. They both indicate that in the northern hemisphere by day, the surface wind veers and increases in speed becoming closer to geostrophic values, whilst the wind higher up in the friction layer (say 1500 ft) will back and decrease.

At night the surface wind backs and decreases in speed (and can in fact become calm under an inversion). Whilst the 1500 ft wind will veer and increase and can become geostrophic as the depth of the friction layer is reduced. In the southern hemisphere veer and back changes are reversed.

In practical terms a pilot approaching to land on the same runway by day and by night will notice a marked difference in aircraft handling as dictated by the diurnal variation of the wind velocity.

Sea Breezes

When the pressure gradient is slack and there is a clear sunny day, for example anticyclonic stable weather, then near the coast there will be much unequal heating of the land and sea. The land will heat rapidly and the insolation will cause the air to rise so that the pressure value at say 1000 ft above the land will be increased. Effectively the pressure surface over the land has been lifted. There is very little sea surface heating and so here the pressure surface will not move. Hence at about 1000 ft there is relatively high pressure over the land and this will cause movement of the air at this level from land to sea. The result of this drift is that the surface pressure on the land will fall, whilst the sea surface pressure will be slightly increased. The result is a wind from sea to land — a sea breeze. The average speed in temperate latitudes is some 10 kn and the extent some 10 nm either side of the coast. This 10 nm, can in mid-summer on some occasions extend to 40 to 50 nm inland. Initially the direction of this breeze will be at right angles to the

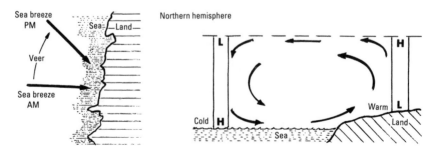

Figure 11.10. Mechanics of a Sea Breeze

coast, but as the air is subject to a longer fetch as the day progresses, geostrophic force will come into play causing a veer in the northern hemisphere and a back in the southern hemisphere. This change in direction is often greatest around 1500 hours when insolation is maximum and can be so marked that at this time the breeze direction is almost parallel to the coast. Diagrams showing the mechanics of a sea breeze are at Figure 11.10.

In tropical regions the pressure gradients are slack and thus near coasts the sea breezes are frequently dominant with speeds averaging 20 kn because of the greater insolation.

Practical Effects

In the evening the sea breeze will peter out as the insolation is lost. The temperature situation is then reversed, the sea temperature holding fast, whilst the land cools rapidly. This causes a reversal of flow at height and at the surface so that a light wind blows from land to sea. This is the land breeze and quite often during the evening change-over from one type of breeze to the other there can be gusty conditions. The differing temperature effects are much less marked with the night land breeze and therefore the expected speed is about 5 kn and the extent only some 5 nm across the coast.

The orographic lifting as the moist sea breeze crosses a coast causes small CU to form and this is a good navigation aid to pilots looking for a coastline — it is the cloud formation that shows the location of the coast. At airfields subject to land/sea breezes it is reasonable for a pilot to expect take-off and landing direction to be towards the sea by day and towards the land at night. The sea breeze must bring a reduction in temperature together with an increase of humidity as it crosses the coast. If the sea breeze first comes inland with a markedly lower temperature it is sometimes referred to as a 'Sea Breeze Front'. Often when sea fogs form off a coastline, the sea breeze can bring the fog inland causing a sudden reduction in visibility.

Katabatic/Anabatic Winds

A katabatic wind is a wind which blows down a hill or mountainside at night. Consider Figure 11.11A. The side of the hill will cool at night, particularly if there is a clear night sky. The air in contact will be cooled by conduction and will thus be denser and heavier than the free air at the same level. Thus it will flow down the hillside. Free air will replace the descending air, be cooled in turn and descend. The result is a wind which will blow downhill reaching a speed of some 10 kn. The flow of air can cause a 'sink' of cold air in

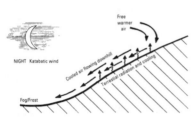

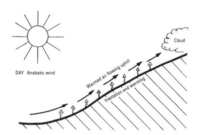

Figure 11.11A. Katabatic Wind   Figure 11.11B. Anabatic Wind

the bottom of the valley and this assists the formation of fog at night and early morning. The katabatic effect is very widespread geographically, for example tests have shown that they occur throughout the year in the valleys of Wales. The effect can be noticeable with only a gentle ground slope, and this can lead to frost pockets in areas where winter temperatures are above zero °C.

Figure 11.11B shows an Anabatic wind formation where the slope of a hill, particularly if it is south facing (northern hemisphere) obtains a high degree of insolation. The surface air is then heated by conduction, is warmer than the free air alongside and lighter and thus flows up the hillside. The wind thus formed is light, rarely more than 5 kn and quite often the lifting can result in a small fair weather CU above the hill. Both these winds are most likely when the pressure gradient is slack, thereby allowing conduction effects to be greater. Additionally a high pressure gradient causing a more normal wind could mask katabatic and anabatic effects.

Fohn Wind
There is a local wind which blows down the lee side of a mountain referred to as a Fohn wind. This is a wind which occurs in the Southern Alps of Europe. It is a warm dry wind which can result in an increase of temperature of some 10°C from the windward side of the mountain to the lee side. A similar wind to the east of the Rocky mountains in Canada is called the Chinook and this can provide a temperature increase of over 20°C. It is particularly important as it clears the ice and snow from the prairie provinces allowing spring sowing of corn. There is also the Santa Ana of the high Sierras in California and to the east of the Andes in South America.

The wind itself is a normal wind blowing against a mountain. It is made very special because, the air lifted by the wind, can cool at the SALR on the upwind side and be heated at the DALR on the lee side of the mountain. The result is a warm dry wind. Consider

Figure 11.12 and note the basic conditions, a stable atmosphere and a strong moist wind blowing against the mountain. The lifted air will quickly become saturated and thereafter cloud will form and the air will cool at the SALR (1.5°C per 1000 ft). Near the mountain top and, most likely, just over the top where the orographic uplift is reduced, precipitation occurs. The air now on the lee side will, because of the stable conditions, descend following the line of the mountain. The precipitation will quickly cause the descending air to become dry (i.e. not saturated) and therefore the air will heat adiabatically at the dry rate of 3°C per 1000 ft during the descent. Thus the wind on the downwind or lee side is very much warmer and dry. In summer the wind will tend to give clear skies, but in winter fog can form after the air has picked up water vapour again and then traversed a cold snow covered surface. The onset of a Fohn wind can cause a sudden drop in surface pressure due to the introduction of warm air and this can affect QFE values for airfields on the lee side.

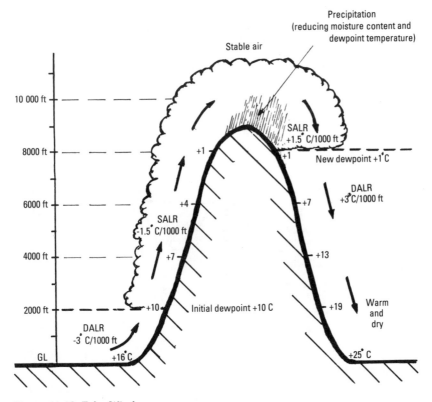

Figure 11.12. Fohn Wind

Valley or Ravine Wind

If a wind is constricted by blowing down a valley or ravine then it will increase in speed. A good example of this is the Mistral which blows down the Rhone valley in southern France between the

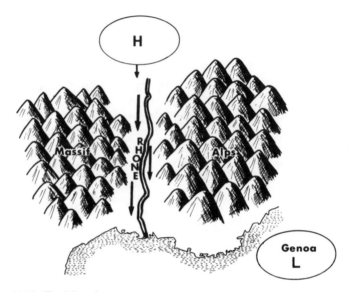

Figure 11.13. The Mistral

Figure 11.14. Reversal of a Valley Wind

French Alps to the east and the Massif Centrale to the west. This can produce surface windspeeds gusting to 70 kn and in winter can quickly bring cold air down the valley giving large CU and heavy snow showers. Figure 11.13 refers. If there is a narrow range of mountains with a valley then it is possible for a small change in the non-valley wind to cause a 180° wind change in the valley itself. This is shown at Figure 11.14 and it will be appreciated that for airfields located in such a valley, a sudden complete reversal in wind direction could adversely affect safety of aircraft taking-off or landing.

Low Level Jets
The term jet for low level winds is really a misnomer as a jet stream implies a wind at high level. Nonetheless there are some special high speed winds in the friction layer or just above which are super-geostrophic. They are formed by large scale interaction of the airflow around anticyclones with mountain barriers. The jets cover very wide areas some hundreds of square miles and speeds can be up to 100 kn. There are two particular known areas where these jets occur. Over Kenya, the Horn of Africa and the Indian Ocean to the east of these regions. Secondly in Australia to the west of the Dividing Range of mountains in Queensland and the Northern Territory.

The area of the low level jet off Africa is shown at Figure 11.15. The flow is some 450 nm in length, 150 nm wide and around 3000 ft to 7000 ft. The jet blows in summer being most frequent from June to August. The southerly wind around the west end of the sub-tropical high in the Indian Ocean is obstructed and deflected away from the highlands of Ethiopia and the African horn. This results in a strong southwesterly flow with a maximum speed of 100 kn at 3000 ft.

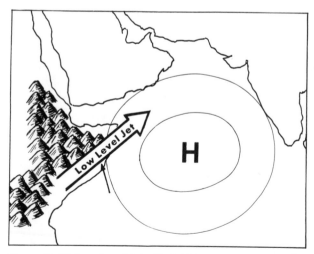

Figure 11.15. Low Level Jet – East Africa

The Australian low level jet has a similar type of formation but is confined to the land area. The orientation of the wind to the mountains is different to the African case. It produces a wind origin which is southwesterly around the east of the subtropical high pressures which are in mid continent in the Australian winter — June to September. The flow then becomes concentrated in a narrow stream and increases in speed due to the barrier effect of the mountains to the east and becomes south-easterly. The very

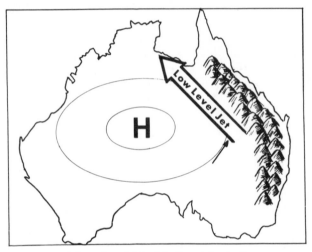

Figure 11.16. Low Level Jet – Northeast Australia

strong surface inversion caused by the high pressure and the clear night skies shields the flow from surface friction effects giving a wind up to 50 kn from the inversion up to 3000 ft. The jet details are shown at Figure 11.16. It is of interest that in both these cases, the increase of windspeed to super-geostrophic increases geostrophic force assisting the wind in the northern hemisphere case to turn right off the mountains, i.e. to become southwesterly and the Australian jet to turn left off the mountains and become south-easterly. There are no doubt other cases of low level jets which are formed in similar circumstances.

Trade Winds and Monsoons

The winds which blow from the subtropical anticyclones towards the heat equator are centred on about 15°N and S latitudes and are called trade winds. The usual reason given for the name is due to the captains of sailing ships travelling to the East, who discovered that these winds could assist quicker passages and were hence good for trade. Originally, the word 'trade' meant to blow constantly from one direction.

The subtropical highs in the northern hemisphere give an outflow towards the heat equator which is north easterly — the north east trade winds. When these have crossed the geographic equator, the geostrophic force will turn the wind to the left in the southern hemisphere providing a northwest wind. The trade winds in the southern hemisphere blow anticlockwise from the subtropical highs giving south easterly winds towards the heat equator. Again there is a reverse of the geostrophic force and when the winds have crossed the geographic equator they are turned to the right in the northern hemisphere giving a southwesterly wind. Where the trade winds meet over the oceans the winds become light and variable. This region, which extends some 5° either side of the heat equator is called the 'doldrums'.

The word monsoon means season and originally referred to the northeast wind over the Arabian sea in winter and the southwesterly over the same area in summer. These, and other seasonal winds are caused by the differential heating of large land and sea areas. The cold centre of Asia in winter causes high pressure and as a consequence, a northeasterly wind covering southeast Asia. The heating of the same area in summer causes low pressure and the air, with trade wind origins from south of the heat equator, becomes the southwesterly monsoon. Other moonsoons include the northwesterly of North Australia in January and the southwesterly monsoon of West Africa in the summer, both of which have origins and combine with the trade winds. Monsoons and trade winds are dealt with more fully in Chapter 18.

Chapter 12
Visibility

There are three aspects of visibility which apply to aviation. These are flight visibility which is simply the horizontal visibility at the flight level, slant or oblique visibility from the air to the ground and the visibility as reported by ground stations. The ground or surface visibility is the most widely used in weather reports and forecasts and will be examined initially.

Visibility is defined as the furthest horizontal distance that a dark object can be seen by an observer with normal eyesight. A dark object is sensible to use for measurement purposes as a white painted object for example, would give an over-optimistic value of the distance that one could see. The visibility in metres is measured at eye level, say some 5 ft above the ground and therefore it is possible for a high value to be reported whilst at the same time there is a shallow layer of fog below eye level. This can cause confusion as a visibility of some 10 km can sound excellent to a pilot. However, if there is a 3 ft thick layer of shallow fog covering the runway it could make landing hazardous. A similar situation could apply if there was loose snow being blown across the runway. For these reasons the term CAVOK used in airfield reports and forecasts which has the colloquial meaning ceiling and visibility OK, has a full meaning as follows:

No cloud below 5000 ft or below the lowest minimum sector altitude, whichever is greater:
No CB, thunderstorms or precipitation:
Visibility 10 km or more, no shallow fog or low drifting snow.

At night visibility is measured using lights of known power at special distances viewed through a series of filters. The resulting values are the daytime equivalent visibilities.

When discussing visibility, reference is really being made to the clarity of the air, or how obscured it is. Reasons for obscurity are in two categories; water and ice crystals in the air and solid particles such as dust, sand and smoke. The solid particles lead to the term haze. The water or ice crystals can be in the form of precipitation and this has an immediate effect on visibility. Two of the worse conditions in this category are drizzle where the myriad of tiny water droplets reflect light in all directions including into a pilot's eyes, and driving snow which can produce the appearance of short white lines in the air. Water and ice crystals can be in suspension in the air and thus cause mist and fog. Mist is defined as relative humidity greater than 95 per cent with very small water droplets and a visibility of 1 km or more. Fog is visibility reduced by water droplets in suspension to values less than 1 km. Ice fog is fog composed of ice crystals and freezing fog is composed of super-cooled water droplets which will freeze when coming into contact with a solid surface. The expression smog is also used and this is a fog which is composed of a mixture of smoke and fog. It is prevalent in large industrial cities — the most notorious in this respect is Tokyo.

Haze and particularly smoke haze, mist and fog occur in stable conditions where winds are light. An exception to this concerns dust/sand haze which can form in association with CB clouds where conditions must be unstable. The stability conditions with smoke haze, mist and fog often extend to an inversion at low level. Reference to Figure 12.1 shows carbon particles trapped under the

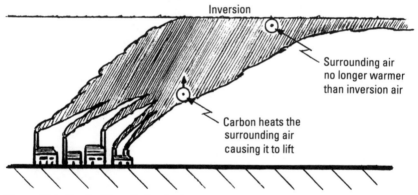

Figure 12.1. Smoke Haze Under An Inversion

inversion leading to a layer of smoke which can be very persistent.

Haze caused by dust is very common in the subtropical anticyclonic areas of the world where the climate produces deserts. In these regions the desert dust can occasionally be lifted up to tropopause heights over very wide areas and lifting to 10 000 ft plus is common. This lifting is caused by strong surface winds and convection. The diurnal variation of surface wind and the reduction of convection after sunset can cause the haze to reduce in height or disappear.

Hill Fog

If there is cloud on the sides or top of a hill or mountain then to an observer in the valley it is called cloud. To an observer on the hill it is fog. A pilot flying over such an area can refer to it as low cloud but more particularly with safety in mind the term used is hill fog — indicating that the top of hills is hidden from view. This is displayed at Figure 12.2. This fog infers a visibility of 200 m or less. Hill fog

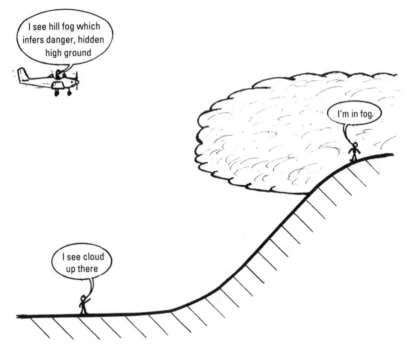

Figure 12.2. Hill Fog

can form by the lifting of other fog types. If radiation fog which forms in a valley is cleared by a strong wind, this will transpose the fog to low ST cloud. Where this drifts over a nearby hill, the result will be hill fog. In a similar manner, sea fog off a coast can be brought inland and lifted. It can then drift over nearby coastal hills becoming low ST and hill fog.

Radiation Fog

This is the most common type of fog. It forms inland, particularly in polar maritime air at night and early morning in autumn and winter. As the name implies the fog is caused by radiation that is terrestrial radiation, which cools the ground and the air in contact by conduction. If the air is cooled below dewpoint, then condensation occurs and the result is either dew on the ground or fog. The radiation and cooling is more likely to be effective if there is a clear night sky and very light winds. Figure 12.3 shows radiation fog

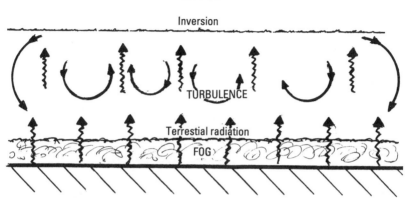

Figure 12.3. Formation of Radiation Fog

formation. If there is no wind to cause turbulence then dew or frost will form (frost by sublimation at temperatues below 0°C) but if there is turbulence caused by a wind or by early morning convection then the water droplets will be kept in suspension. Additionally the turbulence will bring warmer air from the inversion above into contact with the cold ground to be cooled in turn enabling the fog to thicken. This inversion is invariably present when there is a clear night sky resulting in low surface temperatures from the cold ground whilst some of the terrestrial radiation is heating the air above. Additionally the inversion and cooling at the surface can ensure that conditions are stable in the lower layers.

The ideal conditions for the fog to form are a clear sky, a light wind — two to eight kn — and a high relative humidity so that a little cooling will be sufficient to cause saturation and condensation. The fog can form in anticyclones, ridges of high pressure and cols where the first two ideal conditions are to be expected. Further, in these three pressure systems conditions are stable (this only applies to a col in winter). Sometimes all the necessary conditions apply except that conditions are calm, then there is likely to be dew or perhaps mist by the end of the night. At dawn with the first thermal turbulence, the mist can be quickly transposed into thick fog. This situation often applies in the UK. Pilots can arrive at a mist-covered airfield first thing in the morning and be lulled into thinking this will quickly clear with sun-up. By the time their aircraft are ready for flight there can suddenly be thick fog. The other reason for fog to be more likely at dawn is because the lowest temperature is at this time.

Although this fog is most likely to form in autumn and winter when temperatures are low and hence relative humidity is high, it can occur at any time of year, but it clears more quickly in the warmer seasons. In this connection, it is the lower value of solar radiation in autumn and winter which makes the fog more persistent. The fog can be cleared by a strong wind which will lift the fog to form ST cloud. It is also cleared by insolation which will lift the fog away and also evaporate the lower layers. In UK the normal expectation is clearance by between 1000 and 1100 hours. If returning to an airfield at night or early morning when radiation fog is present, there is a recommendation that pilots fly to an airfield on a hill. Alternatively it can be efficacious to fly to a coastal airfield where the warming influence of the nearby sea can give clear conditions.

Advection Fog
This is movement fog and it is caused when warm moist air flows over a cold surface. The cold surface can be either land or sea as displayed at Figure 12.4. The cold surface must be at a temperature

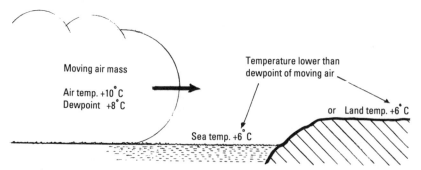

Figure 12.4. Formation of Advection Fog

lower than the dewpoint of the moving air for saturation and condensation to occur. It is unlikely that transported air will be more than a few degrees warmer than the surface over which it passes and therefore this air must have a high relative humidity. The actual speed of the moving air can be up to 15 kn. Above this figure turbulence cloud is probable. Advection fog over the UK and northern Europe is most likely over the land in winter and early spring and over the sea in late spring or early summer when the sea is coldest. The most common wind directions are southwesterly bringing tropical maritime air or northeasterly bringing relatively warm air from the Scandinavian region over the cold North Sea. This can help to produce very poor visibility along the east coast of England and Scotland referred to as Haar conditions.

Nearly all sea fogs are caused by advection. Two good examples are the extensive and persistent fogs which occur near the Newfoundland banks or shallows off northeast Canada and over the sea around the Kamchatka peninsula off the coast of northeast Russia. In both these cases air lying over a warm sea current from the south is moved by the wind over a cold sea current from the north. All advection fogs are very persistent and some can last for weeks on end. They are cleared by strong winds which will lift the fog to form ST cloud or, more usually, by a change in wind direction which will bring a different type of air mass into the region.

Steaming Fog

This is also referred to as Arctic Smoke and as this name implies it occurs at high latitudes. It is in fact a type of advection fog except that in this case the air from very cold land is moving over a warmer sea. Normally this process would result in the formation of CU cloud as previously explained. However, where the air is very stable and cold, the small amount of evaporation off the sea is sufficient to cause saturation. The small amount of lifting from the warmer sea then causes condensation and fog to form. At these high latitudes and low temperatures the fog is ice fog and the formation is by sublimation. It has a white appearance, hence the term arctic smoke. It can have considerable depth — up to 500 ft — and is very persistent. It occurs particularly over the sea off north Norway, Iceland and Greenland. Merging of this fog with a snow surface can make it especially difficult for a pilot to assess where the horizon should be, such conditions are known as a 'white out'.

Frontal Fog

Frontal fog occurs at warm fronts and occlusions; it does not form at cold fronts because of the instability. The basic cause of the fog is the precipitation from NS cloud which saturates the air underneath, lowering the cloud base on to the surface. The evaporation of standing water on the ground from other precipitation besides that from NS assists the fog to form. It can form along a narrow strip

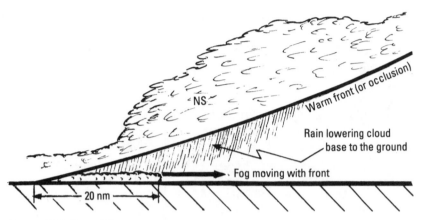

Figure 12.5. Frontal Fog

some 20 nm wide which will then move with the passage of the front. An explanatory diagram is at Figure 12.5.

Visibility From the Air

Visibility from the air is termed downward, slant or oblique. This is shown by Figure 12.6. The only method of reporting the value of oblique visibility is by reference to the distance along the ground between a point directly beneath the aircraft and the furthest point on the ground which the pilot can see. This value is reduced if the pilot is looking towards the sun. At night the value can be increased by looking towards the moon because this relatively gentle light reflects well from water surfaces and from the tops of railway lines.

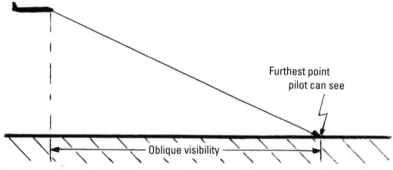

Figure 12.6. Slant or Oblique Visibility

Visual Illusions

Illusions in normal cruising flight are far less important than those which occur at low level and particularly on the approach to land. However, in cruise it is possible for a pilot flying between 'streets' of clouds to align his wings with the cloud lines with the illusion that thereby he is flying straight and level when in fact he could be in a one wing low situation. If there is rain on a windscreen it can act like a lens. If an aircraft is on the approach, the approach lights will appear larger than they should thus giving the illusion that the aircraft is closer to the threshold of the runway than it is in fact. With a clear windscreen, rain between the aircraft and the approach lights in a similar situation can reduce the glow from the lights, thereby making it appear that the threshold is further away. If a heavy rainstorm is moving towards an aircraft there can be the impression that the horizon is moving lower. This illusion can be enhanced on the approach by a pilot's wish to stay below cloud. If a pilot is entering cloud top during a descent, or fog during approach to land there can be the firm impression that the nose of the aircraft has lifted. Reaction to this and the other illusions can cause hazardous situations.

Approaching to Land with a Shallow Fog Layer

Suppose that it is winter at night time and an aircraft arrives over an airfield where there is a shallow layer of radiation fog — say 50 ft deep. The pilot looking down from overhead has a clear view of the airfield as depicted by the runway and taxi lights. Despite the fact that the control tower has reported visibility as 200 m, the pilot commences an approach. During the final part of the descent the aircraft enters the top of the fog layer and the pilot now has a visibility virtually the same as that reported by the tower. He can become disorientated and now loses sight of the runway. The above scenario has occurred many times with tragic consequences.

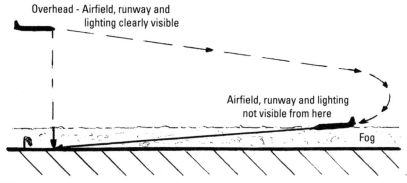

Figure 12.7. On the Approach with a Shallow Fog Layer

Note that the nose-up illusion could also have been experienced. Whilst radiation fog at night has been mentioned, a similar situation can occur in daylight and with other types of fog. Figure 12.7 displays the situation.

Visibility with a Deep Haze Layer

If there is a deep haze layer, say some 3000 ft thick and an aircraft is being flown inside the haze, then any increase of height will reduce the oblique visibility. This is shown at Figure 12.8A. If on the other hand the aircraft is being flown above the haze layer and again the pilot wishes to see as much of the ground as possible, his oblique visibility will increase if the aircraft is climbed to a higher altitude. Figure 12.8B refers.

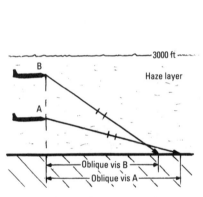

Figure 12.8A. Oblique Visibility from Inside a Haze Layer

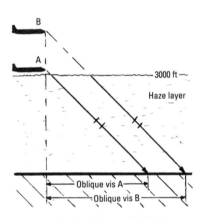

Figure 12.8B. Oblique Visibility from Above a Haze Layer

The effects of the haze when it is some 3000 ft deep and an aircraft is making approaches at 3°, less than 3° and more than 3° to a runway, are displayed at Figures 12.9A, B and C. It can be seen that if the approach is less than 3° the pilot will enter the layer further from the runway and his oblique visibility will not enable touch down point to be acquired. Alternatively, if the approach is more than 3° giving a steeper approach angle, then the pilot's ability to acquire touch down point will improve. If this departure is extended to maintain an altitude to be overhead the airfield, this will provide the best runway view of all. Clearly, if the approach is initiated inside the haze then the oblique visibility should improve during descent. Any loss of ground view can be compensated for by maintaining height for a while so that the angle of approach is steepened.

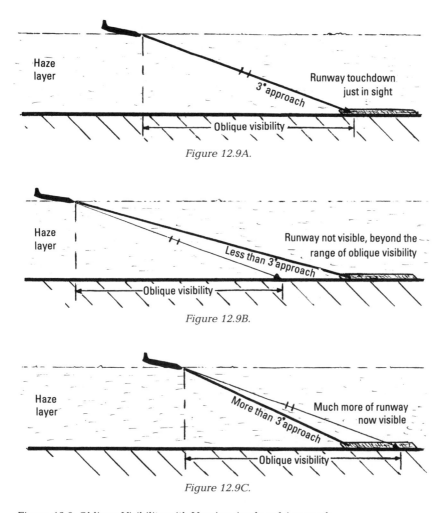

Figure 12.9A.

Figure 12.9B.

Figure 12.9C.

Figure 12.9. Oblique Visibility with Varying Angles of Approach

Runway Visual Range

This is a system of providing an oblique visibility value related to what a pilot might see on the approach as he crosses the runway threshold. It is defined as the maximum distance that a pilot in the threshold area at 15 ft above the runway can see marker boards by day or runway lights at night, when looking in the direction of take-off and landing. RVR is only of use when there is obscurity at low level. It is therefore given to a pilot when the normal ground visibility is 1500 m or less or when fog is reported or forecast. The value is passed before take-off and in the terminal area. It can also be given in aerodrome half-hourly reports. RVR values can be obtained by a ground observer or by use of instruments.

The Instrument Runway Visual Range (IRVR) system employs three transmissometers which measure the values. These are located at touchdown, mid-point and stop-end zones of the runway respectively. Hence three RVR values can be given, e.g. RVR 600, 500, 550, 28L which decodes to values of 600 m at touchdown, 500 m at mid-point and 550 m at stop-end of runway 280 left. The system uses automatic supression which blanks out mid-point and/ or stop-end values when:

a) They are equal to, or higher than, touchdown value unless they are less than 400 m.
b) They are 800 m or more.

When touchdown and only one other value is passed, the second value is prefixed mid-point or stop-end as appropriate. Some further details of Runway Visual Range are given in Chapter 19.

Optical Phenomena

There are a number of different optical phenomena. Many of these are beautiful but have little effect on aviation meteorology. For example, rainbows, which are caused by the refraction of the sun's rays by raindrops together with reflection. Other effects, basically caused by refraction, reflection and diffraction can provide useful information, or at least make the pilot aware that these effects are normal and do not necessarily constitute a hazard.

The Halo

This is a circle of light, or more than one circle around the sun or moon. Usually the circles are white but other colours can sometimes be seen. On occasions there can be one halo and then parts of a second halo appearing as an arc or arcs outside the first ring. Halos form by sun or moonlight refracting and reflecting through a sheet of ice crystals. Hence they are seen with cirrostratus cloud or with ice fog.

The Corona

Whilst the basic halo has an angular diameter of some 22° the corona usually has a much smaller diameter and is therefore closer to the edge of the sun or moon. In fact a corona around the sun is less likely to be observed for this reason. They are caused by the diffraction of light through water droplets and are most likely with thin AS. The size of ring is not an infallible method of differentiating between a halo and a corona. A better method is by noting the order of different colours. The corona sequence is always the brownish red of the aureole followed by violet changing to red.

Brocken Spectre
If there is mist on one side of a mountain and not on the other, an observer with his back to the sun can sometimes see coloured rings of light around the shadow of the observer's head in the mist. A similar situation can apply when flying with the shadow of the front of the aircraft clearly visible on a cloud layer. This effect is also known as 'Glory'.

Mirage
The mirage is caused by the refraction of sunlight through different density layers close to the ground. The mirage indicates large temperature gradients, for it is these that cause the different densities and variable bending of the light rays. If the density is greater on the surface, as with inversion conditions, the light rays are bent downwards. This produces a clear image which can be either erect or inverted. This is called a superior mirage. The inferior variety is more common and occurs with the hottest temperature on the ground — hence the lowest density. The refraction is upwards giving the appearance of a water surface and even trees and buildings. The image is often inverted. This type is often seen over desert areas and over hot road surfaces.

Aurora Borealis
This is visible light from the atmosphere at high latitudes. It is caused by streams of highly charged particles leaving the sun. These are deflected by the earth's magnetic field and then precipitate causing vertical streaks of light, or 'drapery'. They produce a glow at the northern horizon and are sometimes referred to as 'Northern Lights'. They can affect visibility from the air in northern latitudes. (It is also a sign of disturbances in the earth's magnetic field with possible short term changes in the value of magnetic variation).

Effect of Ice Fog
If the sun is viewed at dawn through ice crystals the light will appear very red due to refraction. This fact can be of use to determine that ice fog is between an observer and the low altitude

sun. An additional indicator in this case would be a pale sky above the region where ice fog is suspected. This paleness being caused by the reflection into a clear sky, off the top of the ice fog.

Green Water
There have been pilot reports of seeing a wall of green water. The situations have occurred flying at heights below a few thousand feet adjacent to large CB cloud. It is possible that strong upcurrents supporting very large concentrations of droplets so that they are almost stationary, are the primary cause. Unequal refraction of light through these droplets could then produce a strong green colour. This is a warning of intense CB/thunderstorm activity and the associated hazards.

Chapter 13
Air Masses and Fronts

Air Masses

The term air mass supposes a large volume of air and this can be hundreds or thousands of miles across, where the temperature and humidity in the horizontal are more or less constant. The air masses form where there is high pressure so that basic air movement is slow, particularly near the centre, thus allowing the air over a period of time, to absorb the conditions of the surface over which it is resting. The surface itself must therefore be of a fairly uniform nature for this standard absorption to occur. The air moving away from these high pressure areas can therefore have basic properties which can effect the regions over which they pass. All air leaving these high pressure areas must be stable at the source but this condition, together with original temperature and humidity are subject to change with movement away from the source. All the subtropical high regions of the world are sources of air masses. Being subtropical they must be warm and if the source is the ocean, then the air will also be moist. This leads to an air mass name of Tropical Maritime: basically warm wet and stable at source. If the subtropical high source is over land then the air mass name is Tropical Continental: basically warm dry and stable at source.

When the outflow from the subtropical highs is towards the lower latitudes i.e. towards the equator, then the Tropical Maritime air is called Equatorial. The Equatorial air mass almost immediately becomes unstable due to the surface heating, it is also usually moist with a high temperature.

At the poles the high pressure produces air masses called Arctic or Antarctic. Whether the source is land or sea is of little moment as the source will be ice covered. The conditions at source will be cold, dry and stable.

The cold anticyclones which are permanent in winter only, produce Polar Continental air. The sources being Siberia and the north of North America. Hence the source conditions are very cold, dry and stable. There are also high pressure areas in the north of the North Atlantic and North Pacific oceans. These produce Polar Maritime air which at source is stable cold and moist.

Air Masses Affecting UK and Europe

Air leaving the air mass source regions can be considerably modified by the surfaces over which they move. These modifications can best be appreciated by examining examples. Therefore a study of the air masses effecting the British Isles and Europe is pertinent. Reference is made to the diagram at Figure 13.1. It will be seen that

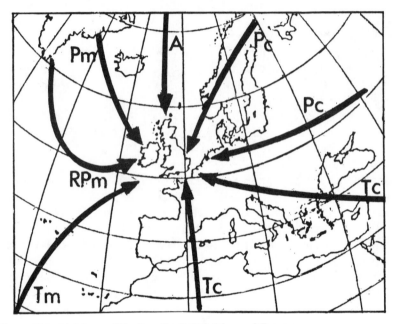

Figure 13.1. Air Masses Effecting the British Isles and Europe

almost all the basic air masses, Polar Maritime, Polar Continental, Tropical Maritime, Tropical Continental and Arctic are involved, together with an additional item, Returning Polar Maritime. Equatorial air masses do not apply to these latitudes.

Polar Maritime

The source region for Polar Maritime is the northern North Atlantic including the Greenland Iceland region where the air is stable, cold with a high relative humidity and a low absolute humidity. The outflow is a cold moist northwesterly flow which is warmed in the lower layers as it moves south and its absolute humidity is increased from the warmer sea. The result is unstable moist air and the development of CU CB with showers, sometimes hail and thunderstorms and good visibility except in showers. These conditions are more likely to apply where there is also orographic lifting over the northwest coasts of Scotland and Northern Ireland. In winter with the passage of the air over snow covered Scotland it is possible for the air to become stable again, resulting in low ST giving light snow and poor visibility. Similarly over England at night in winter with clearing skies, terrestrial radiation can produce a low level inversion, cold surface conditions and a light wind leading to the development of radiation fog. This is the most likely air mass to produce this fog type.

Polar Continental
The origins of Polar Continental air are Siberia and northern Russia in winter. The air at source is stable, very cold and dry. Most frequently the outflow provides a very cold dry easterly wind which gives good flying weather — no cloud or precipitation and good visibility except that smoke from industrial areas can be brought to the western regions and to the UK. If the centre or centres of high are further to the north, then the outflow can be from the northeast with the result that the cold dry air will then pass over the relatively warm North Sea. The air will then be warmed in the lower layers, become unstable to a degree (not so unstable as polar maritime which has a longer sea passage) and absorb water vapour. The result can be SC over the North Sea and German and Dutch coasts. The SC can develop into large CU along the east coast of England and Scotland with heavy snow showers. Sometimes these conditions can spread further inland. When this occurs radiation fog can occur at night when the cloud clears and the air becomes stable again in these inland areas.

In summer, the cold anticyclones over Asia disappear to be replaced by low pressure. If, however, high pressure occurs over Scandinavia (this may be a development from a temporary cold anticyclone) then this air will be stable, warm and dry. The outflow will be northeasterly over the cold North Sea of early spring and summer. It will be cooled in the lower layers by this passage and water vapour will be absorbed from the sea. The resulting very stable flow with a very high relative humidity leads to Haar conditions along the coasts of northern England and Scotland. The conditions are very low ST drizzle, advection fog and generally poor visibility, which can be very persistent whilst the wind is in the north east. In northern England the term 'Sea Fret' is sometimes used instead of Haar.

Tropical Continental
The source of Tropical Continental air is North Africa and southeast

Europe producing a warm dry stable southerly or southeasterly airflow. This air mass effects the region mostly in summer and brings clear stable warm conditions to UK with good visibility apart from dust haze, which can be brought from the Sahara. Moving north the air will be cooled, thereby aiding stability. Sometimes the southerly flow picks up water vapour from the Mediterranean sea but this is usually deposited as rain showers on the Massif Centrale in France before reaching England.

Tropical Maritime
The Azores subtropical anticyclone is the origin of Tropical Maritime air. At source the air is stable and warm with a high absolute humidity and a moderate relative humidity. The airflow is a moist warm southwesterly and as the air moves north it is cooled in the lower layers, adding to stability and increasing the relative humidity. Despite the temperature reduction this air is relatively warm. The resulting cloud type on crossing coasts is of the turbulence variety ST or SC with a very low base giving drizzle or light precipitation and poor visibility. Advection fog due to passage over cold surfaces can occur over the sea areas in the southwest channel in late spring and early summer and over the UK land in winter and early spring. Hence overcast gloomy weather but with temperatures above the average over the normal expectations.

In high summer insolation and the subsequent convection can result in clearance of the low cloud, increasing temperatures and sometimes some fair weather CU can develop.

Arctic
The source is the Polar ice cap (in the western hemisphere this merges with the snow and ice fields in the far north of Canada). The basic conditions are similar to Polar Maritime; stable, cold and with a low absolute humidity. It provides a very cold northerly flow. This becomes unstable as it moves south and it also picks up moisture from the seas to the north of Scotland. It can be established at any time of year but more particularly in winter when there is a blocking anticyclone to the west of Ireland which will result in northerly winds over mainland UK and also the nearby continent. Large CU, heavy snow showers and sometimes blizzard conditions apply, although the degree of cloud and precipitation becomes less with movement further south. During seasons other than winter, a distinctive fall in temperatures applies with the northerly wind and showers are of rain. The north of Scotland and East Anglia are easily exposed to this northerly flow.

Returning Polar Maritime

This is Polar Maritime air which has moved well to the south, e.g. to the south of the North Atlantic and then approaches the UK and France from the southwest or the west. The original Polar Maritime air becomes unstable initially and then in moving north from the southwest, the lower layers up to say 1000 ft and 2000 ft become stable again. Meanwhile the higher layers remain unstable. The resulting air mass, stable at the bottom and unstable above is open to strong uplift if initially the air can be convected through the bottom stability. This can occur in high summer — August/early September — when the land has been subject to heating for a lengthy time. Passage of this air over UK and France can then result in CU CB and much thunderstorm activity, including hail and heavy showers.

Fronts

Introduction

A front is the name given to the surface of separation between two air masses of different temperature. Hence when two air masses meet a front must be established. Along a front the warmer air, being less dense, should lift over the colder air and thus the frontal surface can be active with much cloud and precipitation. The ground or sea position of the frontal surface is shown as a frontal line on synoptic charts.

Where the main air masses of the world meet there must therefore be global fronts. Other fronts can occur where there are relatively minor confrontations between different air masses. The global fronts include:

a) The Intertropical Convergence Zone.
b) The Mediterranean Front.
c) The Polar Front.
d) The Arctic Front.

The average position of the fronts in January and July are shown at Figures 13.2 and 13.3 respectively.

The Intertropical Convergence Zone.

This is also known as the ITCZ and unlike normal fronts it has considerable width, up to 300 nm and is a broad zone of separation between the equatorial air masses either side of the heat equator. The equatorial air is conveyed by the northeast and southeast trade

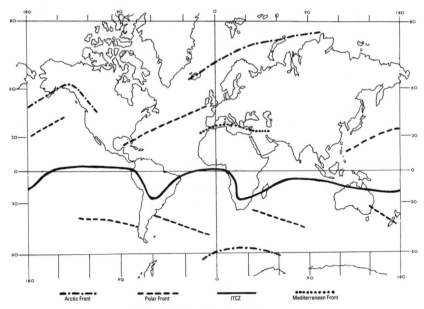

Figure 13.2. Average position of Global Fronts in January

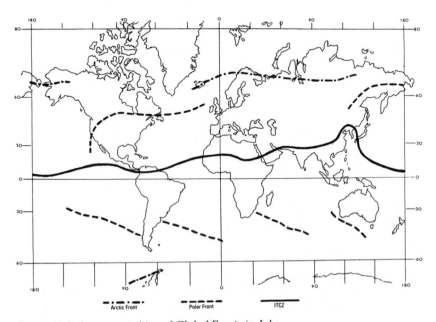

Figure 13.3. Average position of Global Fronts in July

114

winds from the subtropical anticyclones. It is therefore subject to a marked seasonal shift. The zone is also referred to as the equatorial trough and is a region of extensive instability weather.

Mediterranean Front
This is the boundary between Polar Continental/Maritime air from Europe to the north and Tropical Continental air from North Africa. The front extends on a west east line along the middle of the Mediterranean sea. It exists in winter only, when the sea is a region of low pressure. Depressions form on the front and then move west to east over the sea.

Polar Front
This is the frontal surface between Polar and Tropical air masses. The polar air from the high latitude sea areas of the Atlantic and Pacific oceans meeting the air moving to higher latitudes from the subtropical anticyclones. The front extends across the Atlantic and Pacific oceans from 35°N to 65°N, the actual position varying throughout the year. The position in the Southern Hemisphere is around 50°S and here the position is less variable due to the more constant temperature with latitudes in this hemisphere.

A series of waves are always forming on this front which cause depressions which contain their own portions of the Polar Front proper.

Arctic Front
The boundary between Arctic and Polar air masses is called the Arctic front. It lies at higher latitudes than the polar front. Depressions form on the front effecting the land regions at latitudes greater than 65°, however occasionally in winter effects can be experienced at latitudes a little lower than this.

Frontal Factors
Mention of the term front usually conjures up a vision of masses of cloud and precipitation, active weather and varying winds. This is not necessarily the case and the effect of fronts can be almost placid. Consider the diagrams at Figure 13.4. It supposes that there is constant pressure in the warm region and the slope of the front into the cold air results in increasing pressure away from the front in the cold air. The result of this would be no wind on the warm side of the front and a geostrophic wind parallel to the front on the cold side. The result of this air movement parallel to the front is little or no lifting and little in the way of weather.

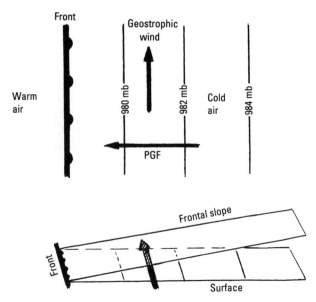

Figure 13.4. Air Moving Parallel to a Front

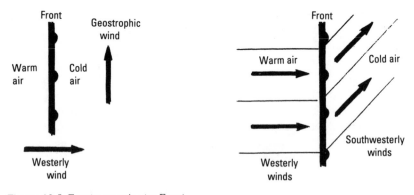

Figure 13.5. Frontogenesis at a Front

Suppose now a westerly wind is superimposed on this arrangement as shown at Figure 13.5. This would provide a westerly wind on the warm side and a southwesterly wind on the cold side. The resulting isobars would now provide a change of direction at the front, i.e. a trough will form. However, despite the trough and the resulting surface convergence this can be relatively meek in terms of lifting and the release of latent heat to accentuate the production of cloud and weather. Again, therefore, with the wind geostrophic, activity is limited. A rapidly falling pressure in association with the trough will deny geostrophic conditions, winds will blow across the isobars and this will considerably increase convergence levels at and above the surface and cause real weather activity. This fact of falling pressure increasing convergence and effectively narrowing the front is called 'Frontogenesis'. In practice overland there is usually weather at a front, for the chances of surface winds being geostrophic are unlikely.

The opposite situation where pressure is rising will result in equilibrium being restored and no real new weather being produced. This rise or steadying in pressure is termed 'Frontolysis'.

From the foregoing the importance of the isallobaric effect as indicated by pressure tendency readings will be evident.

Minor Fronts

These are only minor as a distinction from global and can and do have a profound effect on weather in a region. Very frequently these fronts are contained inside depressions and the fronts themselves are portions of global fronts. Sometimes the fronts are simply dividing surfaces where warm or cold air is invading a region where temperatures are opposite. Again these fronts are surfaces of separation which can spread from sea or ground level right up to the tropopause. All the fronts move at right angles to themselves and the speed of movement can be estimated from the isobar interval measured along the frontal line.

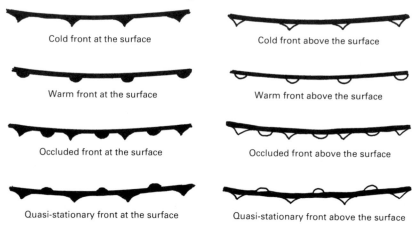

Cold front at the surface   Cold front above the surface

Warm front at the surface   Warm front above the surface

Occluded front at the surface   Occluded front above the surface

Quasi-stationary front at the surface   Quasi-stationary front above the surface

Figure 13.6. Fronts on a Synoptic Chart

Cold Front

The surface of separation where cold air is replacing warm air is called a cold front. Figure 13.6 shows how various fronts are displayed on charts. The cold front travels faster than a warm front because the air behind it is dense and heavy and thus the warm air ahead is simply displaced upwards. The warm front is impeded by the heavier air ahead and thus its speed is reduced. Measurement of the speed of movement of a cold front is often necessary in order to provide an estimate of when a front with its accompanying

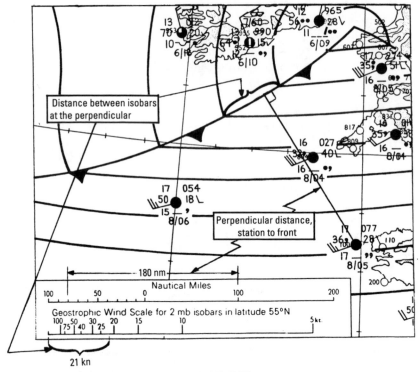

180 nm at 21 kn is approximately 8 Hr 20 Min.
ETA of front at the station is the time of the synoptic chart plus 8 Hr 20 Min.

Figure 13.7. Movement and ETA of a Cold Front

weather will arrive at an airfield. The problem is outlined by the synoptic chart at Figure 13.7 which shows a perpendicular drawn from a station to the front. The length of this line represents the distance to to be travelled by the front. The perpendicular also defines the portion of the front between adjacent isobars, which will arrive at the airfield. The speed can be found by measuring the distance along the front between the two isobars and using this as a geostrophic interval with the geostrophic wind scale on the chart. Knowledge of distance and speed will enable time and ETA front to be found as shown at Figure 13.7.

Warm Front
The surface of separation where warm air is replacing cold air is called a warm front. It is displayed on charts as shown at Figure 13.6. The procedure for estimating the arrival time of a warm front at an airfield is the same as for a cold front, except that the warm front speed is slower and therefore the estimate of speed found on the geostrophic wind scale is reduced by a third: i.e. the warm front speed = the speed found on the geostrophic wind scale x 2/3.

Other Fronts
The Occluded Front occurs where a cold front catches up with or overtakes a warm front. This happens particularly in polar front depressions. They are drawn on charts as shown at Figure 13.6. Initially the occluded front will travel at the speed of the cold front but normally the speed reduces with time.

The Quasi-Stationary Front is a front where movement is very small and indeterminate or it is stationary. The method of chart display is at Figure 13.6.

Chapter 14
Depressions

Polar Front Depressions

Depressions which form on the polar front produce very active weather from the surface and throughout the flying atmosphere. These are the most common depressions and they form in the temperate latitudes where the majority of aviation routes are flown. They are therefore, the most important type of depression. The lows form on the polar front in both hemispheres. Examination of the North Atlantic polar front and the way the depressions develop is representative of formations elsewhere. The average position of the Atlantic polar front is from Florida to southwest UK in winter and from Newfoundland to north Scotland and on to Bergen in Norway in summer. The reason for the seasonal movement is that in winter the outflow from the North American high meets the tropical maritime air well to the south, around the Florida region. Thereafter, as the North American high recedes with winter

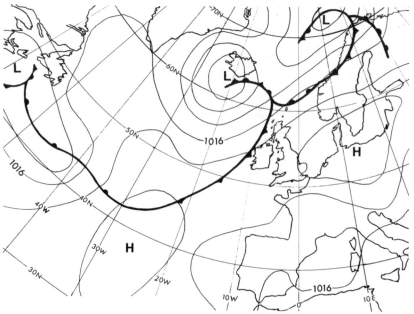

Figure 14.1. The Atlantic Polar Front

changing to Spring the cold outflow then originates in arctic Canada. Additionally the subtropical high origin of tropical maritime air will move north with movement of the heat equator. At the same time in the east of the Atlantic the meeting of polar and maritime air will also gradually move north with movement of the subtropical high. Eventually by July, the front will reach its summer positioning, retreating south again in the Autumn. An Atlantic synoptic chart for 5 July 1987 is shown at Figure 14.1. The position of the polar front is displayed by the warm and cold front lines stretching across the ocean from west to east. South of these frontal lines the air is tropical maritime, whilst to the north the air is polar maritime in origin. Suppose some of the tropical air moves into a region previously covered by polar maritime air. This movement may be caused by a sea current crossing the polar front and thereby taking the warm air on its surface as well. The movement can also be caused by a normal pressure system wind. Referring again to Figure 14.1, the air on the west side of the central anticyclone in the middle of the chart will be moving north with the clockwise wind direction around the high. This will also take warm air into the cold area. The advective movement of warm air into a cold surface area must cause lifting. The result of this will be divergence at height

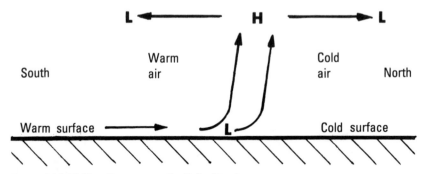

Figure 14.2. Falling Pressure on the Polar Front

and a fall in surface pressure, Figure 14.2 refers. The fall in surface pressure will cause more warm air to flow into the newly formed low. In turn this will be lifted adding to the divergence at height thus causing the depression to deepen. A portion of the polar front proper will be trapped inside this depression, passing through the centre of low as shown by the development diagrams at Figure 14.3. The leading portion of the polar front in the depression is now a line where warm air (tropical maritime) is replacing cold air, hence this is a warm front. The trailing portion of the polar front is

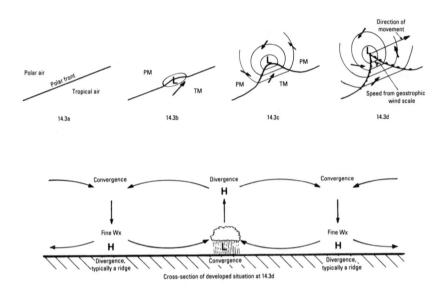

Figure 14.3. Formation of a Polar Front Depression

now a boundary where cold air (polar maritime) is replacing warm air. Hence this is a cold front.

The developed depression can extend to the tropopause with much cloud and weather activity. This will certainly happen whilst the centre of low is deepening and there is thus 'frontogenesis'. In side elevation, viewing the depression from the surface to the tropopause, the stability clouds formed by the lifting of air at the warm front and the instability clouds at the cold front can be appreciated. Figure 14.4 refers and shows a slope to the warm front of about 1 in 150 — becoming steeper with height and the slope to the cold front as the denser air pushes in, of about 1 in 50. The expected cloud sequence from the surface at the warm front is: NS, AS, CS, CC, CI with perhaps some ST at the surface due to turbulence and sometimes there is also AC. The clouds at the cold front are the expected instability CU and CB. Sometimes if there is a stability layer, then NS can form at the front. In the warm sector which is tropical maritime air, the typical ST SC turbulence cloud should be present. These polar front lows are often referred to as warm sector depressions for obvious reasons and they are unique in this respect.

Movement of Polar Front Depressions

The polar front depressions form in the west of the ocean and then move across the Atlantic from west to east under the influence of

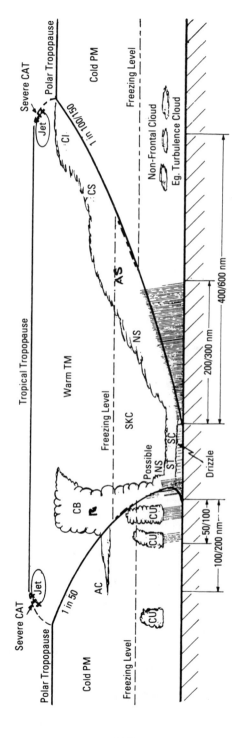

Figure 14.4. Side Elevation of a Polar Front Depression

the upper winds. One depression forming after another along the polar front line. This can be clearly seen at Figure 14.1 where three separate polar front depressions are drawn, with the newest low to the south of Newfoundland and the most developed low to the northwest of Norway. The speed and direction of movement can be assessed by reference to the isobars in the warm sector. The direction is parallel to the first isobars in the warm sector. The speed can be found by taking the geostrophic interval between isobar number one and isobar number two for measurement on the geostrophic wind scale. It should be noted that the individual frontal movements referred to in the previous chapter, include movement of the whole depression. The movement is shown at Figure 14.3.

Sometimes an anticyclone can form to the west of Ireland. This will effectively block the movement of polar front depressions to the UK and Europe. The depressions will then move with the anticyclone clockwise flow to the north or northwest. This type of high pressure is referred to as a 'Blocking Anticyclone'.

Weather with Passage of a Polar Front Low
The weather changes at the surface can be assessed by reference to the final plan diagram at Figure 14.3 and the side elevation diagram at Figure 14.4. These changes can be registered by reference to the two polar maritime air situations and the one tropical maritime region as follows:

a) Ahead of the warm front.

b) At the warm front/In warm sector.

c) At/Behind the cold front.

AHEAD OF THE WARM FRONT:

Surface W/V	–	Southerly — a slight backing may occur just ahead of the front.
Temperature	–	Steady low apart from normal land/sea differences.
Dewpoint	–	As above, but a rise often occurs just ahead of the front.
Pressure	–	Falling steadily.
Cloud Cover	–	Increasing to 8/8.

Cloud Types	–	In sequence CI CS AS NS with non-frontal turbulence cloud probably present at all distances from the front. Sometimes a little AC is present.
Cloud Base	–	Starting at 16500 ft plus for CI and then descending through medium and low levels to 1000 ft or less at the front.
Weather	–	Light intermittent from AS becoming light continuous. Moderate continuous from NS.
Visibility	–	Can be good initially but decreasing steadily as cloud base lowers and precipitation increases. Poor at the front.

AT THE WARM FRONT/IN THE WARM SECTOR

Surface W/V	–	Sharp veer to southwest or west at the front then steady.
Temperature	–	Sudden rise at the front then steady.
Dewpoint	–	As above.
Pressure	–	Stops falling — steady.
Cloud Cover	–	8/8.
Cloud Types	–	NS at the front with ST then ST or SC or both.
Cloud Base	–	Very low — usually a few hundred feet a.g.l.
Weather	–	Moderate continuous at the front then drizzle or light — sometimes nil but gloomy weather. Frontal fog can occur either side of the front.
Visibility	–	Very poor.

AT/BEHIND THE COLD FRONT

Surface W/V	–	Sharp veer at the front to northwest and can veer slightly thereafter. Gusts and squalls can occur particularly at the front.
Temperature	–	Sudden fall then steady.
Dewpoint	–	As above.
Pressure	–	A steady rise.
Cloud Cover	–	8/8 at the front reducing to 6/8 then 4/8 thereafter.
Cloud Types	–	Mainly CU and CB but additionally NS sometimes occurs at the front if there is a stability layer present. The tops of any CB can be effectively CI. Non frontal Turbulence ST or SC may also be present.

Cloud Base — Low at the front because of the precipitation but rising thereafter.

Weather — Showers can be heavy with hail, the amount reducing after frontal passage. Thunderstorms are probable at the front and possible thereafter but dependent to a degree on the time of year.

Visibility — Good except in showers and becoming excellent well behind the front.

Occlusions

The cold front in a polar front depression normally travels faster than the warm front. As a consequence the cold front overtakes the warm front later in the life of the depression. Typically after some 70° of meridian movement. It will be recalled that when the depression forms there is polar air ahead of the warm front and behind the cold front. During movement of the depression the temperature of the two volumes of polar air can change, dependent on the surfaces over which they travel. If, for example the polar air ahead of the warm front is over the warm land of Europe in summer whilst the polar air at the rear is over the Atlantic, this latter air will be colder. A cross section view of the occlusion so formed is at

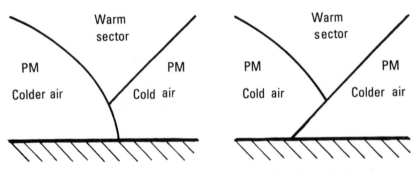

*Figure 14.5. Cross Section of a
Cold Occlusion*

*Figure 14.6. Cross Section of a
Warm Occlusion*

Figure 14.5. The colder air behind the cold front will undercut the air ahead of the warm front. The result will be a lifting of the warm sector and only a cold front will be apparent at the surface. This formation is called a cold occlusion. In these circumstances the cloud from the two fronts will be mixed but overall conditions are more likely to be akin to cold frontal weather. In a winter situation it is likely that the polar air over Europe will be colder than the air at the rear of the cold front over the Atlantic. In this case the less cold air will lift over the colder air ahead of the warm front. The occlusion in this case is termed warm. Again the warm sector is lifted above the surface but in this instance only a warm front is apparent at the ground. The weather will be mixed but it is more likely to provide a wider precipitation belt than the cold type. A cross section view of the warm type occlusion is at Figure 14.6.

Occlusion Weather

It will be noted that there will be two frontal lifting triggers at work. The lifting along the occluded front and the lifting higher up of the warm sector. The cloud amounts and precipitation can therefore be substantial. This together with the mixing of warm and cold front clouds can cause generally active bad weather. Additionally an occlusion usually forms towards the end of the active period of the depression when its movement is slowing e.g. a day or so before frontolysis. Hence the bad weather can last some time. In exceptional circumstances this can result in 24 hours or more of rain and occasionally the occlusion can even reverse in direction.

A particular flying hazard is CB or a thunderstorm embedded in NS or AS, so that the CB encounter is unexpected. This can occur in both types of occlusion although it is a little more likely with the cold type. Over Europe in winter cold polar continental air from Siberia can be ahead of the warm type occlusion. This can cause temperatures below freezing at low level ahead of rain falling from the NS cloud. This can cause the further hazard of rain ice.

In time with frontolysis new activity ceases and the occlusion produces only a little cloud and light precipitation as the depression dies.

Back Bent Occlusions

Sometimes an occlusion can form a loop through the depression centre. This can happen if the depression is moving quickly whilst the occluded fronts have a slower movement and lag behind. A plan view of a back bent occlusion is at Figure 14.7. At both sections of the occlusion and in the area in between, the conditions can become very unstable leading to CU CB and thundery weather.

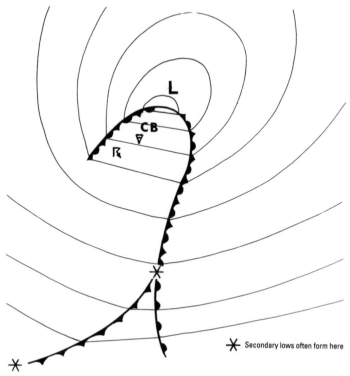

Figure 14.7. A Back bent Occlusion

Secondary lows often form here

Time Periods

Growth of a polar front depression to the time of producing the lowest pressure at the centre is about 4 days. The dying away as the depression fills can take 10 days or more. Eventually it is absorbed into some other pressure feature.

For Europe a typical life span involves the following:

a) Formation and growth near the east seaboard of the USA/ mid Atlantic.
b) Lowest pressure and occlusion near the 0° meridian.
c) Passage and filling over the North Sea/Scandinavia/ Eastern Europe and Russia.

The depressions form in 'families' one behind the other and are usually separated by a ridge of high pressure or a temporary anticyclone. The younger family members often start their formation at the end of a trailing cold front. Sometimes they form as a secondary low at an early occlusion point.

Southern Hemisphere

The polar front moves very little seasonally because of the comparative reduction in the ratio of land to sea. As a result the front lies roughly adjacent to the 50° south parallel of latitude throughout the year. In the east of South America polar air can sometimes move north causing a wave in the polar front in this region.

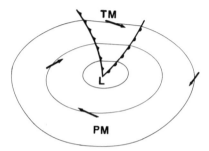

Figure 14.8. Typical Polar Front Depression in the Southern Hemisphere

It will be apparent from Figure 14.8 that the fronts inside a polar front low will be extending towards the equator as in the northern hemisphere but the orientation will be different. The opposite rotation of the winds in the southern hemisphere will result in surface winds ahead of the warm front, at the warm front/in warm sector and at/behind the cold front being respectively northerly, northwest or west and southwest.

Orographic Depressions

These are sometimes referred to as lee lows and are formed on the lee or downwind side of a range of mountains. If a wind is blowing at a large angle against such a mountain range then much of the air will be held back by the mountains and some of it will find a passage through valleys or around the ends of the range. The result is a lack of air just on the downwind side of the mountains. In consequence a low forms, air will move into the low causing lifting, divergence at height and the low then develops into a full depression. This is displayed at Figure 14.9.

The associated weather can fall into one of three general categories:

  a) If the air is dry or if there has been a Föhn wind then good weather — no cloud or precipitation.

129

b) If the air is moist then even if it is stable, the lifting against the mountains can cause convective instability with CU cloud. Passage of this cloud-laden air over the depression can result in additional lifting and CB as well as CU.

c) Sometimes a cold front with its unstable polar maritime air behind is taken over the mountains and lifted again by the depression. The result is widespread CB with very heavy showers and thunderstorms.

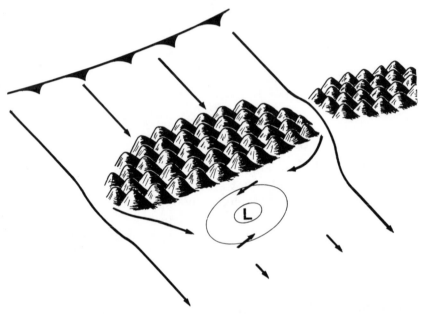

Figure 14.9. The Orographic Depression

These lows can be experienced south of the European alps with a northerly wind thus affecting routes to Italy, Greece, Turkey and Egypt. With a southerly wind in summer, the south of Germany can experience these conditions. They also occur east of the High Sierra mountains in California thus affecting routes from the west coast to Washington and New York.

Thermal Depressions

Thermal depressions are formed by heating of the surface air resulting in strong convection, an increase of relative pressure at height above the convection, followed by divergence at this level with a consequent reduction in surface pressure. Inevitably the reduction in surface pressure will result in the surface air behaving cyclonically acting under the influence of pressure gradient and geostrophic forces and such friction as applies in the local area. This formation and the air movements involved are shown at Figure 14.10.

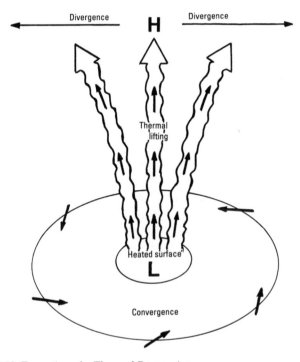

Figure 14.10. Formation of a Thermal Depression

If the thermal low forms in stable conditions then upper level divergence can be at a low level with little weather activity, particularly if the air is dry. However, even in a basically stable atmosphere, if there is sufficient moisture to cause early saturation and a low cloud base then the subsequent lifting can cause convective instability. The resulting weather is the same as expected for unstable conditions; CU CB cloud with showers which can be heavy with the possibility of thunderstorms and hail, visibility good except in showers. Flight conditions can be turbulent with clear icing above the freezing level, which can be severe.

Thermal depressions forming at different latitudes and over land or sea can have differing characteristics although, with the exception of 'dust devils' the weather is in accord with the listing above.

131

Dust Devils

These form over deserts and other dry areas where there is stability. Hence they are relatively shallow in depth. There is no cloud in these lows and therefore the only weather of significance is poor visibility due to the lifted dust and sand causing haze and low level turbulence which can be a hazard on the approach. These dry storms are usually very local in character and often move away from their origin under the influence of winds and local pressure variations.

Polar Air Depressions

These occur in the mid-latitudes when polar maritime air moves to a lower latitude. The result is heating of the lower layers of the air followed by convective lifting. When this passage is over a warmer sea the lifting can be widespread and instability can develop and a thermal low will result. The depressions often occur in the North Atlantic and Pacific oceans in the winter time, when the relative temperature increase as the air moves is highest. In addition to the normal thermal low weather, there can be a series of cold fronts as the polar maritime air continues to feed into the thermal low area. The depressions tend to move with the airflow and occasionally they can move close to the polar front. When this occurs, some tropical air can move into the low and then layer type cloud and more general precipitation can occur. They can also form by air moving from the cold land over the warmer sea. These can occur at high latitudes. The resulting instability can occasionally cause these storms to be vigorous, resulting in gales and heavy snow showers.

Thermal Lows Over Land in Mid-Latitudes

These are a summer phenomenon and give the expected thermal low weather. They occur inland due to convection. Sometimes they start to form close to a coast by orographic means, the insolation and convection further inland together with the moisture from the coastal area causing full thermal low development, which can be very active. The storms with their thunderstorms move with the general air circulation. An example of this occurs when summer thermal lows over Northern France bring thunderstorms to South East England. These lows also form extensively over any heated land area.

Thermal Lows Over Inland Seas

In winter inland seas are warm relative to the surrounding land areas. The temperature difference in mid-latitudes is marked and results in low density and low pressure in the air over the sea surfaces and relatively high density and pressure over the nearby lands. This results in cold dry air moving over the warm sea surfaces, lifting and the development of thermal lows. These are particularly common over the Caspian, Black and Mediterranean seas in Europe and Asia, also over the Great Lakes of North America. In this latter case the storms can be particularly violent. In the Mediterranean they are more likely in the middle and eastern regions of the sea. The storms then move in an easterly direction under the influence of the upper winds and provide winter precipitation for many of the arid desert areas bordering the Arabian Gulf.

Thermal Lows Over Land in Low Latitudes
Anywhere in the tropics and certainly near the geographic or heat equator, lows will develop provided there is moisture. Frequently these form as a series of CB clouds and thunderstorms which occur daily. A good example of this situation is at Singapore. Islands in the tropics are also breeding grounds for thermal lows and often provide the only weather and rainfall other than that afforded by sea breezes.

In central Africa the thermal lows which develop in the upper Niger basin become the tornadoes of West Africa at the equinoxes when the wind is from the east.

These lows develop very rapidly after sunrise and thunderstorms are inevitable with CB cloud tops often well in excess of 50 000 ft.

Thermal Lows Over Sea in Low Latitudes: The Tropical Cyclones
These extreme cases of thermal depressions are covered in the chapter on Aviation Hazards.

Easterly Waves
In the tropics in association with the equatorial trough and the trade winds, the easterly flow of air applies at all heights in the troposphere. Wave characteristics can develop in the easterly flow in both hemispheres. These are found in the region between the equatorial trough and the subtropical highs. At the centre line of these waves, something akin to a trough line can emerge. An example is shown at Figure 14.11. Convergence occurs in the air moving to the north, on the east side of the wave resulting in instability through a deep layer and large scale thunderstorms can

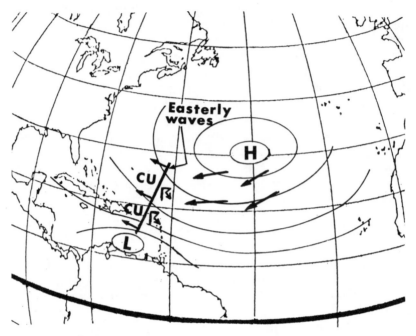

Figure 14.11. Easterly Waves

result. Elsewhere in the easterly flow any lifting can be restricted to the lower levels by subsidence.

A weak low centre is sometimes evident on the lower latitude side of the wave. This can develop into a tropical cyclone. Easterly waves are more frequent in summer. Although the West African Tornadoes which can result from the waves over land occur in the spring and autumn.

Chapter 15
Upper Winds

Upper Level Pressure Systems

At the upper levels above the equatorial region anticyclones can be expected due to the lifting of warm air and the subsequent low rate of reduction of pressure with height. This will include high pressure above the Hadley cells. For similar reasons upper level depressions can be expected above the polar regions. In the middle latitudes therefore, the expected zonal flow of wind — that caused by the main pressure systems, should be westerly. It will be recalled that on a smaller scale, and mostly in the lower troposphere, depressions can be expected above surface anticyclones and the latter above the surface depressions although this is not always the case. These smaller changes in mid-latitudes can cause north/south perturbations in the zonal flow, which result in ridges and troughs in a small wave pattern. An example of what could occur over the North Atlantic with surface polar front lows and ridges is shown at Figure 15.1. The ridges extending from the lower latitudes and the

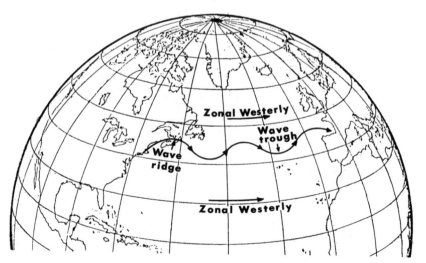

Figure 15.1. Upper Zonal Flow Over the North Atlantic with Perturbations

troughs from the higher latitudes. The waves so formed are relatively short, say 30° of longitude and move rapidly in concert

135

with the surface system movements. There are longer wave effects, again resulting in north/south perturbations. These are caused by long wave orographic troughs developing to the east of the large north/south mountain ranges such as the Rocky mountains and the Andes. In these cases the wave lengths are of the order of 50° to 100° of longitude. They effect wind flow worldwide and not only in the originating areas. At any one time there are approximately four long waves around the world.

It will be apparent that the surface enclosed pressure systems with their origins largely based in the great variation in surface temperatures and pressures, are not always repeated at height. It can be expected that at the upper levels troughs and ridges are far more likely and this particularly applies in middle latitudes.

Constant Pressure Charts/Contour Charts

Synoptic charts produced for mean sea level display the varying pressures at this level together with isobars. For the upper levels, a reverse approach is used whereby pressure is constant all over the chart and the varying heights of a particular pressure surface are displayed. These charts are called constant pressure, or contour charts. The latter name because lines are drawn on the charts

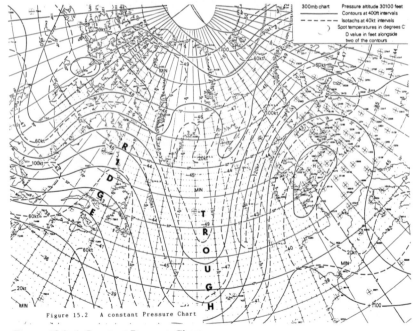

Figure 15.2. A Constant Pressure Chart

joining places where the height of the particular pressure surface is the same.

Any line drawn on a constant pressure chart must, by defintion, be a line of constant pressure. The contour line is a case in point, but additionally it is a line of constant pressure at the same level and therefore it is an isobar. An example of a 300 mb chart is shown at Figure 15.2. The solid black lines are the contour lines/isobars. The ridges extending from the low latitudes and the troughs from the high latitudes can be clearly seen.

Constant pressure charts can be drawn for a number of different pressure surfaces. The most common charts are for:

Pressure	Nominal equivalent heights	Average pressure altitudes in mid-latitudes
700 mb	10 000 ft	9 900 ft
500 mb	20 000 ft	18 300 ft
300 mb	30 000 ft	30 500 ft
250 mb	35 000 ft	34 000 ft
200 mb	40 000 ft	38 400 ft
100 mb	50 000 ft	53 100 ft

Nominal heights are widely used and as aircraft fly at pressure altitudes, the constant pressure chart system is sensible.

The winds at all levels above a few thousand feet are caused by the same forces which affect air movements at lower levels, apart from friction. Hence the forces of Pressure Gradient, Geostrophic and Cyclostrophic still apply. However, it will be noted from the pressure considerations that the cyclostrophic force becomes of reduced importance as enclosed pressure systems are less common. Upper winds are therefore most often close to geostrophic and the geostrophic formula for windspeed still applies where:

$$V = \frac{PGF}{2 \, \Omega \, \rho \; \text{sine latitude}}$$

Since ρ, the density, reduces with increase of height, the speed will increase accordingly.

By use of the contour lines and invoking Buys Ballot's Law, the upper winds at the level of a constant pressure chart can be found thus:

The upper wind blows parallel to the contour lines such that with your back to the wind in the northern hemisphere the region of low contour height (and thus low pressure) is on your left. Speed is proportional to the distance between the contour lines. In the southern hemisphere, the low contour height would on the right.

The chart at Figure 15.2 shows dashed lines. These are isotachs, which are lines joining places where windspeed is the same. They replace the geostrophic wind scale used on mean sea level charts. Using Figure 15.2 it can be estimated that the 30 000 ft wind at 40°00′N 50°00′W is 320/60 (the lowest contour height being to the north). Other information includes the location, shape and maximum speed of jet streams as shown by the isotachs. There is a good example of this with a southwesterly jet passing to the north of Scotland with speeds up to 120 kn. The temperatures shown are spot temperatures at the chart level.

Radiosonde
The radiosonde is used to provide upper air information. This is used to produce constant pressure charts. It in fact produces data

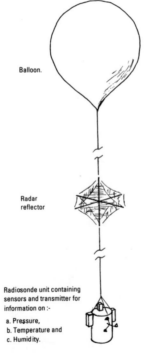

Balloon.

Radar reflector

Radiosonde unit containing sensors and transmitter for information on :-

a. Pressure,
b. Temperature and
c. Humidity.

Figure 15.3. A Radiosonde

on a 12-hour interval basis of pressure temperature and humidity. The radiosonde comprises a small radio transmitter suspended from a hydrogen balloon which emits a carrier wave. The carrier is modulated by introducing in turn, three sensing elements into the carrier wave circuit. After release from the ground the sensors continuously measure pressure, temperature and humidity. The balloon takes the device up to some 150 000 ft (46 km) transmitting the whole time. Around this level the balloon bursts and the radiosonde then breaks up as it falls into denser air.

Transmissions are received at a ground station and decoded into normal values. The sites from which 12-hour releases are made include ships and ground stations. In the UK there are nine ground sites, whereas in a large country such as the USA there are hundreds of sites.

During operation the radiosondes are tracked by radar enabling upper winds to be measured and height to be monitored. These devices are not a danger to aircraft but sometimes they can be seen ascending within sight of an aircraft. A drawing of a radiosonde is at Figure 15.3.

The Thermal Wind Concept
A further method of finding the upper wind is by reference to the difference in wind between one level and another. Consider the

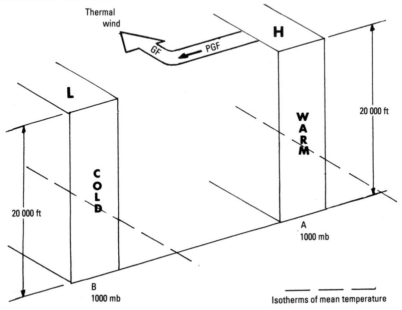

Figure 15.4. Thermal Wind Concept

diagram at Figure 15.4. Surface pressures at A and B are the same, hence there is no wind between A and B. Above A there is warm air and therefore at any height above A pressure will be higher than at the same level in the cold air above B. The higher pressure will cause pressure gradient force and geostrophic force to apply, resulting in a wind which is blowing parallel to the two columns of air. There could be a difference between the surface pressures at A and B causing a geostrophic wind (nominally above the friction layer at 2000 ft). If this was so then by the addition of this wind to the thermal wind, the total upper wind could be found. An example

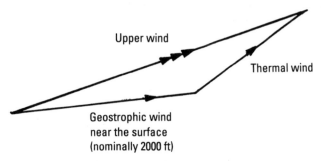

Figure 15.5. Vector Diagram of Surface, Thermal and Upper Winds

of the vectorial addition of the two winds is shown at Figure 15.5. This difference in wind between the two levels is called the thermal wind.

Thus, if the wind at one level is known, then by adding vectorialy the thermal wind between this level and a higher level, the upper wind can be calculated. This can be a continuous process allowing winds to be found for any level.

The value of the thermal wind can be gauged from a formula for 50° latitude: For a difference in mean temperature of 1°C per 100 nm below a level, the thermal wind speed is approximately equal to the thickness of the layer in thousands of feet. Thus at Figure 15.4, if the difference in mean temperature between column A and column B is 5°C and the two columns are 100 nm apart, then the thermal wind speed is 5 × 20 = 100 kn. It can therefore be deduced that the thermal wind is also the wind caused by the difference in mean temperature between two columns of air in the horizontal.

The thermal wind can be found by reference to the isotherms of mean temperature drawn between one pressure surface and another. It was noted that the thermal wind at Figure 15.4 blows parallel to the columns of air, i.e. parallel to the isotherms of mean temperature with the lowest mean temperature on the left in the northern hemisphere. In the southern hemisphere the lowest mean temperature would be on the right.

Thickness Charts

Figure 15.6 shows two pressure levels, 950 mb and 500 mb and the

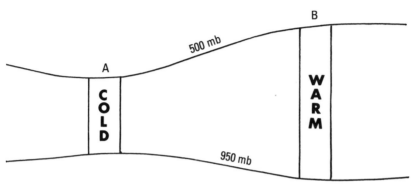

Figure 15.6. Thickness between Two Pressure Levels

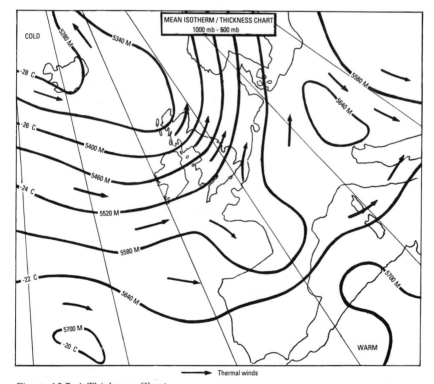

Figure 15.7. A Thickness Chart

varying thicknesses of the two levels is apparent. The difference in thickness is less at 'A' than at 'B' and this can only be because the mean temperature in column A is colder than at B. There is therefore a direct relationship between the isotherms of mean temperature and the isopleths of thickness — in fact they are coincident. The thermal wind therefore blows parallel to the isopleths of thickness with the lowest thickness values (lowest mean temperatures) on the left in the northern hemisphere and on the right in the southern hemisphere. Speed of the wind is proportional to the distance between the isopleths. Hence thickness charts are used for finding the thermal wind. Additionally they indicate where there are cold and warm pools of air and this assists forecasting. An example of a thickness chart is shown at Figure 15.7 together with thermal wind directions.

Thermal Winds — Global
In the troposphere the expected colder air above the polar regions and the warmer air above low latitudes will produce thermal winds which are westerly. This is in accord with the mid-latitude zonal wind.

Above the tropopause in the stratosphere the vertical temperature situation changes and lower temperatures should be over the lower latitudes. It therefore follows that a small easterly component to the wind will develop. The effect of this will be to mitigate the expected increase of westerly speed due to the reduction of density with height. Any westerly speed reduction due to this reversal in mean temperature should only become apparent at levels above 50 mb (say, 70 000 ft).

It has already been mentioned that despite a westerly zonal flow in the troposphere, there will be north/south perturbations and some of these can be caused by surface pressure systems and the consequent pressure changes above. These changes above can be controlled not only by the air rising and descending causing high pressure above the lows and low pressure above the highs, but additionally, by the thermal component above these features. For example, if there is cold air being lifted above a surface depression then it is likely that pressure at height will also be low compared with pressures at the same level. Similarly, if warm air is made to descend to a surface anticyclone then at height the pressure may also be high. This in fact is the case above the subtropical anticyclones.

Despite the above caveats and the perturbations caused by the long waves, in general it can be expected that with increase of

142

PLATE I **HIGH LEVEL LAYERED CLOUD**

CI – CIRRUS is a stability cloud which forms some 400 nm to 600 nm ahead of the surface position of a warm front. It is sometimes referred to as 'Mare's Tails'. It is composed entirely of ice crystals. When cross banded with one axis running NW/SE it indicates the position of a jet stream and CAT. (In the southern hemisphere an axis would run SW/NE.)

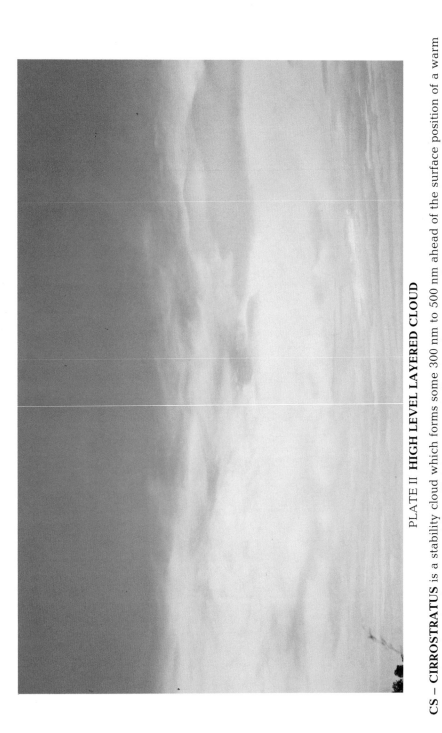

PLATE II **HIGH LEVEL LAYERED CLOUD**

CS – CIRROSTRATUS is a stability cloud which forms some 300 nm to 500 nm ahead of the surface position of a warm front. When this cloud is seen to follow CI, it is a strong indication that a warm front is approaching. This is particularly so if in addition the surface wind is southerly and the pressure is falling. The cloud is composed entirely of ice crystals and the sun shining through these crystals can produce a halo.

PLATE III **HIGH LEVEL LAYERED CLOUD**

CC – **CIRROCUMULUS** is a stability cloud sometimes associated with frontal activity. It is composed entirely of ice crystals. There is no icing in any of these high level clouds, the ice crystals will not adhere to an airframe. There is no precipitation from any of the high level clouds.

PLATE IV **MEDIUM LEVEL LAYERED CLOUD**

AS – ALTOSTRATUS is a stability cloud which forms some 200 nm ahead of the surface position of a warm front. It is also present in the intertropical convergence zone when stability layers are present. It gives only light turbulence, light continuous precipitation and light rime icing. The composition is a mixture of water droplets and ice crystals. This picture shows Altostratus (Thin).

PLATE V **MEDIUM LEVEL LAYERED CLOUD**

AS – ALTOSTRATUS often merges with CS at the upper level and with NS at the lower level in frontal situations. The Altostratus (Dense) shown here is difficult to distinguish from NS except by the cloud base and the type of precipitation.

PLATE VI **LOW LEVEL LAYERED CLOUD**

NS – NIMBOSTRATUS can exhibit characteristics more akin to CU whilst its general height band is from the surface to 6500 ft. It can extend well into the AS levels. It occurs regularly at and ahead of warm fronts. It also forms in the inter-tropical convergence zone when stability layers are present. NS is composed of water droplets and provides moderate continuous precipitation. It can give moderate to severe clear airframe icing as well as rime. It can cause rain ice ahead of a warm front or occlusion. At an occlusion NS can sometimes have CB and thunderstorms embedded.

PLATE VII **MEDIUM LEVEL LAYERED CLOUD**

AC – **ALTOCUMULUS** is a stability cloud composed of water droplets and ice crystals. It can form in association with fronts, as AC Lenticularis with mountain waves and as AC Castellanus in the cumuliform category. The cloud does not have sufficient depth to provide precipitation of any significance. This picture shows a typical 'Mackerel' sky where the cloud forms in 'streets' parallel to hills or mountains.

PLATE VIII **MEDIUM LEVEL LAYERED CLOUD**

AC – ALTOCUMULUS (Lenticularis) forms over hills and mountains and indicates low level stability and the presence of mountain waves. The air is lifted over the high ground and cloud forms. It then deforms by evaporation on descending down the lee side of the high ground thus producing the lens shape.

PLATE IX LOW LEVEL LAYERED CLOUD

ST – STRATUS is a stability cloud formed by turbulence and is often in broken form when it is called Stratus Fractus. It has a very low base and can interfere considerably with circuit flying. It can also be formed by the lifting of fog. The composition is water droplets and the precipitation is drizzle. It can cause light rime icing.

PLATE X **LOW LEVEL LAYERED CLOUD**

ST – STRATUS (Cap) refers to stratus which forms over the top of high ground. It often drifts to the down wind side of the high ground hence forming a 'cap'. It is an indicator of strong low level stability and of the presence of mountain waves.

(Original photograph by Captain Julie S. Simmonds)

PLATE XI **LOW LEVEL LAYERED CLOUD**

SC – STRATOCUMULUS is a stability cloud formed by turbulence and is sometimes referred to as a roll cloud. Above SC there is usually a temperature inversion and very smooth air. It gives light precipitation or drizzle and light to moderate rime icing. Its composition is water droplets. It can sometimes be seen just ahead of a thunderstorm CB.

PLATE XII CUMULIFORM CLOUD

CU – CUMULUS is an instability cloud which is often isolated particularly when formed by convection. It can be quite small and is then referred to as Fair Weather CU as displayed here. If this type is seen in the early morning it can well develop into large CU or CB later in the afternoon.

PLATE XIII **CUMULIFORM CLOUD**

CU – **CUMULUS** can be very large in the vertical and extend up to some 25 000 ft from near the surface. It is common at cold fronts, at the intertropical convergence zone and in tropical cyclones. Precipitation is in the form of showers which can be heavy. Turbulence is usually in the moderate to severe category. Airframe icing can be moderate to severe of the clear type. A line of CU can sometimes be seen along a coast or over a range of mountains.

PLATE XIV CUMULIFORM CLOUD

CU – CUMULUS of the large variety can join together to form a thunderstorm cell. The main features of the cell are strong upcurrents and severe turbulence in and around the cell. The upward growth can be clearly visible.

(Original photograph by Captain Julie S. Simmonds)

PLATE XV CUMULIFORM CLOUD

CB – CUMULONIMBUS is the danger cloud formed when there is instability through a considerable depth and sufficient water vapour available. It can extend from near the surface to the tropopause and above. This picture shows CB without an 'anvil' top.

(Original photograph by Captain Julie S. Simmonds)

PLATE XVI CUMULIFORM CLOUD

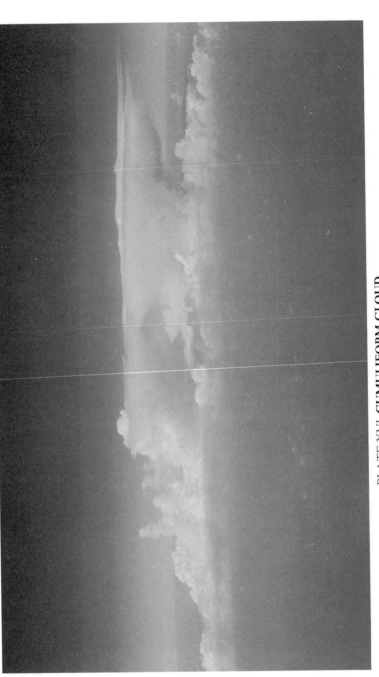

CB – CUMULONIMBUS is the cloud which can produce thunderstorms and hail. Precipitation is in the form of heavy showers. The hazards in CB include severe turbulence, heavy hail, lightning and severe icing. Under the cloud, squalls, microbursts and windshear can be expected. It is formed by convection, at cold fronts and in the intertropical convergence zone. It is the main weather factor in tropical cyclones. The picture shown above is of CB with anvils formed orographically over a mountain range.

(Original photograph by Captain David M. A. Wells)

PLATE XVII **CUMULIFORM CLOUD**

CB – CUMULONIMBUS can form in a line at a cold front or occlusion as shown above. The CB actually form along the frontal surface. There can be squalls under each CB thus forming a line squall.

PLATE XVIII CUMULIFORM CLOUD

AC – ALTOCUMULUS (Castellanus) forms when a stable atmosphere in which normal AC is produced suddenly becomes unstable. Hence linear formations suddenly develop 'towers' as the instability takes hold. There can be moderate to severe turbulence in these formations. This cloud indicates the probability of thunderstorm formation within the next 24 hours.

(Original photograph by Captain David M. A. Wells)

PLATE IXX **EXCEPTIONAL HAIL DAMAGE**

Port and Starboard Engine Intake Areas – The photographs here and overleaf are published by the kind permission of the United States Marine Corps and McDonnell Douglas Aircraft Company. They show exceptional hail damage to an AV-8B Harrier II aircraft. The pictures reflect not only the robust construction but also the fine skill of the pilot in recovering the aircraft.

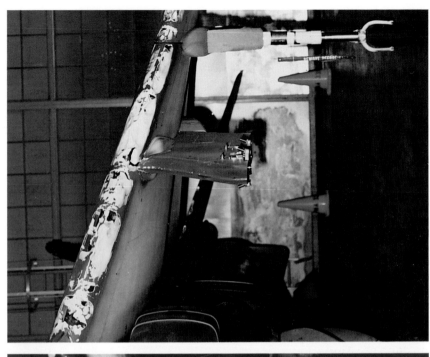

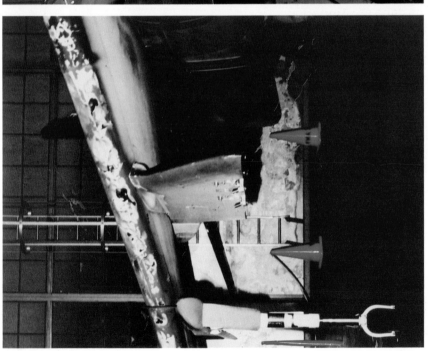

PLATE XX   EXCEPTIONAL HAIL DAMAGE

Port and Starboard Wing Leading Edges.

height in middle latitudes in the troposphere the wind will become progessively more westerly.

Within the tropics, Buys Ballot's law no longer applies and the upper winds tend to become more easterly from the surface with increase of height. These easterly winds accord with the low level and high level anticyclones associated with the subtropics which on the lower latitudes side must give an easterly zonal wind. These easterlies have a pressure, rather than a thermal content and have seasonal movements northwards in July and to the south in January.

At the higher latitudes in winter there are strong westerly winds which increase in strength as the temperatures are kept low deep into the stratosphere by polar night cooling. In summer with the higher temperatures in the polar stratosphere the westerlies are reduced and reverse to easterlies with further increases of height deeper into the stratosphere. Care should be taken to note that the lower stratosphere in the polar regions means only some 24 000 ft to 30 000 ft. Therefore these stratospheric upper winds can easily apply to modern jet aircraft.

Wind Charts
Constant pressure charts are the basis for finding upper winds together with thickness charts. This information together with accurate reports from aircraft is used to provide the forecast wind charts where wind velocities and temperatures are plotted at main latitude and longitude intersections. In some countries, forecast documentation for pilots include constant pressure charts.

Jet Streams
When thermal effects are very strong jet streams can form. These can be likened to a hollow flat tube through which air passes at high speed. One open end of the tube being an entry and the other an exit for the passing air.

The World Meteorology Organisation defines a jet stream thus:
> A strong narrow current concentrated along a quasi-horizontal axis in the upper troposphere or stratosphere, characterised by strong vertical and lateral wind shears and featuring one or more velocity maxima. The windspeed must be greater than 60 kn.

Typical dimensions for a jet are 1500 nm long, 200 nm wide and 12 000 ft deep. Diagrammatic representations are at Figure 15.8

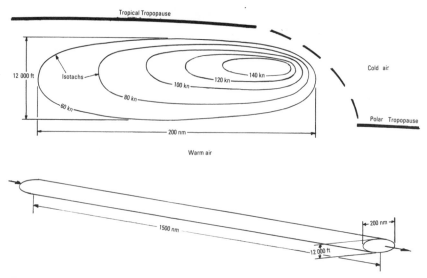

Figure 15.8. Jet Stream Diagrams

which show the general shape together with typical isotach values in a cross section diagram. The isotachs show that there are very strong windshears on the cold or polar side of the jet and above the jet core too. In these areas therefore and particularly on the cold side there is strong clear air turbulence.

Jet streams in the troposphere have a general westerly direction and speeds well above 100 kn are common. In the region of east Asia and Japan speeds can be up to 300 kn.

There are two main locations for tropospheric jet streams. These are the subtropical jets and the polar front jets. In both cases the jet streams form in the warm air below the tropical tropopause.

Subtropical Jets

These are caused by the strong mean temperature gradients on the higher latitude sides of the subtropical anticyclones and the cause is associated with the Hadley cells. The jets are more or less permanent but move seasonally with movement of the subtropical anticyclones. They occur in the approximate latitude bands:

25° to 40° in winter

40° to 45° in summer

The diagrams at Figure 15.9 show the warm descending air from the Hadley cells with the colder air on the polar sides thus causing the strong thermal effect and the jet stream. The location with respect to the heat equator is also shown in plan. The diagrams

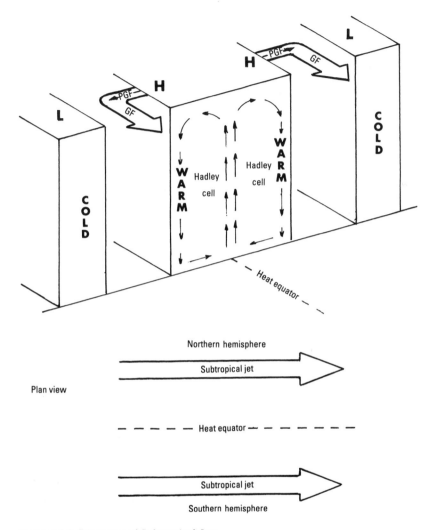

Figure 15.9. Diagrams of Subtropical Jets

show that the jets are located in the warm air with the higher pressure above the warm subtropical anticyclone. Thus in the northern hemisphere the direction of the pressure gradient force will be to the north. The moving air is then turned to the right by geostrophic force producing a westerly subtropical jet. In the southern hemisphere the pressure gradient force is to the south and the geostrophic force turns the moving air to the left, again producing a westerly subtropical jet.

Polar Front Jets

At the polar front there is the meeting between polar and tropical air and therefore a strong north/south thermal gradient. This produces a westerly jet stream in both hemispheres in accord with Buys Ballot's law. The polar front is frequently separated into different segments and contained within polar front depressions. A cross section of a polar front low is at Figure 14.4. The basic skeleton of this cross section is shown at Figure 15.10 and it will be

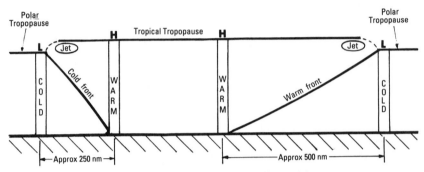

Figure 15.10. Polar Front Cross Section Showing Different Mean
Temperature Values and Jets

noted that there is a distinct increase in the mean temperature of a column of air in the warm sector compared with the two columns in the polar maritime air ahead of the warm front and behind the cold front respectively. The resulting strong thermal components cause jet streams to form in the warm air below the tropical tropopause. It will further be apparent that the jet is more likely, or, likely to give a stronger wind, in association with the cold front because of the shorter horizontal distance between the warm and cold columns.

The plan diagram of a polar front low at Figure 15.11 shows that the two separate jets are in fact one jet stream lying roughly parallel to the frontal surfaces. The portion of the jet in association with the warm front is some 400 nm ahead of the surface warm front position and is parallel to the front. This results in a general northwesterly jet. The jet behind the cold front surface position by some 200 nm, is again parallel to the front and usually from a generally southwesterly direction. (In the southern hemisphere, again the jets are parallel to the fronts, but the usual directions are changed in accord with Buys Ballot's law: southwesterly ahead of the warm front and northwesterly behind the cold front). The isopleths of thickness are indicated to show the thermal winds. Care should be taken when viewing this plan diagram which can give the impression that the jets are in the cold air. This is not the

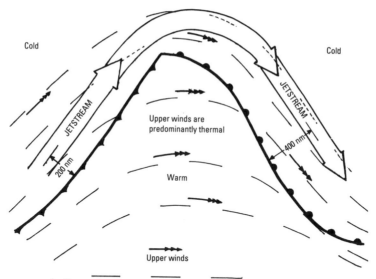

Isotherm of mean temperature (isopleths of thickness)

Figure 15.11. Plan View of Jets and Upper Winds in a Polar Front Depression

case as the slope of the fronts allows the plan position to be transposed to the warm air at height.

It will be recalled that with passage of a polar front low from the west, the surface winds veer from southerly through to northwesterly in the northern hemisphere. The upper winds however back with passage of a polar front low from the west, changing from northwesterly through westerly to southwesterly behind the cold front. This can be appreciated from Figure 15.11. (In the southern hemisphere the surface winds back whilst the upper winds veer).

Referring back to the constant pressure chart at Figure 15.2 the 30000 ft southwesterly polar front jet behind a cold front can be seen passing to the north of Scotland. Similarly, the northwesterly jet ahead of the next warm front can be seen to the east of Newfoundland. These polar front jets move with the lows and are therefore not as permanent as the subtropical jets. They are more numerous and tend to be stronger in the winter months. The reasons are that there are more fronts in winter and also during this season there are greater mean temperature differences between the continents and the oceans.

Other Jet Streams

Besides the main jet stream locations, there are upper level winds well in excess of 60 kn in association with increasing wind strength with increase of height, when mountain waves are formed and these can spread into the stratosphere.

The previously mentioned zonal easterly winds in low latitudes can sometimes produce tropospheric easterly jets in the summer hemisphere, although these tend to be fragmented in location. In the stratosphere the easterly winds become jets with speeds of 75 to 100 kn. These are positioned in both hemispheres but are more pronounced in the summer hemisphere.

Chapter 16
Aviation Hazards

Introduction
Meteorological aviation hazards now vie in importance with those based in engineering and therefore their significance cannot be overplayed. It is unlikely that that the reader will fully appreciate the following sections without knowledge of the preceding chapters. The hazards include:

a) Wake Turbulence.
b) Mountain Waves.
c) Rotor Streaming.
d) Low Level Windshear (including Microbursts).
e) Clear Air Turbulence (CAT).
f) Cumulonimbus — Thunderstorms.
g) Tornadoes.
h) Airframe and Enging Icing.
i) Tropical Cyclones.

WAKE TURBULENCE
Wake vortices, sometimes referred to as wing tip vortices, produce two counter-rotating cylinders of air trailing behind an aircraft. They are caused by air from under the surface of a wing where pressure is relatively high, moving to the upper wing surface where pressure is low. This initial movement is then given length by the local airflow over the wing. In stable conditions when winds are light, the vortices can slowly descend to around 1000 ft below the flight path and remain suspended in the air for some minutes. Near the ground they can move sideways and outward from the track of the generating aircraft. Referring diagrams are at Figure 16.1. The vortices can be quickly dispersed if the atmosphere is unstable and winds are strong, under these conditions they last for seconds only.

The degree of turbulence in the vortices is affected by a number of factors including the state of the ambient air, but in general the heavier the aircraft the greater the turbulence generated. The turbulence effects are most marked at low level, just after take-off

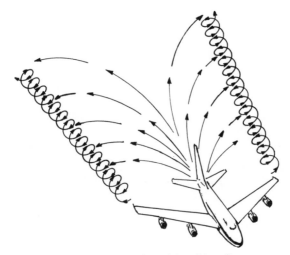

General view of Vortex flow pattern

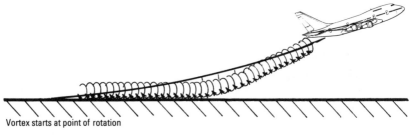

Vortex starts at point of rotation

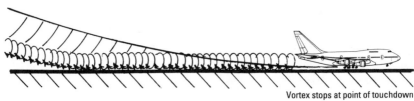

Vortex stops at point of touchdown

Figure 16.1. Wake Turbulence

when the vortices first form and during the approach. There can thus be a problem for a lighter aircraft about to take-off behind a heavier aircraft. Any case of an aircraft following too closely behind a heavier aircraft at low level, or even crossing a vortex can produce dangerous turbulence. This is particularly so when the air is stable and winds are light. The recommended spacing on the approach between a leading heavy aircraft (136000 kg or more maximum TOW) and a following light aircraft (7000 kg or less maximum TOW) is 6 nm and 3 minutes. If there is high relative humidity, the adiabatic cooling as the air moves around the wing to the lower pressure on the upper surface can cause condensation and the vortices to be clearly visible.

MOUNTAIN WAVES

Mountain waves are also known as standing waves. They can occur above and downwind of a mountain range and at all heights in the aviation atmosphere. They are formed by the whole troposphere from ground level on the upwind side of a mountain range moving together in one general direction, roughly at right angles to the range (say within 30°). This total movement can only apply if the atmosphere is stable, if the ground level wind is 15 kn or more, and the speed increases with increase of height. Additionally if there is particularly stable air, and this may be in the form of an inversion or an isothermal layer, just above the mountain range. The airflow will then tend to follow the outline of the mountain range. The result is a wave formation occurring over the mountains and this basic oscillation is repeated in the atmosphere downwind. The consequent mountain waves are sometimes in existence hundreds of miles downwind with a major range such as the Andes. An average distance for effective waves is 50 to 100 nm downwind as well as above the range itself. Vertically they can extend above the tropopause.

The lowest level wave can produce marked downdraughts and updraughts just downwind of the mountains and this can be an area of severe turbulence. An aircraft flying parallel to and just downwind of the range could be in a dangerous situation. Further, it can be hazardous for an aircraft at low level being flown from the downwind side towards the mountains. It can then be subject to severe up and downdraughts.

At the higher levels there is a form of very severe turbulence which is comparatively rare. However, there have been well documented cases of aircraft being subject to waves which are breaking, similar to waves breaking on a sea shore. In these conditions the airframe integrity can be at risk.

The increasing wind strength with increase of height almost inevitably leads to a jet stream which can extend into the stratosphere. Around the edges of the jet, turbulence can occur caused by rapid wind shears. Frequently this is outside cloud and is therefore classified as clear air turbulence (CAT). Mountain waves will often cause lenticular cloud to form and this is the prime indicator that mountain waves are present. The air passing through the wave causes cloud to form on the lifting side of the wave and to gradually evaporate on the descending side. Other indicators include a cap cloud of stratus resting on the top and downwind side of the mountains. In the region of the strong down and updraughts on the lee side of the mountains, rotors can form. These are rotating cylinders of air which then add to the turbulence in this area. Additionally a roll of stratocumulus often develops in this region. The presence of ragged edges to the lenticular clouds and the existence of roll clouds in the rotor zone give warnings of severe turbulence. A diagram of mountain waves showing cloud types and the areas of turbulence is at Figure 16.2.

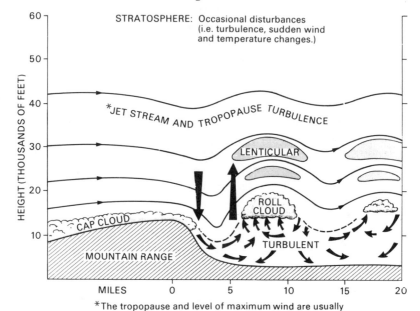

*The tropopause and level of maximum wind are usually located somewhere within this layer

MODEL OF A WELL-DEVELOPED MOUNTAIN WAVE SHOWING TYPICAL FEATURES

Figure 16.2. Mountain Waves

If the presence of mountain waves is suspected then the effects can be mitigated by:

a) Arranging to cross the mountain range at right angles.

b) At low level arranging never to approach or penetrate the rotor zone downwind of the range. Never flying parallel to and downwind of the range.

c) Flying as high as possible and at least 4000 ft above the mountains. If an obvious stable layer is present allow a clearance of 5000 ft on either side of the base of the layer.

152

d) Flying at the recommended turbulence speed for the aircraft type.
e) Accepting that waves may be present, even if there are no cloud indicators. This can be the case if the air is dry.
f) Taking particular care in mountainous areas where mapping heights can be inaccurate.
g) At high level noting that the speed difference between cruise and stall is small and therefore wave turbulences can give control problems. Additionally by recognising that when flying downwind in a wave, the higher relative speed can place greater loads on an airframe.

ROTOR STREAMING

Rotor streaming is a severe form of travelling turbulence which can occur downwind of a mountain range in conditions where basic mountain waves are unlikely.

As with mountain waves, a rotor zone can form just downwind of the mountains, but in certain conditions the rotor zone can then stream downwind taking its severe turbulence with the movement. The conditions necessary for this streaming to occur are stable air, strong winds at right angles to the mountain range (within 30°) for a restricted height comparable to mountain height and for lighter winds to apply above this level. The rotors can exist from ground level up to three times the height of the mountains and sometimes move downwind. They can cause extreme turbulence up to some 50 – 100 nm downwind of the range. A diagram of rotor streaming is at Figure 16.3.

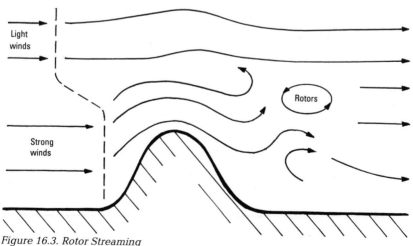

Figure 16.3. Rotor Streaming

LOW LEVEL WINDSHEAR (INCLUDING MICROBURSTS)

The term wind shear supposes a change in windspeed and/or direction with change of height. However, low level WINDSHEAR is a severe hazard and more complex. It only applies in the most dangerous portions of a flight profile, i.e. along the final approach path, along the runway during approach and take-off and during the initial climb-out.

In essence windshear is a sudden prolonged and large change in windspeed and/or direction which can occur in the horizontal or vertical. It can cause an aircraft to be displaced abruptly from the intended flight path such that substantial control action is necessary. Vertical updraughts and/or downdraughts can also cause shear. Severe windshear can make it very difficult for a pilot to maintain a required climb-out or approach profile, or a required target airspeed. Its effects can be very dangerous with large passenger aircraft which are subject to inertia.

Why should the question of inertia arise? Consider the diagram at Figure 16.4. Above the shear line the aircraft is settled down on the 3° approach path and the pilot has selected an appropriate power setting. On passing the shear line the headwind will drop to 10 kn and the airspeed will immediately fall from 120 to 100 kn and there will be a loss of lift. If it is a light aircraft then the effect of the reduced headwind will be a sudden increase in groundspeed. Therefore the tendency for the aircraft to depart below the approach path due to reduced lift, will be corrected by the increasing speed relative to the ground. There may be some need for small speed adjustments dependent on the degree of shear and the actual weight of the aircraft. Beyond these points there are few problems for the pilot. If alternatively the aircraft is a large modern jet, say 200 000 kg plus take-off weight, then after passing the shear line there will be the same sudden reduction in airspeed and lift. However, because of the inertia of the large aircraft the groundspeed will remain the same for some minutes and therefore the aircraft will depart below the approach path with a steepening descent angle. The groundspeed will gradually increase as the descent steepens but the aircraft may now be in severe danger of striking the ground or some prominent feature on the approach. Clearly the closer the shear occurs relative to the ground the greater the danger will be. Early application of large amounts of power are necessary to forestall the danger. This inevitably entails early appreciation of the problem. A sudden increase in a tailwind

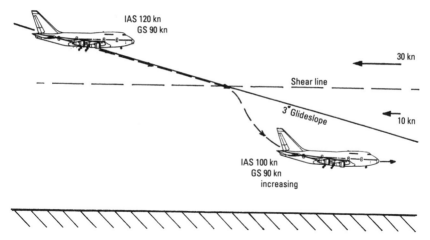

Figure 16.4. Windshear with a Loss of Airspeed and Lift

can produce the same effect and whilst this is an unlikely scenario for an approach or climb-out, it can occur with some thunderstorms.

The opposite case, where an aircraft passes a shear line and there is a sudden increase in headwind is shown at Figure 16.5. Here there is a sudden increase in lift and the heavy aircraft will depart above the approach path. This is a safe situation but of course some power adjustments will be necessary to regain the line and continue the approach. As before there is little effect on a light aircraft and the effects are power beneficial. A sudden decrease in tailwind would have similar effects on airspeed and lift. There are four particular meteorological situations where windshear is likely.

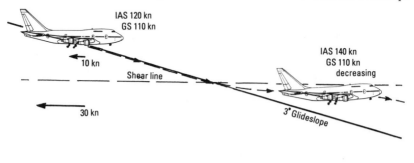

Figure 16.5. Windshear with a Gain in Airspeed and Lift

Inversions

A high speed low level wind sometimes forms in a strong inversion of shallow depth. Additionally, an inversion can separate a strong wind (say geostrophic) from calm or light winds beneath where the air has become stable. These occurrences often develop with a clear night sky which enhances terrestrial radiation and causes the inversion to develop. This is a relatively common situation in anticyclones. A relevant detailed diagram is at Figure 16.6.

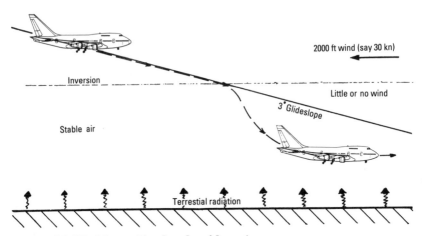

Figure 16.6. Windshear with a Low Level Inversion

Thunderstorms or CB

In thunderstorms or CB substantial shafts of air may be encountered, with no warning, which can be moving either vertically up or down. Such shafts may be virtually side by side, and the shear will then be very marked and violent. Entering a vertical up-draught or downdraught from a horizontal airflow, the aeroplane's momentum will at first keep it on its original path relative to the new direction of flow. In addition to a loss of airspeed, it will also be realised that the shift of relative airflow will affect the angle of attack of the wing, which may result in either an increase or decrease in angle. A slight increase of angle may not cause much concern. However if the aircraft is already on the approach with a high angle of attack, an increase might put the wing near the stall, and any decrease will bring about a loss of lift. Neither result is desirable when near the ground. Normally the risk of a downdraught will be more likely than an updraught when below 1000 ft.

Microbursts

These are powerful downdraughts of air which can descend from a CB centre with speeds as high as 60 kn down to a level as low as 300 ft. These will produce vortices from the ground in all directions. The result is that an aircraft approaching the area will experience a marked headwind followed by a severe downdraught followed again by a negative headwind (or tailwind). The effects on immediate airspeed and rate of descent are displayed at Figure 16.7 which indicates that the microburst is somewhat similar to a bomb burst. The microburst can be 'wet', i.e. associated with heavy precipitation which can be seen on the weather radar, or dry when the precipitation droplets have evaporated. In this case there will be no show on the weather radar but fallstreaks from the precipitation which does not reach the ground, 'Virga', is an indicator. The dry case is more likely to produce severe conditions. There have been well documented cases in the USA where the speed change from one vortex to the other exceeds 200 kn. These strong microbursts are more likely with air mass thunderstorms passing over dry near-desert regions. Here particularly, the evaporation of precipitation causes virga involving the absorption of large amounts of latent heat. This increases density and pressure at a low level thus enhancing surface divergence and the speed of downdraughts. Clearly in these extreme cases it is unlikely that any aircraft could survive. Hence the microburst is the most potentially dangerous of all the windshear cases. Microbursts only occur when the downdraught is concentrated in a shaft in the cloud some two nm wide and when it is particularly strong. They

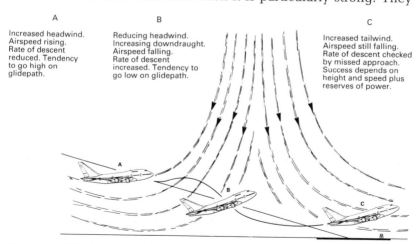

A
Increased headwind.
Airspeed rising.
Rate of descent
reduced. Tendency
to go high on
glidepath.

B
Reducing headwind.
Increasing downdraught.
Airspeed falling.
Rate of descent
increased. Tendency to
go low on glidepath.

C
Increased tailwind.
Airspeed still falling.
Rate of descent checked
by missed approach.
Success depends on
height and speed plus
reserves of power.

Figure 16.7. Effects of Flight Through a Microburst

are uncommon in the UK and Europe but are relatively frequent in the USA.

Fronts

If a front has strong convergence and with a marked temperature change across the front, say 5°C or more, then it is likely that the isobars will be sharply inclined at the frontal surface. The result is a large windshear in direction as an aircraft passes through the frontal surface. Typical situations for cold and warm fronts in plan and side views are shown at Figure 16.8. In the cold front case displayed, the aircraft is descending on the approach and is experiencing a westerly headwind which rapidly becomes a northwesterly beamwind on crossing the frontal surface: In consequence there will be an immediate reduction in airspeed and lift. In the warm front case displayed, the aircraft is experiencing a westerly tail wind which rapidly becomes a southerly beamwind on crossing the frontal surface: In consequence there will be an immediate increase in airspeed and lift. Clearly the loss of lift case is the more dangerous. This can occur with both types of front. In the warm front case at Figure 16.8 this could occur if the approach was in a southerly direction through the frontal surface.

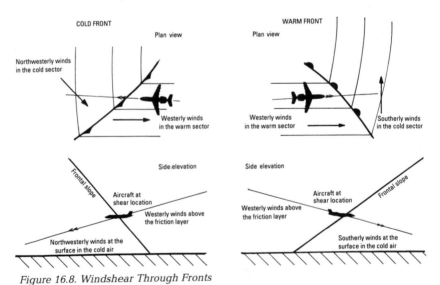

Figure 16.8. Windshear Through Fronts

Other less important Causes of Windshear

Ahead of a thunderstorm there is often a Gust Front and this can be encountered up to 25 nm ahead of the storm. It does not always cause shear but because it is due to cold air from the storm at the surface undercutting warmer air above, there is turbulence with a potential for windshear.

A sea breeze front affecting coastal airfields can cause shear when the sea breeze first moves inland across the coast. If it impinges on a thunderstorm it can alter the outflow from the storm and may enhance windshear. Topographical windshear can occur with mountain waves and rotors. Any topographical feature that provides differing winds with a sharp interface can cause shears.

Techniques to Counter Worst Effects

Avoidance by a proper appreciation of the met forecast is the prime requirement. On this basis a delayed take-off or diversion, may be necessary. If already committed and mentally alerted to a possible windshear situation, then an increase in airspeed by up to 20 kn may be efficacious. However, this is dependent on the type of aircraft and for a landing situation, how much airspeed may have to be lost during the final part of the descent.

The rate of shear is important so a slower penetration will result in a lower rate of shear, so the angle of attack can be brought into the argument whereby pitch attitude is increased and power raised to keep a high airspeed. The rapid response of propeller driven airflow over a wing will ease the windshear problem when power is applied. The best technique to counter worst effects for other pilots is early, and if possible detailed reports, of any windshear experienced.

Windshear Indicators

INSIDE THE AIRCRAFT:
   a) Use of weather radar for heavy precipitation returns.
   b) Comparison of INS wind velocity at height with ground reported wind velocity.
   c) Airspeed indicator — sudden changes.
   d) Vertical speed indicator — sudden changes.
   e) Heavy static indicating a nearby CB.

OUTSIDE THE AIRCRAFT
   a) Wind sleeve or smoke indicating a different wind velocity from that at the flight level.
   b) Strong shafts of rain or hail.
   c) Virga.
   d) Rising dust or sand.
   e) Any indicator of a CB (e.g. lightning, St. Elmo's fire).

f) Divergent wind patterns with grass, crops or trees being beaten down or lashed.

Conclusion

Windshear can be extremely dangerous and during the period from 1970 to 1990 a number of total fatalities have occurred many of which are well documented in accident reports.

CLEAR AIR TURBULENCE

Clear air turbulence is turbulence out of cloud which does not include the turbulence in the friction layer. Hence this is turbulence at all heights above a few thousand feet. At the higher levels, CAT can cause loss of control, stalling and airframe damage when it is severe.

CAT is common in association with jet streams, for around the boundaries of a jet, vertically and horizontally, there are strong windshears in terms of wind speed. The turbulence is more severe on top of the jet and more particularly on the cold or polar side. It is also more severe with stronger winds, with jets which are curved and with those which occur above and to the lee of mountain ranges. In this latter instance the vertical movements caused by mountains can speed up the jets and also enhance the shear in speed. Frontal jets can produce more severe turbulence than the subtropical type because they move with the movement of the front. This movement is roughly at right angles to the direction of wind flow. The diagrams at Figure 16.9 show the different features of the turbulence in association with jet streams and fronts. Sharp directional wind shears with upper level troughs and sometimes with upper ridges can cause turbulence. In these instances flight along the trough or ridge line should be avoided if possible. The areas of CAT are shown at Figure 16.10. The same figure also shows turbulence in association with CB cloud. The instability lifting inside the cloud causes air from the sides to enter the uplift area thereby causing turbulence all around the cloud. There is often CAT above a CB cloud. This more frequently occurs where the cloud tops have been restricted due to the dryness of the air above. Therefore the lifting is still present although the water droplets at the cloud top have evaporated. It has been mentioned earlier in this chapter that clear air turbulence must occur with mountain waves if the air is dry and there is thus no cloud. A similar situation applies with rotor streaming. Additionally there will be CAT in association with the upper level jet stream which occurs with mountain waves.

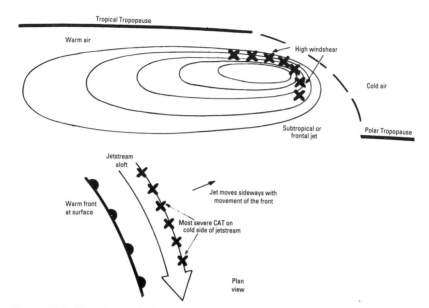

Figure 16.9. Clear Air Turbulence with Jet Streams

To reduce CAT effects it is recommended that aircraft are flown at the 'rough' air speed for the aircraft type and if possible that areas where the terrain drops abruptly be avoided. For the CAT associated with jet streams, with a direct 'head-on' or 'tail-on' jet a

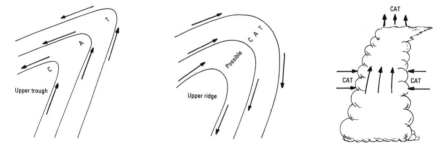

Figure 16.10. CAT with Upper Level Troughs and Ridges and with CB cloud

change of flight level or heading can be efficacious. For a cross track jet a change of flight level only is worthwhile.

CUMULONIMBUS — THUNDERSTORMS
Introduction
The heading to this section has been selected for the particular reason that not all CB cloud becomes thunderstorms further, many

of the hazards of thunderstorms apply equally to CB cloud. Additionally, in flight, to differentiate between a CB cloud and a CB cloud which is also a thunderstorm is often very difficult. The following paragraphs are therefore aimed directly at thunderstorms and well developed, active CB clouds.

Types of Thunderstorm

There are said to be two types of thunderstorms, those caused by frontal triggering and those formed by other lifting processes. This is not a particularly clear division, nevertheless it does underline the main characteristics of frontal thunderstorms. These occur at cold fronts and occlusions in association with depressions and troughs of low. They often occur in a line along the frontal surface and squalls under each cloud can produce line squalls. They can form night and day over land or sea and are more frequent in winter because there are more fronts in winter. The other thunderstorms include the convection type which will only form by day over land in summer. These are isolated and tend to form in the afternoon and dissipate in the evenings. Regeneration can occur at this later time of day by passage of the cloud over surface moist 'hot spots'. These storms form particularly in cols and weak lows where the air has ample time to be heated by surface contact.

Orographic thunderstorms can form by night or day and these can be in a line formation when a range of mountains is involved. Therefore line squalls can be produced. Unless the air is basically unstable, moderate to strong moist winds are usually necessary.

Thunderstorms can form by advection when cold moist air passes over a warm surface. This may suppose a warm land surface by day and maritime air from a cold sea in summer similar to convection. However the more usual case is where cold moist air moves over a warmer sea and this is more likely to produce thunderstorms in winter with a polar maritime air mass moving to a lower latitude. Clearly these storms can occur night or day. They are most likely to form in the unstable air behind a cold front or occlusion. A non-frontal trough of low, strong convergence with moist air can produce convective instability and thunderstorms. These can form along the trough line where the convergence is most concentrated. In many respects these can be similar to frontal thunderstorms.

It should be noted that thunderstorms or CB cloud cannot occur in high latitudes. This is because the low temperatures preclude their being sufficient water vapour in the air at saturation, for the cloud to form.

Development

Thunderstorms are likely to form in CB cloud (and very rarely in thick unstable medium cloud), when the cloud extends well above the freezing level resulting in supercooled water droplets together with ice crystals. This will help towards the electrical potential in the cloud as ice crystals grow by sublimation and the collision with supercooled water droplets. The basic formation of ice by the freezing of water is also known to generate an electrical charge. Instability must also be necessary for the basic cloud to form and as lapse rates greater than 3°C per 1000 ft are rarely found in the free atmosphere, conditional instability must be a prerequisite. In sum therefore the conditions necessary for the development of thunderstorms include:

a) An ELR greater than the SALR through a considerable depth well in excess of 10000 ft and extending several thousand feet above the freezing level.
b) Sufficient water vapour to form and maintain the cloud and to provide early saturation so that full instability quickly develops.
c) Trigger action.

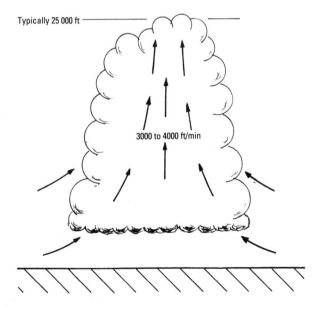

Figure 16.11. Development Stage of a Thunderstorm

During the development stage a number of CU clouds join together to form a CU cell perhaps some 5 nm across. This grows rapidly upwards, the cell containing only up currents at this stage. These may reach speeds of 3000 ft to 4000 ft per minute. The lifting from below together with an influx of air from the sides of the cloud causes turbulence around, as well as under and in the cloud. A diagram of the development stage is at Figure 16.11. A centre pages photograph also refers.

Mature Stage

The mature stage is reached when there is precipitation. By this time, the ice crystals have formed together with large concentrations of water droplets, resulting in precipitation. This will cause down currents which may reach speeds of 2000 ft to 3000 ft per minute. The up currents increasing at this stage to some 6000 ft per minute. These vertical movements cause turbulence inside the cloud. The cloud tops will be close to tropopause height and in low latitudes this can be in excess of 50 000 ft.

Whilst there will be adiabatic heating in the down currents, at the same time evaporation of water droplets and the absorption of latent heat will cause much cooling. The result is cold air being brought to the surface below the cloud. Additionally, squalls, windshear and possibly microbursts can occur under the cloud. The storm will move under the influence of the upper winds and there will be a tilting of the clouds in the direction of the increasing wind with height. The average movement will be in accord with the winds in the 8000 ft to 15 000 ft levels. At the bottom leading edge of the storm there is often a roll of SC and a strong gust or gust front can be experienced near the SC and up to 25 nm ahead of the storm. This is caused by the reaction of a strong downdraught from the leading edge of the cloud with the ground. The gust front can sometimes be the first indicator of an approaching storm. The storm can produce lightning at this stage the discharge being caused by the large variation of static charge in and around the cloud. The lightning can appear in the cloud, from cloud to ground, or from cloud to the air alongside. The sound of the discharge — thunder, travels approximately 1 nm in 5 seconds. Hence by counting the seconds between the lightning flash and the thunder sound, an estimate of the distance to the storm can be made. This could be useful to a pilot on the end of the runway who is uncertain of how close a storm may be. Opening a clear vision panel should enable thunder sound to be heard. A diagram of the mature stage is at Figure 16.12.

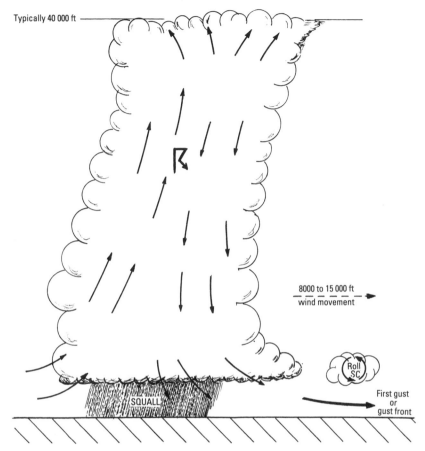

Figure 16.12. Mature Stage of a Thunderstorm

Dissipating Stage

The main indicator of the dissipating stage is the presence of an anvil. The cloud has then produced maximum ice crystals and has been spread out by the inversion at the tropopause and the upper wind at this level thus forming the anvil shape. The cloud at the very top tends to be CI with a fibrous appearance and can reach 55 000 ft plus in low latitudes.

The precipitation diminishes at this stage as the local supply of moist air reduces. However, the cloud form can still produce lightning at this stage.

The most active life of the storm is of the order of 30 to 40 minutes, but the total cell life is some 2 to 3 hours. However, as previously indicated regeneration can occur by downdraughts from adjacent clouds causing convergence and by passage over moist warm areas. In these cases the storms can last for some hours. A good example are the summer convection thunderstorms forming over northern France becoming regenerated over the Channel and then affecting southeast England through to the evening. A dissipating stage diagram is at Figure 16.13. Photographs of thunderstorms in the development and anvil stages, and at a cold front are in the centre pages.

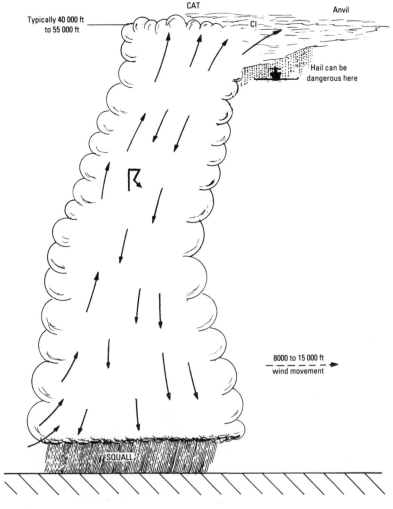

Figure 16.13. Dissipating Stage of a Thunderstorm

SUMMARY OF THUNDERSTORM HAZARDS

Turbulence can be violent in and all around the cloud. Under the cloud turbulence can be particularly dangerous during take-off and landing. It is possible for a pilot to overstress an airframe in these conditions, by strenuous control corrections. Loose articles in cabins can be a danger to passengers and crew. Pressure instruments will inevitably lag and be in error when there are violent vertical movements.

Windshear/Microbursts were covered in the section on windshear.

Hail can be met at any height in the cloud, below the cloud and below the anvil. Severe skin damage can occur when hail is large. Photographs of hail damage are at the centre pages, Plates IXX and XX.

Icing can occur at all heights in the cloud where temperature is between 0°C and −45°C. Heavy concentrations of droplets and large droplet sizes can result in severe clear icing. Carburettor icing can form at temperatures from −10°C to +30°C and be particularly severe from −2°C to +15°C.

Lightning is most likely within 5000 ft of the freezing level. There are three basic effects:

    a)   A pilot can be temporarily blinded (say 20-30 minutes).
    b)   Compasses can become totally unreliable.
    c)   Light airframe damage can be sustained.

Very rarely ball lightning, coloured purple and about the size of a football can be seen in cloud. There have been instances of ball lightning travelling down the inside of a fuselage and exiting near the tail. This passage is alarming to the occupants but not necessarily injurious.

Static causes interference on radio equipment in the LF, MF, HF and VHF frequencies. 'St Elmos Fire' can be caused by static and results in purple rings of light around wing tips, windscreen borders, nacelles and propellers. This is not a hazard but it does indicate that the air is electrically charged so that lightning may well occur.

Pressure Variations can be very local covering only a very small region in or close to a storm. These can result in QFE/QNH to be in error so that altimeter readings can be inaccurate by as much as ± 1000 ft at all heights. These togehter with the instrument lag effects can cause height errors at low level which can be very dangerous. There have been reports of air sinking immediately behind a storm causing a local pressure fall at the surface of several mb.

Water Ingestion can exceed design limits for some turbine engines. This can occur if the speed of updraughts in the storm approaches or exceeds the downward speed of raindrops. An aircraft can then be flying into a 'wall' of water, resulting in flame out and sometimes engine structural failure.

Avoidance

There is a particular problem regarding thunderstorms. It is possible to have experience of flight in or through large CB with only light to moderate turbulence. This can create an impression that the hazards have been over-stated. On later occasions however, this sense of false security can be misplaced with unfortunate consequences. There are therefore some general recommentations regarding avoidance.

It is recommended that any thunderstorm should be avoided by at least 10 nm if it is tall, growing rapidly or has an anvil top. The cloud tops should be avoided by at least 5000 ft which may prove very difficult for present day aircraft. In this case lateral avoidance can be efficacious. The recommended avoidance ranges using returns on airborne weather radars are as follows:

Flight Level	Range
0 – 250	10 nm
250 – 300	15 nm
Above 300	20 nm

TORNADOES

There are two types of tornado; one is the West African and the other are tornadoes at higher latitudes. The latter are associated with severe thunderstorms and take the form of a violent whirlwind. They are usually initiated by a trough of low with very sharply inclined isobars leading to massive convergence. If a CB forms then the lifted air can be given a rotating twist by the differing wind directions along the trough centre line. The resulting lift can raise the spiral of rotating air and divergence at height can then lower surface pressure. The resulting large surface pressure drop can be very local, only some hundreds of feet across, so that it will not be reported synoptically. Diagrams displaying the trough and the spiral lifting as a tornado forms are at Figure 16.14. The lifting is so strong that it can lift water from a sea surface up into the cloud, or dust from the land. This lifting can be in the form of a funnel shaped cloud extending from the cloud base. When this funnel touches the

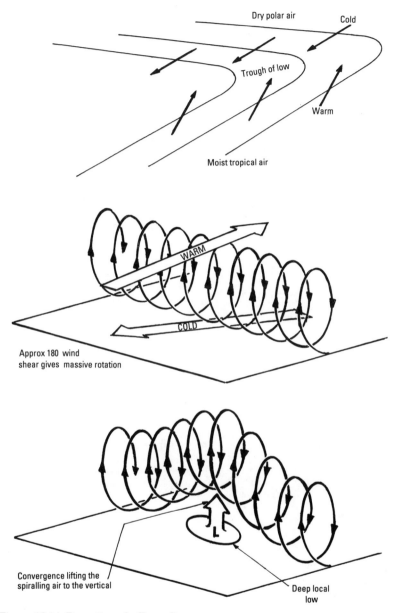

Figure 16.14. Formation of a Tornado

surface it is called a tornado. A picture of a funnel cloud touching the surface from the base of a cloud is shown at Figure 16.15.

At the surface the low pressure in the base of the funnel can

169

cause buildings to explode because of the large pressure differential. The vortex in the form of the funnel can be extremely violent and can extend up to the cloud tops. Thus the normal CB hazards together with the violent turbulence caused by the vortex can make these tornadoes very dangerous. The wind speeds in a vortex can exceed 200 kn and an aircraft entering a vortex at any height, is

Figure 16.15. Photograph of Funnel Cloud

almost certain to suffer structural damage. Tornadoes are common in the USA and can be very severe when air from the Gulf of Mexico meets cold dry air at a trough line, in early summer, in the upper Mississippi river region. They are rare and usually much less severe in Europe, although since 1980 at least one aircraft has been destroyed with total loss of life.

West African Tornadoes
These are thunder squalls with heavy rain which form on a north/ south line in the upper Niger river region in central Africa. They

are effectively a line of convection type thunderstorms forming in the region of the heat equator. In the Spring and Autumn the northeast trade winds and the southeast trade winds respectively move through an easterly direction. The wind thus brings the line of CB with squalls towards the northwest countries of Africa including northern Nigeria, Ghana, Liberia, Guinea and Senegal. These tornadoes can give the usual CB and thunderstorm effects but they are not as severe as the tornadoes of higher latitudes.

AIRCRAFT ICING — AIRFRAME

Introduction

Modern transport aircraft have efficient anti-icing and de-icing systems. However, there can be occasions where the ice build up is so severe that a system becomes less effective in keeping the skin clear of ice. Additionally there are instances where systems malfunction or become inoperative. The systems use a high proportion of aircraft power and affect fuel consumption. The HS146 for example uses some 6 per cent of take-off power to operate all systems continually. A knowledge of airframe icing characteristics can reduce possible hazards.

Effects

Airframe icing can cause a serious loss of performance, control and safety. The effects include the following:

a) AERODYNAMIC
    Ice tends to form in the greatest depth, on the leading edges of wings and tailplanes thereby spoiling aerofoil shapes as shown in Figure 16.16. The result is reduced lift and increased drag, weight, stalling speed and fuel consumption. Control surfaces can be similarly effected and thus control suffers. It is possible for pieces of ice to break off other fuselage surfaces and to jam between the control surface and the wing or tail.

b) WEIGHT OF ICE
    In its severest form ice can adhere at a rate of 1″ in 2 minutes.

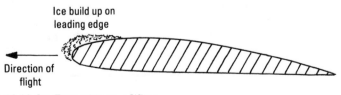

Figure 16.16. Ice Formation on a Wing

The weight plus the rate of formation will not be constant over an airframe. This will cause a wandering centre of gravity, instability and subsequent control difficulties. With time these problems will be aggravated if the ice build-up is allowed to continue. Ice on a propeller will inevitably form unevenly causing a weight differential on the blades. This leads to the engine rocking on its mountings and producing severe vibration.

c) PITOT/STATIC ICING

Ice can block pitot and static inlets causing readings of pressure instruments to be grossly in error. The instruments include altimeter, ASI, VSI and machmeter.

d) GENERAL

A thin film of ice or ice crystals can cause skin friction resulting in a need for a longer take-off run. Windscreens and canopies can be obscured. Undercarriage doors can be iced up in the closed position causing delay in gear deployment. Ice on aerials can cause radio interference and the weight may cause a fixed aerial to break off. Aircraft with tail mounted engines can be damaged by ingress of ice breaking away from the wings.

Conditions Where Icing Can Occur

Water in its liquid state is necessary for ice to form on an airframe. True airframe icing, as distinct from frost therefore, can only occur in cloud precipitation or fog. There will be no icing in the cirrus type clouds as their composition is ice crystals which will not adhere to an aircraft skin. Frost, which is ice crystals can form by sublimation. The ambient temperature should be below 0°C for ice to form and the same condition should apply to the airframe itself. However, instances have occurred where an aircraft has been flying at 30 000 ft or more for some hours, allowing a low fuel temperature to conduct through the wing structure to its upper surface. In these circumstances ice can form at a lower level despite the ambient temperature being above 0°C. This can also cause ice to form with the aircraft on the ground when there is rain drizzle or fog and the aircraft has been on the ground for only a short time.

Supercooled Water Droplets

It is possible for water droplets to stay liquid at temperatures as low as −45°C. If an aircraft comes into contact with these droplets, the surface tension breaks down and the droplets start to freeze. The severity of the icing will partly depend on the size of the droplets. This is controlled by the cloud type and the temperature. Clearly large supercooled water droplets cannot occur in the general run of layer clouds such as stratus because the basic cloud droplets are small. In CU, CB and NS large basic cloud droplets can be expected. The temperature effects are governed by the fact that the lower the temperature the smaller the droplet that can exist in supercooled form. Therefore as the temperature in the cloud reduces from below 0°C so the larger droplets progressively become ice crystals and thus cannot cause airframe icing. Different types of icing occur dependent on the cloud type and the ambient conditions.

Clear Ice (Glazed Ice)
If supercooled water droplets are large and come into contact with an airframe, part of the droplet will immediately form ice. This formation will release latent heat and thus raise the temperature of the rest of the droplet. This can delay the freezing process until this droplet portion has flowed back over the wing or tailplane where it will then become ice. This ice is clear like glass, very tough and it adheres strongly to the aircraft skin.

The amount of the droplet that freezes on impact is related to the temperature of the droplet and the amount of latent heat released, which is almost 80 calories per gm. Therefore the amount of the droplet that freezes on impact is about 1/80th for each 1°C below 0°C. Hence if the droplet has a temperature of −20°C, a quarter would freeze on impact whilst the rest flows back to freeze over the airframe surface. This type of icing can therefore produce a severe modification to the aerofoil shape and all the possible icing effects can apply.

Clear ice will only form in clouds where the basic droplets are large and thus it occurs in CU, CB or NS when the temperatures are between 0°C and −20°C. It is a dangerous form of icing.

Rime Ice
If the supercooled water droplets are small, the total droplet will virtually freeze on impact. The latent heat released will be very small and thus the ice will form more quickly. This ice is opaque and has a light texture which can result in it being compacted by the airflow on a leading edge. However, it normally breaks away relatively easily. It can cause some loss of aerofoil shape and air intakes can be affected.

Rime occurs in any cloud where there are small water droplets at temperatures from 0°C to −45°C. It can therefore occur in any of the layer clouds. Additionally it can form in the heap clouds at levels where temperatures are below −20°C and therefore the supercooled water droplets which may exist must necessarily be small. This type of icing is rarely severe in effects but it can often form together with clear ice. Rime can also occur in freezing fog.

Rain Ice
This type of icing, as its name implies, forms outside cloud in rain. It can form ahead of a warm front or occlusion at low level — say, below 2000 ft and covers only a narrow range of altitudes. If rain is falling from NS and the inversion at the front, into air at a temperature below 0°C, then the rain can become cooled. If an aircraft has been flying in this cold air for sometime and therefore has a skin temperature below zero, the rain impacting on the airframe will cause clear ice to form. This can build up very rapidly thus causing the most dangerous form of icing. It is likely to occur on climb-out or on the approach and is therefore particularly hazardous. The conditions for the formation are displayed at Figure 16.17. If rain ice is suddenly encountered, it may be necessary for a pilot to turn immediately on to a reciprocal heading.

The rain ice conditions frequently occur in winter over North American and in Europe: Particularly where the air ahead of the front is polar continental, thus providing the low temperature air under the frontal surface. Rain ice is far less common over the British Isles but its occurrence can be expected if there is 'black ice' on road surfaces. This is completely clear ice through which the

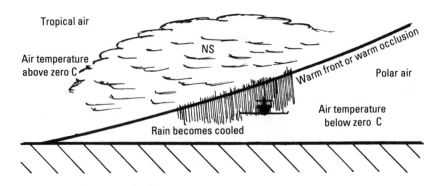

Figure 16.17. Formation of Rain Ice

black road surface is clearly visible. This too can form in rain ice conditions.

Pack Snow
This is icing due to a mixture of snow and supercooled water droplets. It can block air intakes, undercarriage wells and any other aircraft openings. Normally the effects are slight.

Hoar Frost
Hoar frost as its name implies is not airframe icing as such; it is frost which can completely cover an airframe. It is a minor hazard compared with clear and rime icing.

The frost forms in clear air due to sublimation when air in contact with a cold airframe is cooled below dewpoint and below 0°C (this is sometimes referred to as the Frost Point). The water vapour in the contact air then changes immediately to ice crystals. It can form with an aircraft on the ground in a similar fashion to frost on a car in winter. It is necessary for this frost to be cleared before take-off so that windscreens and canopies are clear, to obviate skin friction and a longer take-off run and also to stop radio interference which can occur with frost on aerials. Control hinge points can also become a little stiff.

Hoar frost can form in flight if an aircraft has to make a sudden descent from a high level to a warm moist layer. The very cold airframe can then be in contact with a large amount of water vapour at the lower level and sublimation and frost results. It can also occur if an aircraft has been outside for the whole of a winter night and then early the next morning does a steep climb out, perhaps for noise abatement reasons, through an inversion. The effects are not severe and the frost can be cleared quickly.

Factors Affecting Icing Severity
The main factor is how much free water is available at the right temperature to become ice. With the exception of the form of the airframe, all the factors are concerned with the amount of free water.

Size/Concentration of Supercooled Water Droplets
As previously mentioned, the size of droplets is dependent on the cloud type and the temperature in the cloud. The effect of these factors is tabulated below. Care should be taken where tempeature values are given as these are not finite and a spread of some 3°C should be expected.

Icing Type	Details	Cloud
Moderate/Severe clear ice	Supercooled water Droplets can only be large in CU, CB, NS and then only in the cloud temperature range 0°C to −20°C.	Large CU and CB — severe. Smaller CU, NS with heap type characteristics and ACc — moderate to severe.
Light/moderate Rime	In layer clouds small supercooled water droplets are present from 0°C to −10°C.	Layer clouds light but light to moderate for SC.
Light Rime	In layer clouds at temperatures from −10°C to −45°C supercooled water droplets are very small.	All layer clouds.
Rime	Supercooled water droplets are small in CU CB NS from −20°C to −45°C.	CU CB NS
Nil	Ice crystals will not adhere to the airframe.	CI CS CC

The concentration of water droplets is higher in the heap clouds because of the stronger upcurrents, thus causing greater severity of icing. There should always be a greater concentration of droplets near the base of a cloud, for this is where condensation first occurs. Gravity will also tend to result in a greater concentration near the base.

Proximity to Hills/Mountains

If clouds are formed orographically, or if clouds formed by other triggers pass close to or over hills or mountains, then additional up currents can be caused by the wind against the hills (innocuous NS may become NS with heap type characteristics). The result is larger droplets being supported and a heavier concentration of droplets. Cloud formed orographically in stable air will have a lowered freezing level. This can be a few thousand feet below the forecast freezing level for the area. Hence icing could occur at a lower level than anticipated.

Cloud Base Temperature

The higher the cloud base temperature the greater the amount of water vapour in the air at saturation and thus to become free water in the cloud as condensation occurs. This will apply not only at the

176

base itself, for the free water content will be increased at all levels in the cloud due to the upcurrents. The effect is more severe icing above the freezing level. Although the 0°C isotherm may be as high as 16 000 ft the degree of icing will be severe above this level.

Form of Aircraft
With a low drag aerofoil shape the airflow more closely follows the outline of the airframe, whereas a high drag form will cause the airflow to divert from the outline of the aircraft. Hence there will be more water droplets actually in contact with the airframe in the low drag case. Additionally low drag will normally infer a higher speed and therefore the number of water droplets encountered in unit time will be higher and thus icing rate should be increased. However, if the speed of the aircraft causes kinetic heating so that the skin temperature is raised above 0°C then there will be no icing.

A case in point is Concorde where the skin temperature in supersonic cruise is some +90°C, so no icing is possible. However, in climb-out, descent and subsonic cruise, icing can occur and because of the streamlined shape it is likely to be more severe than with say, a Boeing 747.

★   ★   ★

Icing Description
Airframe icing is described as 'Trace', 'Light', 'Moderate' or 'Severe'. The full meaning of these terms is given in Chapter 19.

Icing Recognition
If an aircraft is being flown in icing conditions then frequent inspection of leading edges, particularly where these are not visible from the cockpit, is a worthwhile discipline. At night a high powered torch used to inspect leading edges for reflecting ice can be efficacious. Pre-flight checks to ensure the whole aircraft is free from ice, frost or snow before taxying are clearly essential in winter conditions.

AIRCRAFT ICING — ENGINE
Introduction
The causes and effects of icing differ for piston and turbine engines. However, in both cases there is the possibility of fuel freezing and therefore it is axiomatic that a pilot must know the fuel

freezing point specification for his aircraft type. The big difference between the two engine types is that icing in piston engines can occur at temperatures as high as +30°C or more, whereas the top temperature for turbine engine icing is around +5°C.

Piston Engine Icing

This is sometimes referred to as induction icing. It can involve three different areas. Impact icing which occurs in the intake area and is akin to airframe icing (for turbo-charged engines this is usually the only icing problem). Secondly fuel icing which is caused by water in the fuel freezing in pipe bends thus reducing the fuel flow to the engine. 'Coring' — this is the name given to a situation where in very low ambient temperatures, the fuel freezes on the inside of induction piping so that only a small conduit is left in the centre of the pipe to allow fuel to flow. Thirdly there is the major hazard of carburettor icing.

Carburettor Icing

This is caused by a lowering of the temperature inside the carburettor so that ice can form. The temperature can reduce due to two causes. The evaporation of fuel which involves the absorption of latent heat from the metal internal parts and the cooling of the air by adiabatic expansion as it passes through the venturi in the carburettor. Thus the inside of the carburettor can become very cold and any water droplets from cloud or fog in the inducted air can quickly form ice. The total reduction in temperature can be in excess of 30°C and therefore icing can occur even in clear air at high temperatures if the relative humidity is 30 per cent or more.

The result of the ice formation can be more severe if the throttle is at a low setting with the carburettor butterfly only partially open. In these conditions complete fuel starvation can occur and engine 'cut-out'. For the above reasons the most severe icing is more likely on the descent on a warm humid day in summer. The icing can occur in the temperature range of −10°C to +30°C with an RH of 30 per cent or more. Hence in the UK carburettor icing can occur at almost anytime. It is more likely to occur if the aircraft is fuelled with MOGAS (4 star car petrol) which can have a higher water content than AVGAS. Extra care should also be taken if there are obvious indications of an increase of water vapour in the air, e.g. mist over water areas, recent clearance of fog, flight between cloud banks or just below cloud, wet ground with dew and a light wind. Carburettor icing is most severe from −2°C to +15°C in cloud, fog or precipitation at any power setting and also in clear air with a

BUILD-UP OF ICING IN INDUCTION SYSTEM

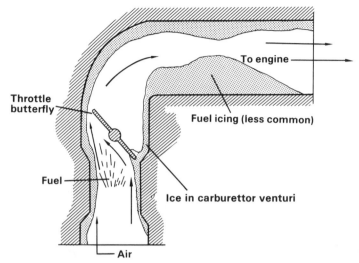

Figure 16.18. Icing in Piston Engines

CARBURETTOR ICING IN AIR FREE OF CLOUD, FOG, OR PRECIPITATION
-risk and rate of icing will be greater when operating in cloud, fog and precipitation.

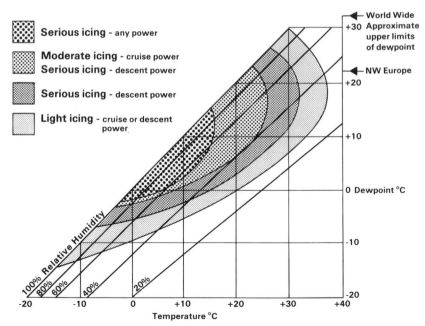

Figure 16.19. Graph of Carburettor Icing Severity

179

high relative humidity. A diagram of icing in piston engines is at Figure 16.18. A graph of the degree of carburettor icing in clear air at varying temperatures and humidities is at Figure 16.19.

Turbine/Jet Engine Icing

The intakes of turbine and jet engines and any struts across the face of the intake can be subject to icing in a similar fashion to airframe icing. If this breaks away and enters the engine proper, blade damage can occur.

Ice in the first stage compressor blade area can form in the presence of supercooled water droplets and generally the greater the engine revolutions the greater the icing. An accompanying high airspeed increases the mass of air entering the engine and thus the water droplet content. Another effect related to high engine revolutions is a pressure reduction inside the intake which can cause an adiabatic temperature fall of some 5°C. Hence icing can occur at high revs. with water droplets in cloud or fog at temperatures up to +5°C. It can be a special hazard with freezing fog. Additionally, these conditions can result in icing in clear air if the relative humidity is high.

Icing at low level during take-off or the approach to landing can be particularly hazardous. The throttle settings are normally high during these portions of a flight profile and thus icing effects can be accentuated. The clear air icing can even occur with the aircraft on the ground if engines are run at high revolutions. Fuel inlet filters can be subject to icing when the fuel temperature is below 0°C after long periods of flight. Engine power indications on the flight deck can be in error if there is ice on engine inlet pressure probes.

In potential icing conditions engine igniters should be used to obviate failures. Most modern engines are fitted with blade heaters to reduce icing effects. If there is severe engine damage caused by icing which results in severe vibration, many modern aircraft have an automatic total engine and intake release system. Drastically, this separates engine and intake from the wing or tail thus ensuring that the integrity of the airframe and remaining engines is maintained.

TROPICAL CYCLONES

Tropical cyclones form over warm seas in latitudes from 5° to 25° in both hemispheres. They do not form closer than within 5° of the geographic equator because of the absence of a geostrophic force. They are most frequently observed between 12° and 17° in each hemisphere. The formation occurs most often close to the ITCZ where the strong convergence and high temperatures produce deep instability. There is evidence that a sea temperature in excess of +27°C is critical. The ability of the warm air to hold masses of water vapour results in large scale CB and provides the release of much latent heat. This heat is the main source of energy for the storms. These revolving storms are given different names dependent on the area where they occur: They are called 'Hurricanes' in the West Indies, the Pacific islands, Madagascar and Mauritius. In the Arabian sea, the Bay of Bengal and the North and East of Australia they are called 'Cyclones'. In the Phillipines, the China seas and Japan they are named 'Typhoons'. In the North West of Australia they are sometimes referred to as 'Willy Willys'. (This name is also used in Northern Australia for local dust devils and for more widespread dust storms.)

The strong lifting causes divergence at heights up to 50 000 ft plus, resulting in a large fall of surface pressure. Whilst a typical surface pressure in the centre of the storm is 950 mb, values have fallen on occasions down to 870 mb. These storms are rarely more than 500 nm across so the pressure gradients are very steep and can cause winds at all levels of 100 kn or more. Despite these strong winds the storm as a whole only moves at around 10 kn and usually in a westerly direction under the influence of the low latitude easterly winds. It is this westerly movement that causes the major storm areas to be on the east side of continents. On crossing the tropic of Cancer or Capricorn they frequently turn to the east — effectively moving around the outskirts of a nearby subtropical high. In the centre of a storm there is strong subsidence due to the fierce rotation effects. This can be likened to a stick being rotated violently in a pail of water causing the surface of the water to depress in the centre. The subsidence covers a diameter of some 15 nm to 50 nm and as the air is descending it prevents cloud formation, thereby leaving a region of clear sky and comparatively light winds in the centre. This is referred to as the 'Eye of the Storm' and shows clearly as a black spot in the centre of masses of white cloud on a satellite or radar picture. An example is at Figure 16.20. The clouds are large CU and masses of CB producing torrential rain thunderstorms, heavy hail storms and extreme turbulence together with the strong winds and squally surface conditions. These storms are exemplified by the hurricanes of the West Indies which form off the coast of North West Africa and then move erratically in a general easterly direction at about 10 kn towards the Caribbean Islands. Here they can produce extreme conditions and some

Figure 16.20. The Eye of a Tropical Cyclone

devastation as they pass over areas of habitation. Approaching the Central American states they tend to turn to the north east as if avoiding going too far inland, but often cross Florida still moving north east thence into the Atlantic. Sometimes they can join in with a Polar Front depression and eventually reach Europe as a particularly active polar front low.

The storms are essentially a summer phenomenon because of the formation close to the ITCZ/heat equator. Therefore the expected main seasons are June to September in the Northern hemisphere (in Southeast Asia and particularly the Phillipines, they sometimes also occur at other seasons including winter) and January to March in the Southern hemisphere.

Since the deployment of satellites, the track of the storms can be followed and forecasts can be made with some accuracy. However, these rely to a large extent on the eye of the storm standing out on pictures. Where clouds at a low level obviate this clarity, forecasting can be more difficult. Pilots should take particular care when flying in storm areas in the summer months. If large values of starboard drift are experienced in the Northern hemisphere the aircraft should be turned until port drift occurs. The aircraft will then be flying away from the storm and it is possible to navigate around the storm edges using this drift watching system. In the southern hemisphere the drift signs are reversed. The Airborne Weather Radar screen will show the strong returns from the masses of CB clouds and returns from hail in particular should stand out to give warning to pilots. It should be noted that whilst the main season for storms is the summer, they are known to occur occasionally at other times of the year. This random occurrence is most common with Typhoons.

Chapter 17
Practical Forecasting
for Pilots

Introduction

This chapter deals with practical forecasting from a pilot's viewpoint using the mean sea level synoptic chart. The detailed forecasting techniques employed by professional meteorologists at main centres, many of which are based on computer modelling are not included here. A pilot should be capable of interpreting a mean sea level synoptic chart and thus to develop landing forecasts and route forecasts for low level flight. Inevitably coverage of these items will also provide a recapitulation of many of the facts and concepts in the previous chapters.

Landing Forecasts

When a landing forecast is required reference should be made to the latest synoptic chart for the landing area concerned. The chart information will be out of time, nevertheless the reports of station circles will be of assistance. The chart will ideally require updating but this could only be achieved by obtaining the latest reports from airfields concerned in the area. Instead of chart updating, the landing airfield position can be updated so that it is akin to its future position in the synoptic environment at the estimated time of arrival — the ETA. Figure 17.1 shows part of a synoptic chart for 0600 hr for a date in April. Suppose that a landing may be made sometime between 0600 and 1200 hr at Shannon airfield. The synoptic position of the airfield is as shown on the chart for 0600 hr. By 1200 hr the approaching cold front will have passed through Shannon and the airfield will then be in the unstable polar maritime air behind the cold front. Its 1200 hr synoptic position can be found as follows:

a) A perpendicular is dropped onto the cold front from Shannon airfield and extended through the front into the area behind.

b) The perpendicular indicates the portion of the front which will passage through Shannon. This portion can be used to find frontal speed — 30 kn.

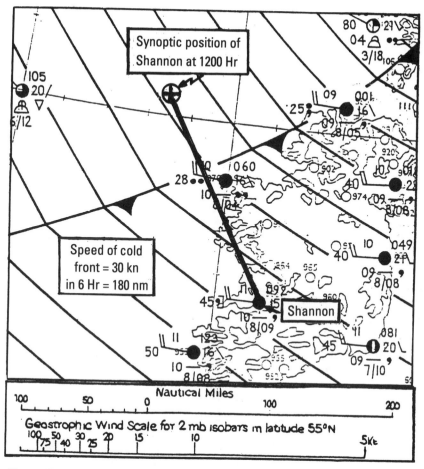

Figure 17.1. Use of a Synoptic Chart for Landing Forecasts

c) The 1200 hr synoptic position of Shannon can be found by multiplying the frontal speed by the 6 hr period of the forecast 30 × 6 = 180 nm. This distance is then marked from Shannon along the perpendicular line, to establish the new synoptic position.

The ETA for frontal passage at Shannon can be found by using frontal speed and the distance along the perpendicular to the front. It is now possible to provide a landing forecast for "In the Warm Sector" and "At and Behind the Cold Front" specifying the times for the two regions. The stations reporting close to the perpendicular line can be used to indicate likely weather to affect Shannon.

Reference to the chart will show that the number of appropriate reporting stations is few in number. Additionally some will be in surface terrain positions different from Shannon. Therefore the basic weather expectations with frontal passage must also be involved. Further, the effect of a later time of day to 0600 chart time has to be borne in mind, as this can affect cloud amount, cloud base and perhaps visibility. The basic procedures outlined above should be within the capabilities of any well trained pilot and can certainly assist where meteorology facilities are not instantly available. The system can be similarly used for incoming warm fronts and occlusions. If there are no fronts in an area then the fact that a non-frontal depression will tend to move towards the region where pressure is falling most steeply can be of assistance. This region can be ascertained by reference to the pressure tendency values at reporting stations on the chart. An average 'track' line for the depression centre can be found and this 'track' line direction can be plotted through the airfield concerned in a reverse direction. By using an average depression speed of say, 25 kn or by making a judgement on the basis of the pressure gradient values adjacent to the 'track' line to the landing airfield, a synoptic position for the airfield at the end of the forecast period can be found. A forecast can then be made with no separate portions except possibly by use of different time periods where appropriate.

Simple Route Forecasting

Perhaps the simplest practical route forecast is one which answers the queries: Where and at what time can I expect to cross the front? (this can be warm, cold or an occlusion). If the aircraft track is within 30° of the perpendicular to the front then a straight forward closing speed can be used, i.e. aircraft groundspeed plus frontal speed, together with distance to the front to find time of crossing. This time can be used to find ETA front and also to find distance to the front and hence a position using solely aircraft groundspeed.

If the track will not meet the front in a perpendicular sense, then a different method is necessary. This entails selecting two positions on the front which will bracket the portion of the front to be crossed. The speeds of the front at these two locations is found and then the frontal portion is marked for convenient intervals ahead, parallel to the front, Figure 17.2 refers. The aircraft track is drawn on the chart and the time the aircraft will meet convenient interval positions is found using aircraft groundspeed. Inspection will then allow an estimate to be made. This should be accurate to within 3 minutes.

An aircraft leaves Brest at 0000 Hr on a track of 325 and with a groundspeed of 200 kn. The portion of the cold front which will be met by the aircraft has a speed of 22 kn. The closing speed is thus 222 kn. Distance to the front is 200 nm. The time to meet the front is therefore 54 min.

The distance along track to the position of meeting the front is therefore 54 min at the aircraft's groundspeed of 200 kn = 180 nm.

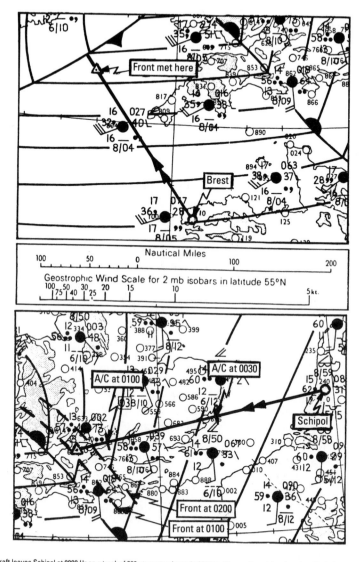

An aircraft leaves Schipol at 0000 Hr on a track of 262 at a groundspeed of 230 kn. The position of the aircraft at 30 min intervals is marked on the track line. The new position of the warm front is drawn for one hour and two hours ahead of chart time.

At 0100 Hr the aircraft is 35 nm away from the 0100 Hr position of the front. This would take 9 min of flight time. During these 9 min the front will have moved some 4 nm closer. Hence the resulting 31 nm of travel will take only 8 min of flight time. The time for meeting the front is thus 0108 Hr. The distance along track is 68 min at the aircraft's groundspeed of 230 kn = 262 nm.

Figure 17.2. Obtaining Time and Position of Crossing a Front

Detailed Route Forecasting

A detailed low level route forecast procedure can be used with the MSL Synoptic chart. The forecast will necessarily take into account the movement of the aircraft and the movement of pressure systems and fronts. Further, the time difference between take-off time and chart time together with ETA and chart time must be important factors.

In order to use reports at station circles on the chart, the synoptic position as distinct from the geographic position of the take-off airfield at the time of take-off and destination airfield at ETA have to be found. The line joining these two positions will then enable a track to be established which is relative to the synoptic situation. This could be referred to as the weather track. Stations reporting close to this track can be used to assist in writing a forecast. Additionally the position of the aircraft at changing weather stages must be considered. One of the more complex route forecasts can be where the aircraft track passes through a polar front depression with its warm and cold fronts. The forecast should then cover the separate weather sectors: Ahead/At warm front: In the Warm Sector: At/Behind cold front. Clearly the times the aircraft is expected to be in these sectors will form part of the forecast. The detailed procedure for establishing the relative weather track and the timing of crossing fronts is as follows:

RELATIVE WEATHER TRACK

a) Find the difference between chart time and ETD.
b) Drop a perpendicular from the take-off airfield to the first front (usually warm) to establish the portion of the front which will pass through the airfield.
c) Find frontal speed.
d) Use time from (a) and speed from (c) to find a distance. Then move the airfield in the opposite direction to frontal movement, along the perpendicular for this distance. This establishes the synoptic position of the take-off airfield at ETD.
e) Find the difference between chart time and ETA destination.
f) Drop a perpendicular from the destination airfield to the second front (usually cold) to establish the portion of the front which will pass, or which has passed, through the airfield.
g) Find frontal speed.

h) Use time from (e) and speed from (g) to find a distance. Then move the airfield in the opposite direction to frontal movement, along the perpendicular for this distance. This establishes the synoptic position of the destination airfield at ETA.

i) Drawing a line between the synoptic positions of the airfields found at (d) and (h) will establish the relative weather track.

POSITION OF CROSSING FRONTS

This is done by finding the actual time of crossing fronts by use of the relative weather track and then relating those times from take-off, along the actual geographic track to be flown by the aircraft. Procedure:

a) Measure the distance along the relative weather track and by equating this to the expected flight time find a relative groundspeed.

b) Measure the distance along the relative weather track to each of the fronts.

c) Using the relative groundspeed and the distance along the relative weather track, compute times to each of the fronts.

d) Establish ETA for each of the fronts. These timings will be accurate timings for the flight.

e) Use the expected actual aircraft groundspeed and the times to each of the fronts to compute distance to each of the fronts.

These distances can then be measured along the geographic aircraft track between the two airfields to find the positions along track where the fronts will be crossed.

These procedures are displayed on the chart at Figure 17.3. Using this chart and flight detail information a forecast for the route can be made. Again it will be necessary to use basic knowledge of weather expectations with frontal passages as well as information from the chart. Surface terrain differences have to be borne in mind, together with weather changes to be expected with diurnal variation of surface temperatures.

It will be noted that Figure 17.3 uses a computer produced MSL synoptic chart. These are in widespread use. The small differences in coded symbols/figures from a normal chart are detailed in Appendix 'A'.

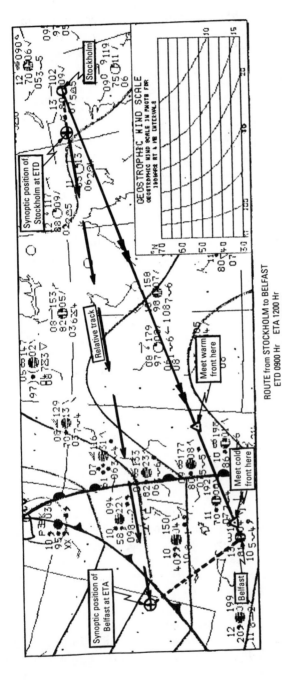

ROUTE from STOCKHOLM to BELFAST
ETD 0900 Hr   ETA 1200 Hr
Time of chart 0600 Hr

Difference between chart time and ETD = 3 hours. The warm front speed is 33 x 2/3 kn = 22 kn. Distance to move Stockholm at right angles to the warm front is 3 hours at 22 kn = 66 nm.

Difference between chart time and ETA = 6 hours. The cold front speed is 32 kn. Distance to move Belfast at right angles to the cold front is 6 hours at 32 kn = 192 nm.

The synoptic positions of Stockholm at ETD and Belfast at ETA are now established. A line drawn between these two positions will indicate the track relative to the synoptic situation.

Relative groundspeed = relative track distance / the 3 hours flight time, = 805 nm / 3 hours = 268 kn. Relative distance to the warm front is 605 nm at 268 kn relative groundspeed = 135 min. ETD 0900 Hr + 135 min gives ETA at the warm front as 1115 Hr. Relative distance to the cold front is 770 nm at 268 kn relative groundspeed = 172 min. ETD 0900 Hr + 172 min gives ETA at the cold front as 1152 Hr.

True groundspeed = true track distance / the 3 hour flight time = 815 nm / 3 hours = 272 kn. Distance to warm front = 135 min at true groundspeed of 272 kn = 612 nm. Distance to cold front = 172 min at true groundspeed of 272 kn = 780 nm.

Figure 17.3. Route Forecast Procedures on a Chart

Note: Meteorological services provide Terminal Airfield Forecasts (TAFs) and area en route forecasts for low level (below 15 000 ft). Significant weather charts are produced for higher levels. Details of all these services are at Chapter 19.

Chapter 18
Climatology

Introduction

Climate can be defined as the long term behaviour of weather. This suggests that statistics are an important tool in climatology. Whilst this must be true, internationally controlled weather statistics are only available from the 1870s. Furthermore, these statistics are for surface weather conditions and do not give a background to weather conditions in the upper air, except by implication. Other information can be gathered from the earliest records of individual countries, and from historical notes such as 'Fairs held on the frozen Thames in London in 1855'. The examination of ice cores from drilling at high latitudes has produced much information about climate in the past centuries.

Studies show that during the past 1000 years there was a warm period where UK temperatures were above present day levels and vineyards were commonplace (about AD 1000 to AD 1300). Similarly there was a small ice age with temperatures below present day values (about AD 1400 to AD 1900). Some of the reasons postulated for the climatic changes include, small changes in the earth's orbit, and long term changes in the interaction between the atmosphere and the seas. Active volcanoes under the sea can radically change sea currents. On a smaller scale, volcanic eruptions producing ash and dust which can be long lasting at high levels in the atmosphere, can effect solar radiation. These factors need to be borne in mind when considering possible climate changes caused by the 'greenhouse effect' mentioned in Chapter 7. It is worth emphasing that the major greenhouse gas is ordinary water vapour, followed by carbon dioxide. The other gases such as methane, nitrous oxide and CFCs, whilst having a greater effect per molecule, are present in much smaller quantities.

Statistics concerned with upper air conditions including wind information in the aviation atmosphere are available only since the early 1900s. For parts of the world where aviation is on a relatively small scale, information is particularly sparse — notably the polar regions. It is incidentally, only since the 1960s that the low level jet stream off the Horn of Africa mentioned in Chapter 11 was discovered. From the foregoing it is clear that changes in climate can occur, but these have in the past been gradual. Further new information for the aviation atmosphere is bound to accrue in the future.

This chapter will cover climate on a latitude or zonal basis together with a study of recent past statistics for the main weather factors. Finally an examination will be made of the expected climate and flying weather in the separate world areas.

General Circulation

In Chapter 6, it was shown that world pressures for a simple globe in an unrefined atmosphere could produce pressure zones based on latitude. These are reproduced at Figure 18.1. This shows the low

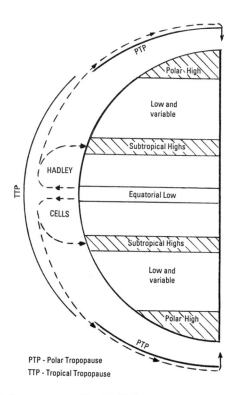

Figure 18.1. World Pressures on a Simple Globe

pressure in the equatorial region with the lifted air producing Hadley cells and the subtropical anticyclones. The high pressure at the poles (caused by the low temperatures and the excess of air at height) and the variable lows in mid-latitudes between the two high pressure systems. Four distinct climate zones could be inferred from the diagram:

Equatorial — Surface air moving in. High temperature causing lifting and instability clouds and weather.

Subtropical — Surface air moving out. Air above descending causing stability and no cloud. Dry desert climate.

Low and Variable — Surface air moving in. Depression weather variable cloud and precipitation.

Polar — Surface air moving out. Air above descending causing stability. No cloud, cold and dry.

Applying earth rotation and thus geostrophic force to the simple globe can give wind directions as shown at Figure 18.2.

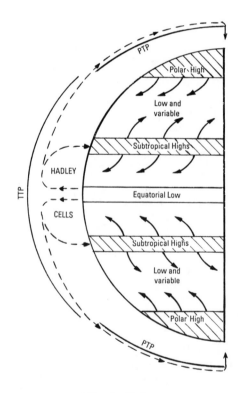

Figure 18.2. Wind Directions on a Simple Globe

The 23½ degree inclination of the earth's axis and the subsequent seasonal variation in earth orientation to the sun can cause important changes. The heat equator will be in the Northern hemisphere June to August and in the Southern hemisphere December to February. The climate zones will move with movement of the heat equator. Furthermore, from March to May and September to November, the heat equator will be close to the geographic equator. The consequences of the heat equator movement will be to produce two more climate zones.

Savannah	– Between the equatorial low and the sub-tropical high which must have equatorial climate in the summer season. Dry desert type in the winter.
Warm Temperate	– The Low and Variable zone is now divided into two. This warm temperate region in the south is due to movement of the subtropical high weather in the summer hemisphere.
Disturbed Temperate	– The higher latitude portion, renamed Disturbed Temperate.

From the preceding chapters it will be clear that movement of the heat equator necessarily causes other main weather factors to move. Amongst these will be the Intertropical Convergence Zone (ITCZ) which was mentioned in Chapter 13 and will be dealt with more fully below.

In summary the main weather items to move due to the heat equator are as follows:

By July the following will have moved to their furthest north:

a) The heat equator.
b) The equatorial rains.
c) The ITCZ.
d) The subtropical anticyclones.
e) The subtropical jet streams.
f) The Polar Front (movement from 50°S is small).
g) The Polar Front jet streams.

By January, all the above items will have moved to their furthest south, due to movement of the heat equator into the southern hemisphere.

CLIMATIC ZONES

The zones are shown by latitude at Figure 18.3.

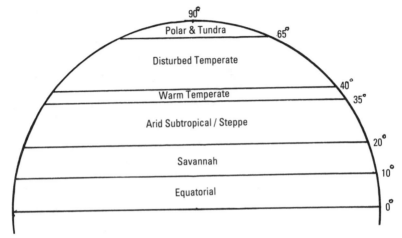

Figure 18.3. Climatic Zones

Equatorial 0°–10°

Surface pressure is slack and the sea breezes become important for coastal regions. There are two main wet seasons at the Equinoxes (March and September) when surface heating is greatest. The weather includes large CU and CB with heavy showers and thunderstorms. Both temperature and humidity are high. Over the oceans the slack pressure produces a band of almost calm surface wind conditions called the 'Doldrums'. Upper winds are easterly, with some easterly jet streams.

Examples of the region are Kenya in Central Africa (The heavy rains at the equinoxes in Kenya are referred to as the 'Long Rains'). Singapore is also in the region and has an almost daily thunderstorm.

Savannah or Tropical Transitional 10°–20°

Dry trade wind conditions can be expected in winter. The winds will be northeasterly in the northern hemisphere and southeasterly in the southern hemisphere. In the summer season the equatorial rains will enter the region. The duration of this wet season reduces with increase of latitude until there is merging with the Steppe type. Summer surface winds become southwesterly in the northern hemisphere and northwesterly in the southern hemisphere. Upper winds are generally easterly. Examples of the Savannah region are northwest Africa including North Nigeria, Ghana, Liberia extending northwards to Mauretania: Northern Malaya and Burma. In the southern hemisphere there is Northeast Queensland, Mozambique and Madagascar.

Arid Subtropical — Steppe 20°–35°

Weather is typical of the anticyclonic type. Descending air stable warm and dry, producing the main desert areas of the world. Deserts include: the Sahara, Arabian, Sind, Gobi, Kalahari and the Gibson and Simpson deserts of Australia. Surface winds are light, but basically northeast in the northern hemisphere and southeast in the southern hemisphere.

Bordering the desert regions there are the steppe regions of treeless plains which have a short rainfall season. In the northern hemisphere this border region is in the north of the deserts in winter (January) and to the south in summer (July). Examples are Algeria and Central South Russia. In the southern hemisphere the border steppe region is in the north in July and to the south of the deserts in January. Upper winds are westerly with the subtropical westerly jet stream in winter. Examples are the Veldt of South Africa and the Nullabar Plain of Australia.

Warm Temperate 35°–40°

This is the Mediterranean type climate with westerly surface winds in winter together with depressions with much cloud and precipitation. In summer warm and dry with only light winds and sea breezes. Upper winds are westerly. The westerly subtropical jet can affect the south of the area in winter together with some polar front jet streams.

In the southern hemisphere examples are Victoria in Australia and the north island of New Zealand.

Disturbed Temperate 40°–65°

The expression disturbed is used to define the many pressure changes that occur in this region. These are mainly caused by the polar front depressions which dominate the weather with ridges or high pressure systems in between. Strong winds including gales are a feature of the westerly surface winds in winter. There is no dry season but the polar front lows are less frequent and at a higher latitude in the summer. Upper winds are westerly. The jet streams associated with the polar front depressions are the dominant feature of the upper winds. In summer the subtropical westerly jet is in the lower latitude area of the zone. Examples of the disturbed temperate zone are Europe north of the Mediterranean Sea and the south island of New Zealand.

Polar 65°–90°
For much of the time this zone will have anticyclonic weather, very cold and dry. During summer depressions can move into the region bringing unsettled weather and precipitation usually as snow. At this season temperatures can rise above 0°C in some areas for a month or two giving a 'Tundra' climate of lichen and moss replacing the snow. In the higher latitudes the ground is permanently frozen — 'permafrost'.
 Surface winds are mainly easterly becoming more westerly in summer as fronts enter the region. Upper winds are easterly in summer and westerly in winter.

Caveat
The zonal weather does not take into account those important variations caused by the differences in the type of surface underlying the air. This will affect surface heating values and thus density and pressure. Tropopause heights will also be affected. Additionally, mountain ranges can cause meridian movement of air and change the direction, speed and location of the upper winds. Therefore the climatic zones are a good guide to climate but do not give a comprehensive picture. It must also be remembered that the form of the earth is closer to a tangerine than a sphere.

DOMINANT WEATHER FACTORS
The high pressure systems of the world produce basically good weather apart from poor visibility. It is, therefore, the low pressure systems which provide nearly all the global weather. The polar front depressions are a dominant factor in world weather in both hemispheres. The basics of these depressions have been dealt with in some depth in earlier chapters, together with the weather which they produce. Other factors which are dominant and have received only a modicum of coverage so far are considered here. They include: The Heat Equator; The Equatorial Trough; The Inter-tropical Convergence Zone (ITCZ); The Trade Winds and the Monsoons. There are interconnections between these factors which bear directly on climate.

The Heat Equator
This is a line on the earth's surface joining places where the surface

temperature is highest at a particular time. Its position is largely controlled by the sun's maximum elevation and the type of surface. In January the sun has a maximum elevation at the Tropic of Capricorn (23½°S). In July the maximum elevation is at the Tropic of Cancer (23½°N). However, the heat equator only follows these positions in a general sense and there tends to be a lag behind the sun's position particularly over the oceans. Here, the movement is most frequently around 10° from the geographic. Over the land areas the lag has less effect and in South East Asia the heat equator extends well above 23½°N because of the type of terrain. The graph at Figure 7.3 refers.

The Equatorial Trough

This is the region of low pressure caused by high temperature leading to convective lifting and the subsequent CU CB cloud with heavy showers and thunderstorms. It must therefore be based on the heat equator. Surface air moves into the trough from the subtropical anticyclones.

The Intertropical Convergence Zone — ITCZ

The zone varies in width from a few tens of miles to 300 nm wide hence it is a zone rather than a front. It is the region where the two trade wind systems meet. The trade winds move from the subtropical anticyclones either side of the heat equator and converge. The centre line of this convergence must be coincident with the centre line of the Equatorial Trough, i.e. the heat equator. The interconnection between these three dominant weather factors is now evident. In fact some authorities maintain that the Equatorial Trough and the ITCZ are the same thing. There is however a tendency for the Trough over land to be more significant than over the sea because of the greater daytime surface temperatures. There is also a greater movement of the ITCZ north and south over the land than over the oceans. Figures 18.4 and 18.5 show average positions of the Heat Equator/Equatorial Trough/ITCZ and the Trade Winds for January and July respectively.

ITCZ Weather

The main weather feature of the ITCZ is large scale CU CB cloud with thunderstorms and heavy showers. There is often widespread AS and NS when stability layers are present and more continuous type rain can then apply. There is no well defined front as with the depressions in mid-latitudes and therefore the zone produces a more congested type of weather than for a normal front. Cloud tops

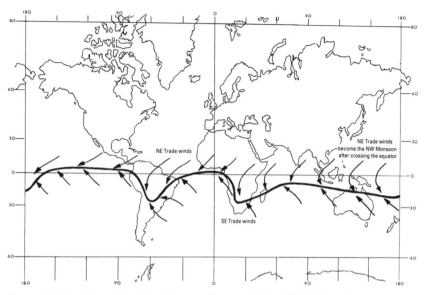

Figure 18.4. Position of the Heat Equator/Equatorial Trough/ITCZ in January

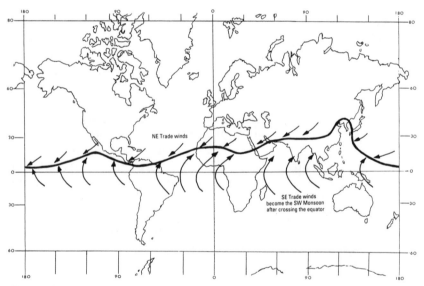

Figure 18.5. Position of the Heat Equator/Equatorial Trough/ITCZ in July

can be as low as 20 000 ft but more frequently cloud extends beyond the 50 000 ft level. The high temperature over sea areas and the other lifting agents provide breeding grounds for tropical storms.

Flying conditions can be very turbulent with severe icing above 16000 ft. The tropopause height in the ITCZ averages between 51000 and 58000 ft.

The Monsoons
These are seasonal winds which combine the trade winds with the outgoing airflows from continents in winter and with the in-flowing air to the same continents in summer. These winds move air from air mass sources which can then be modified by the surfaces under the moving air. The monsoons are inevitably distinguished not only by a particular wind direction but also by the type of weather which accompanies the wind.

The North East monsoon of Asia leaves the Siberian High as a cold dry wind. This stays cold and dry over much of South East Asia. However coastal areas which are facing this wind, notably the east coasts of India, Sri Lanka and Malaya experience CU CB heavy showers and thunderstorms. This is because the monsoon passes over warm seas where much water vapour is absorbed and the convective lifting over the sea is augmented by orographic triggering over the coasts. This is particularly marked over Southern Malaya where the littoral contains a mountainous region. The North East monsoon of Asia also affects North Australia. This wind direction is changed radically soon after crossing the geographic equator. The moving air then enters the southern hemisphere where the geostrophic force turns the moving mass of air to the left. The effect is to transpose the North East monsoon into the North West monsoon of northern Australia. This is a warm moist wind and it brings with it the ITCZ and its weather together with tropical cyclones.

In the North West Africa area the warm dry outflow from the subtropical high over the Sahara gives the North East trade wind. In this case it is again a seasonal wind, but is referred to as the Harmattan. The significant weather factor here is dust which can be carried up to thousands of feet giving very poor visibility.

In summer the South East trade winds leave the southern hemisphere subtropical anticyclones as warm moist air. These cross the geographic equator into the northern hemisphere where the geostrophic force turns moving air to the right so that the direction becomes southwesterly. The January high pressure over Asia has now disappeared due to the rising surface temperature. The result is the Asia low of summer. The low pressure further enhances the movement of the air from the southwest so that the South West monsoon of summer is established. The long sea passage in the

Southeast Asia region and the lifting on the ITCZ with this southwesterly monsoon brings widespread CU CB heavy showers and thunderstorms. Additionally the lifting at the ITCZ contributes to the breeding of tropical cyclones.

The summer southwest monsoon is also established over northwest Africa, in the 20°N region by July. Again the ITCZ is part of the monsoon. Here the weather tends to be more predominantly CU, CB, heavy showers and thunderstorms. It is not a tropical cyclone area.

GLOBAL CLIMATE FACTORS

Temperature

Worldwide surface air temperatures are governed in the main by latitude, season, land/sea surface, the effect of topography and by sea currents. The detailed effects of latitude, season and the type of land surface have been covered in earlier chapters. Taking these factors as understood, the remaining items are the closer examination of the differences with land and sea surfaces, topography and sea currents.

The average mean sea level temperatures for January and July are shown at Figures 18.6 and 18.7 respectively. Land temperatures have been corrected to sea level so that a common base applies.

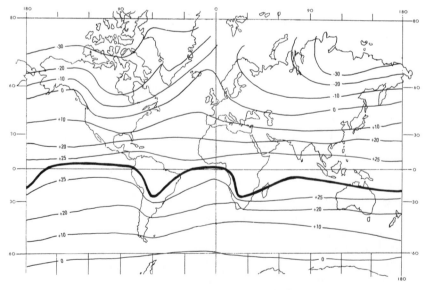

Figure 18.6. Average Mean Sea Level Temperatures in January

202

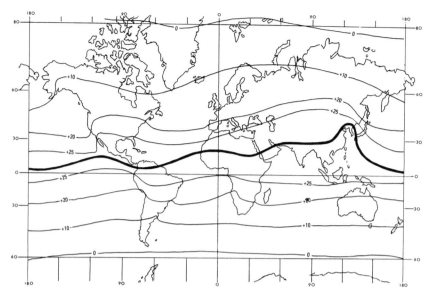

Figure 18.7. Average Mean Sea Level Temperatures in July

Land and Sea Surfaces.

The land heats and cools rapidly. Therefore high temperatures occur early in the summer months and cold temperatures early in winter. The heating of the sea is much slower and therefore temperatures are still cold in early summer. By the end of summer temperatures are at their highest and relatively high temperatures are retained by the sea for sometime into autumn and early winter. For these reasons it is to be expected that any isotherms of mean monthly temperature will be at a lower latitude in summer over the sea. Similary in winter the isotherms are at a lower latitude over the land. This is shown at Figures 18.6 and 18.7.

The large land masses of Asia and North America are thus centres of very low temperatures in winter and high temperatures in summer. It is colder in Siberia in winter, than it is at the North Pole. In summer the temperatures in Siberia are equivalent to those in Southern England despite the latitude being almost 20° higher. The range of annual temperatures over these large northern hemisphere land areas is therefore high compared with the oceans. This range can be in excess of 50°C compared with some 10°C over the oceans. The large African continent is not affected in the same way because of its disposition about the geographic equator and the traverse of the ITCZ/heat equator north and south through most of the continent. The same applies to the largest and most northern

203

part of South America. It will also be noted that the annual temperature range in the equatorial region is only some 5°C.

Figures 18.6 and 18.7 show the isotherms in the southern hemisphere to be more or less parallel to the lines of latitude. This accords with the predominantly ocean surface. Furthermore, this comparative lack of land must result in warmer winters and colder summers than in the northern hemisphere.

Topography

Coastal mountain ranges can have a profound effect on temperatures. In summer the cooler sea air can be held back by the mountains so that temperatures inland are higher. In winter, temperatures on a coast will be warmer because of any incoming warmer air from the sea. Additionally the mountains can restrict the outflow of cold air from inland. Typical of mountains with these effects are the north/south ranges along the western coasts of North and South America and the Great Dividing Range of Australia. The east/west range of southern Europe provides similar effects. The inland range of Southern Asia, including the the Himalayas, holds back the Polar Continental air from the north so that the Indian sub-continent is much warmer in winter than would otherwise be the case.

Two particular mountain areas are worth special mention. The Zagros mountains of the Iran/Pakistan region can provide coastal effects similar to those mentioned earlier. In addition, in the Baluchistan region the bare rock mountains facing south to the sea can attain very high summer temperatures. Similarly high summer values are also found in the southeast-facing bare mountain area of China.

All the mountain regions provide Anabatic, Katbatic and Fohn winds of varying values. These can have marked effects on temperatures. This is exemplified by the Fohn winds of Canada to the east of the Rocky mountains — the Chinook winds — where temperatures can be raised by up to 25°C for a few weeks. The opposite of the mountain effects are where there is relatively low lying ground, such as the north European plain. Here the summer winds from the Atlantic are unrestricted and temper what would otherwise be high temperatures. In winter the relatively warm air off the Atlantic has a free passage and can provide warming, particularly in the west.

Sea Currents

A map showing the main sea currents is at Figure 18.8; significant sea currents are as follows:

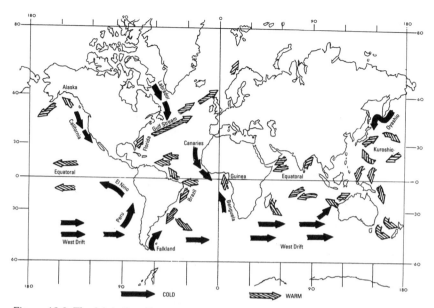

Figure 18.8. The Main Sea Currents

a) The Gulf Stream with its extension towards Norway and the Barents Sea. The flow transports masses of warm water northeast. This raises sea temperatures and nearby land to well above the expected latitude values. The winter effects are very beneficial as otherwise ports in the British Isles and Norway could be icebound.

b) The Kuroshio current is the Pacific equivalent of the Gulf Stream. In winter it has a warming effect on the cold monsoon which is northwesterly in this area. This warming is one of the reasons for the higher temperatures on the east coast of Japan compared with the west.

c) The Labrador, California, Canaries, Benguela, Peru, Falkland and Oyashio cold currents, all help to reduce coastal temperatures. They also cause extensive advection sea fogs and stratus.

d) The northern part of the Peru current is exceptionally cold. The southerly winds displace the top layer of water, allowing very cold water from below to reach the surface. This region of the current is referred to as El Nino. In recent years there has been speculation that climate in a global sense could be affected by the temperature value and extent of El Nino.

205

Upper Air Temperatures

The average lapse rate in the troposphere is 2°C per 1000 ft. Using this rate as a norm, it is clear that the upper air temperature must initially be controlled by the surface temperatures. The height of the tropopause over the tropics is greater than over the poles. Therefore the lapse rate applies over a greater depth of air and despite the higher surface values the temperatures at the tropical tropopause are lower than those at the polar tropopause. This is shown diagrammatically at Figure 18.9. The figure also shows that

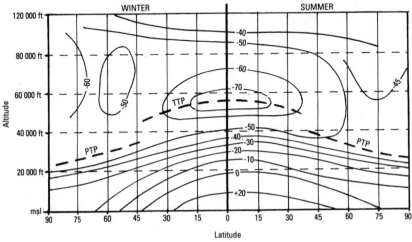

Figure 18.9. Upper Air Temperatures

in the lower stratosphere, around 80 000 ft, the temperatures increase from the equator to the poles in summer. In winter the higher values are in the middle latitudes with decreasing temperatures towards the equator and the poles.

Tropopause Heights

As previously indicated, the tropopause heights are governed in the first instance by latitude. Overall, the expected range by this control is 24 000 to 58 000 ft. However, variations in surface temperature in a longitude sense must also affect the heights. For example, Siberian values should be, and are, lower than expected in winter and higher than expected in summer. Tropopause heights will vary with the type of air mass and therefore air mass movements can bring changes to tropopause height expectations. In general Tropical Tropopause heights throughout the year are within the range; 48 000 to 58 000 ft. For the Polar Tropopause the values are within the range 24 000 to 45 000 ft.

Whilst tropopause heights are important as a guide to the upper limits for clouds it should be borne in mind that this limit can be broken through, particularly if the air at this level is relatively moist.

Icing Limits

The height of the 0°C isotherm is the lower limit for airframe icing. In the region of the heat equator, this height is 16000 ft, and exceptionally 18000 ft. In winter it can normally be expected that the position of the 0°C isotherm at sea level will be between 40°N and 50°N. In summer the expected latitude range is 70°N to 80°N. In the southern hemisphere the 0°C isotherm is at sea level at around 60°S throughout the year. The upper icing limit of −45°C will be close to the 40000 ft level at the heat equator, decreasing to 18000 ft in the polar winter and to 37000 ft in the polar summer.

Pressure

Surface Pressure

The surface values must largely accord with the surface temperatures. There are exceptions to this caused by Hadley cell movements and by the passage of frequent low pressure systems through some areas. The average mean sea level isobars for January and July are shown at Figures 18.10 and 18.11 respectively.

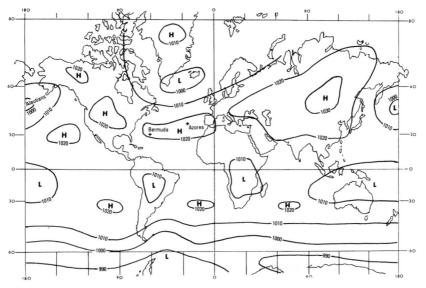

Figure 18.10. Average Mean Sea Level Pressures in January

207

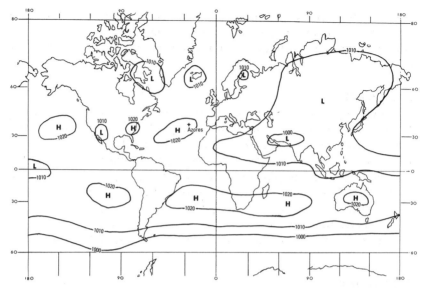

Figure 18.11. Average Mean Sea Level Pressures in July

For January the subtropical anticyclones are clearly displayed over the sea in the southern hemisphere. In the northern hemisphere there is the Atlantic subtropical high over the Azores extending to the Bermuda high. The Pacific subtropical highs are also evident. The two major cold anticyclones of Siberia and North America are established at this season. As expected there is the low pressure belt around the equatorial region at all seasons. The lows of mid-latitudes are transient and therefore only show statistically in the areas of most frequent passage. These are the Iceland low for the Atlantic and the Aleution low for the Pacific.

In July the subtropical highs have moved further north and the Australian subtropical high is now in the centre of the continent. The Siberian and North American anticyclones disappear and the same regions are now areas of low pressure due to the high land temperatures. The transient lows of the northern hemisphere have moved northwards resulting in statistical lows to the west of Greenland and over Iceland. The Aleution low is no longer statistically relevant.

At all seasons, the isobars for the southern hemisphere south of 40° North are more or less parallel to the lines of latitude. This accords with the almost total sea surface. Additionally, in this hemisphere the transient lows passage close to the 50° South parallel of latitude with no particular area of frequent passage. This again results in the parallel isobar situation.

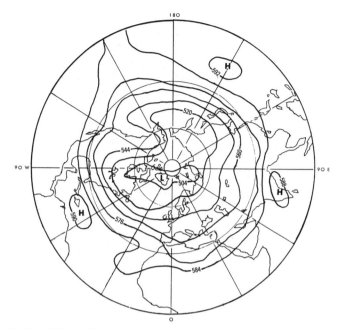

Figure 18.12. A 500 mb Constant Pressure Chart for January

Figure 18.13. A 500 mb Constant Pressure Chart for July

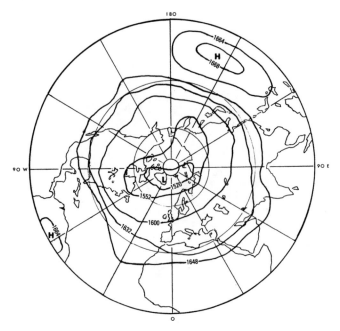

Figure 18.14. A 100 mb Constant Pressure Chart for January

Figure 18.15. A 100 mb Constant Pressure Chart for July

Upper Level Pressures

Constant pressure charts for northern hemisphere upper levels averaged over a ten-day period for January and July 1988 are shown at Figures 18.12 to 18.15. The charts show contour heights in terms of decametres. Averaging over a number of years can hide significant pressure factors, therefore in some ways these ten-day charts in one year are preferable. Obviously care should be taken in drawing firm conclusions on the restricted samples here. Nevertheless general inferences can be drawn from the charts. Figures 18.12 and 18.13 are for the 500 mb level (some 18 000 ft) for January and July respectively. It can be seen that at these heights the surface polar high is no longer evident. Neither are the surface winter cold anticyclones over Russia and North America. However, the warm subtropical highs are still clearly defined. In the lower latitudes, there is almost a complete absence of contours indicating very small pressure gradients. This accords with the expected near-constant surface temperatures and horizontally in the layers above, particularly for July. Figure 18.12 for January shows a far larger range of contour values and closer contour spacing indicating stronger winter winds.

At higher levels the effects of surface pressures and particularly the differences due to oceans and continents should be much weaker. Figure 18.14 for 100 mb in January clearly shows this trait. Only the Pacific subtropical high is discernible. The contours show a distinct polar low pressure area with the contours providing a quasi-circular pattern. This results in strong westerly winds right down to some 25°N.

A study of the July chart at Figure 18.15 indicates that surface influences still apply. The subtropical highs are just evident at these levels. There are some separate small low centres around the pole. However, the overall pressure gradient picture for the entire hemisphere appears slack. Contour heights range from 16 400 to 16 800 metres. (The January range is 15 200 to 16 680.) There is thus evidence that in July winds are more variable and less strong at the 100 mb level, than in January.

Wind

Surface

Surface wind diagrams are at Figures 18.16 and 18.17 for January and July respectively. The winds largely follow the expectations from the pressure systems. Hence the subtropical highs in the northern hemisphere should, and do, produce northeast winds on

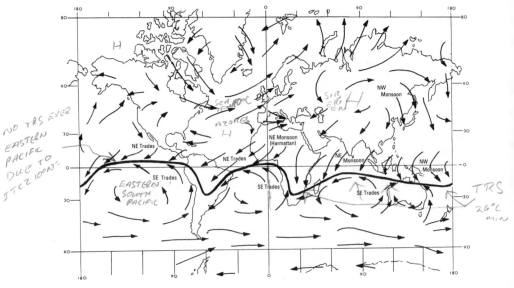

Figure 18.16. Surface Winds in January

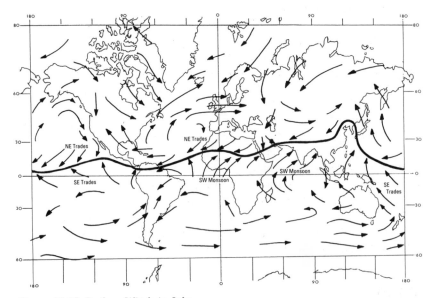

Figure 18.17. Surface Winds in July

the low latitude side and southwesterlies on the higher latitude sides. The latter join with the westerlies on the southern side of the mid-latitude low pressure systems. At the northern side of these lows easterly winds apply.

In the southern hemisphere, the basic pattern is similar except that the subtropical highs produce southeasterly winds on the low latitude side and northwesterlies on the higher latitude side. These join with the westerlies on the northern side of the mid-latitude lows. Easterly winds apply on the southern side of these lows.

Whilst the foregoing is in accord with pressure expectations and does apply, there will inevitably be differences in practice that are outside these main streams. Important differences will include the effect of local pressure changes at the place and time: sea breezes which become very important at low latitudes and at higher latitudes in summer. Even more dominant are the monsoons of Asia, Northern Australia, North West Africa and North America. The influence of the monsoons on the basic wind pattern can be seen at Figures 18.16 and 18.17.

Upper Winds (300 mb to 200 mb)
Simplified diagrams of the global upper wind directions for January and July are at Figures 18.18 and 18.19. They are based on the expectations from upper pressure systems, thermal wind effects and jet stream positions. The diagrams show the following main wind systems:

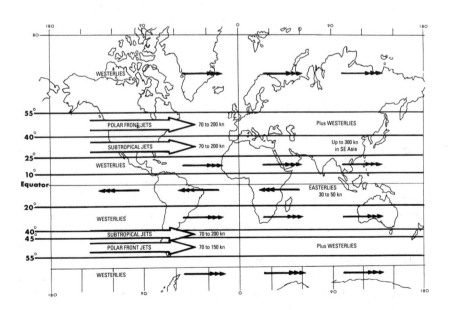

Figure 18.18. A Simplified Upper Wind Diagram for January

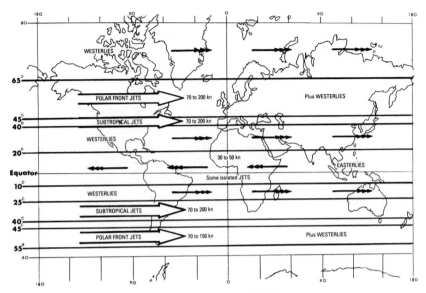

Figure 18.19. A Simplified Upper Wind Diagram for July

a) *Easterlies* within 10° of the geographic equator at all times: Extending to 20° in the summer hemisphere.

b) *Westerly* subtropical jet streams within the band 25° to 40° in winter. In summer from 40° to 45°.

c) *Westerly* polar front jet streams 35°N to 55°N in winter moving north to 45°N to 65°N in summer. In the southern hemisphere 45° to 55° throughout the year.

d) *Westerlies* at the poles.

e) *Westerlies* light to moderate between the main streams.

At the 300 mb to 200 mb levels the upper winds are of particular importance to aircraft cruising conditions. Whilst the simplified diagrams give basic upper zone flow expectations, they are a guide only. In practice the pressure conditions at the time, topographical effects and actual frontal positions can cause radical changes. Additionally upper level troughs and ridges can cause strong north/south winds. Figure 15.2 shows examples of these.

The Subtropical Jet Streams (STJ)

These provide westerlies with speeds which vary with season. Generally speeds are greater in winter because of the greater disparity in mean temperature below a level over land and sea. Hence speeds of the order ot 100 to 200 kn can be expected over

214

the North Atlantic and Pacific Oceans in winter. Speeds will be reduced from these values in summer. Over Europe in winter the jet is established in the eastern Mediterranean sea between Egypt and Cyprus with speeds up to 200 kn. To the west the stream continues to Morocco and the Atlantic jet. To the east it extends to Arabia, the Arabian Gulf, India and the Far East. In summer over Europe the jet speed is dissipated to some extent by the effects of the southern mountains so that winds speeds rarely exceed 40 kn to 50 kn. In effect therefore, the jet does not exist far beyond Bordeaux to the east. In winter the jet is positioned south of the Himalayas across India. Further east it covers southern China and further north and east in the region of the most southern part of Japan. Here the subtropical jet combines with the Polar Front jet. Additionally the surface wind is northwesterly. The joining of all these winds results in a westerly jet (nominally subtropical) which can reach speeds of 300 kn.

In the southern hemisphere the jet averages 120 kn over Australia and New Zealand. It can reach 200 kn on occasions. Elsewhere and particularly over the southern Pacific Ocean there is some evidence of speeds up to 120 kn. Over South America there is little evidence that the subtropical jet has significance.

The Polar Front Jet Streams (PFJ)
These are relatively short term compared with the subtropical jets. They can occur along the basic polar front itself. More frequently they occur as individual jets in association with polar front depressions. In these instances whilst the general direction is expected to be westerly, directions can vary dependent on the bearing of a front. The jet will normally take up a position parallel to the front. Hence if the front — be it warm or cold — is lying along a north south axis, then the jet stream will be northerly or southerly. The speeds of polar front jets are usually around the 100 kn level.

Westerlies at the Poles
The westerlies apply in the winter months. In spring they tend to decrease becoming more variable including easterly directions in the summer. Speeds at this season are reduced from the winter values.

Weather
Introduction
Weather as a global climate factor in this context includes average cloud amounts, precipitation, thunderstorms and visibility.

Average Cloud Amounts

The cloud amount or degree of overcast is of importance to any pilot in a terminal area. The cloud amount is largely governed by three main factors; the amount of lifting, the humidity and the general type of cloud produced. There will be variables controlled by the time of day and the season.

Around the heat equator there is strong convective lifting, assisted by frontal lifting on the ITCZ. With the exception of large land areas straddling the equatorial regions, e.g. parts of Africa, there are nearby sea and river basin areas so that humidity is high. However the type of cloud produced is mainly of the cumuliform type. The clouds will have great depth, but the degree of overcast is not as large as may be at first considered. Furthermore, at night the cloud tends to dissipate as convection ceases. Hence on a 24 hour statistical basis, the cloud amount is relatively low.

At higher latitudes in the subtropical zone any lifting is restricted by subsidence and cloud cover is low. These are the desert areas of the world.

Beyond the subtropics are the temperate zones and the polar regions. Here the dominant lifting agent is frontal and polar frontal primarily. This produces widespread stability cloud as well as cumuliform and thus the degree of overcast is high. With the polar front clouds forming over the oceans there is ample moisture and cloud amounts are often greater over the oceans and nearby coasts than at continental locations. Lifted fog can assist the overcast and also fog of some depth. Here the appearance of the top of the fog is the same as ST cloud. This greater depth of fog is more likely in the polar regions. At night the frontal activity continues so that large cloud amounts can apply throughout the whole 24 hours. For any individual area within the frontal activity area, there will be seasonal variation. This will apply in the warm temperate zone as a decrease in summer and in the polar regions as an increase in summer.

The monsoon regions of South East Asia, North West Africa and North Australia have the greatest cloudiness in summer. In winter the outflow from the centre of the continent is dry and cloud amounts are smaller. The question of the base of the overcast will always bear on aviation. As a general rule it can be expected that cloud bases will be lower as latitude increases. This is purely on the basis of the decrease in temperature causing higher relative humidities.

Precipitation

There is a connection between the amount of cloud cover and

precipitation. However this is by no means a direct correlation. The amount of precipitation is controlled by the depth and type of cloud as well as the amount. In the equatorial zone of strong convection and convergence with the ITCZ, the cloud type is mainly CU CB and the precipitation is in the form of heavy showers. Rain/hail can be expected at all seasons. At places where there is a distinct gap between the two passages north and south of the ITCZ there can be two periods of extra strong rainfall. Kenya is a case in point.

There is a secondary maximum precipitation area in the latitudes of polar front activity. Here the precipitation can be over longer time periods due to the predominance of stability type clouds.

There are other areas where precipitation is heavy and not strictly in accord with climatic zone considerations. In general precipitation will be somewhat greater over oceans than continents because of the availability of moisture. It will also be greater over islands in oceans because of orographic lifting and the daytime convection. The west coasts of continents will have much higher precipitation in the region of the temperate westerly winds. Examples are the British Isles, Norway, western North America, Chile and New Zealand. High mountain barriers along these coasts enhance cloud formation and precipitation. The Rocky mountains of North America, the Andes of South America and the Southern Alps of New Zealand are prime examples. High rainfall is also the result of lifting of the summer southwest monsoon against the Himalayas to the north of the Indian sub-continent. The climatic zone where precipitation is least include the subtropical desert areas and the higher latitude regions beyond 65°. In this latter region the cloud amounts were said to be large. However, the depth of cloud is necessarily thin. This is because of the low values of absolute humidity at saturation caused by low temperatures. Hence whilst the number of days when precipitation occurs may be many, the actual amount is small. Other areas where conditions are almost arid are the lee side of mountain ranges. Such areas are sometimes referred to as being in the 'rain shadow'. A good example is the Patagonia desert in the shadow of the Andes in South America. There are also the regions to the east of the Rocky mountains in North America. Any rain shadow area can be subject to Fohn effect and to the air becoming dry due to the heavy precipitation on the windward mountainside.

Thunderstorms

Thunderstorm formation is generally associated with areas of strong convection and frontal activity. This is overlaid by the regions where tropical revolving storms occur. The prime areas for thunderstorm activity are therefore in the equatorial zone and close to the ITCZ. These include the East Indies and notably Java and Sumatra where the incidence of storms can exceed one day in three and there is little seasonal variation. Other areas of high activity in summer include Central America, the West Indies, New Mexico, Equatorial Africa and Malaya. In the southern hemisphere summer, Madagascar, central and western Brazil and northern Australia are regions where activity can approach one day in three.

In the temperate latitudes summer surface heating can result in frequent storms in the centre of the USA and to a smaller extent in central Europe. Whilst there are thunderstorms in these same latitudes caused by cold frontal lifting, the incidence is relatively low. Thunderstorms do not occur in the polar regions and even large scale CU are restricted by the low absolute humidity at saturation.

Visibility
Radiation fogs are particularly common in temperate regions with a main season in autumn and winter. They can occur at lower latitudes but clear very quickly with early morning insolation. Sea fogs can be common where cold sea currents are adjacent to coastal areas. Any warmer winds can then result in extensive advection type fogs. Particular areas are California (California cold sea current), Morocco (Canaries current), South West Africa (Benguela current), Chile (Peru current), Newfoundland (Labrador current), and Kamchatka (Oyashio current). Details of the above currents are shown at Figure 18.8. Any transport of warm moist air over a colder surface can cause advection fogs. For example, the coasts of the British Isles and North West Europe can be affected with a southwesterly wind from the Azores high.

Dust storms and haze are prevalent in the low latitude arid regions. These include: Central and South West Asia (Sind and Arabian deserts), North Africa (Sahara and Sudan), South West Africa (Kalahari), Central Australia (Gibson and Simpson), South America (Chile and Patagonia), Central and South West USA (Arizona, Colorado, and Mohave). The extensive depth of dust haze in these areas can, on occasions, effect aircraft in flight up to and above the tropopause.

Volcanic ash can reduce visibility in flight over a wide area above and downwind of an eruption. Furthermore the effects can last for months on end. Volcanic dust, as distinct from the larger ash has been known to persist for years and to extend into the stratosphere. The ash can be a particular hazard by causing jet engine flame out. Active volcanic areas include Iceland, Japan, Sumatra (Krakatoa), Sicily (Etna), Italy (Vesuvius), North West Canada, Central America and Ecuador.

CLIMATE IN ROUTE AREAS

Introduction
Many of the major aviation routes worldwide are now standard. For example London to New York and Singapore to Tokyo. Other routes are being changed to some degree by the extended range of modern aircraft. The present importance of the Arabian Gulf area as a refuelling stop is being reduced, although passengers travelling to and from the region will continue to require air traffic. In the future non-stop routes from London to Cape Town and London to Sydney, or something akin to these distances, will be possible. In the examination of climate for route flying, it is therefore preferable to concentrate on route areas rather than on routes *per se*. Nevertheless some mention of a basic route will sometimes be efficacious.

In addition to normal surface climatic conditions, pilots will be particularly concerned with visibility, surface and upper winds, freezing levels and icing. Upper winds considered here are at the 300 to 200 mb level. A decode of the symbols used in the figures which follow is at Appendix 'B'.

Tropopause Heights
It was mentioned previously that these are variable with a number of factors within any area. For this reason tropopause heights are not listed under the individual route areas. They are given here as average heights for particular latitude bands as follows:

0° to 30°	–	48 000 to 58 000 ft
40° to 60°	–	30 000 to 45 000 ft
70° to 90°	–	24 000 to 30 000 ft

Africa
Routes for the African continent cover two main areas. Through North West Africa from Algeria to Nigeria and on the east side of Africa from Egypt south to South Africa.

Geographic Considerations
The climatic zones include Equatorial, Savannah, Arid subtropical/

219

Steppe and — at the higher latitudes — Warm Temperate. There is almost a duplication of climatic zones north and south of the Equatorial zone. There are no extensive mountain chains dividing climates. There are vast plateaus above the 3000 ft level particularly in the south. The Atlas mountains in the north and the highlands of Ethiopia and around lake Victoria are the cause of some orographic lifting.

In the north the continent is dominated by the Sahara desert. This is a source of dust which can reduce visibility over large areas. The Canaries current has a cooling effect on airflow along the northwest coastal regions.

Pressure Systems
There is a portion of the winter subtropical high in the north Sahara which is a source of tropical continental air. The equatorial trough/ITCZ has a major effect on climate. In January it is positioned across Zimbabwe and Mozambique. Then moving north it crosses Tanzania, reaching Uganda and Kenya at the spring equinox in March. It continues north reaching Ethiopia and the Sudan. Its maximum northerly position, some 200 to 300 nm north of Khartoum around 20°N is reached in July. In the west, the ITCZ is over

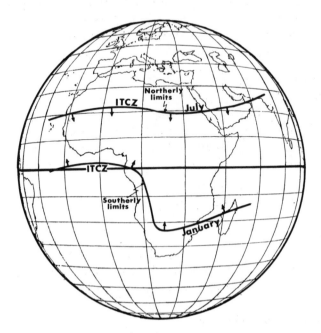

Figure 18.20. ITCZ Positioning over Africa

Nigeria in May. It continues north through Ghana, Ivory coast, Guinea and Senegal to southern Mauretania. It extends to some 200–300 nm north of Dakar in Senegal to be around 20°N in July. On both sides of the continent the ITCZ then moves south over the same countries. In the west it clears the 5°N south-facing coast to an ocean position in October. In the east it is in the Kenya area in October/November. Then continues south to be over Zimbabwe/ Mozambique around 20°S in January once more. The ITCZ positioning is shown at Figure 18.20. In the southeast of the continent, Mozambique is sometimes effected by Tropical Cyclones in the January season. The subtropical anticyclone in the southern Indian ocean provides on shore east and north east winds along the east coast.

North West Africa
The region includes the area from the Mediterranean sea to Nigeria west of 10°E. It includes Algeria, Morocco, Mauretania, Senegal, Guinea, Sierra Leone, Liberia, Ivory Coast, Ghana and Nigeria.

Weather South of 20°N
January (winter). The ITCZ is south of the region. There is little or no cloud or precipitation. This is the dry season and is widely affected by very poor visibility. The warm dry dusty Harmattan wind from the Sahara can reduce visibility from November to April. Visibility is frequently below 5000 m and sometimes below fog limits. The cold Canaries current off the west coast can cause the Harmattan to pick up moisture and produce advection fog. This can then be drawn into the coastal regions by sea breezes.
July (summer). The surface wind veers from March/April to the east and then to the southwest in summer. This brings the ITCZ into the region with the southwest monsoon from May to July when it reaches some 20°N. This is the wet season with CU CB and heavy showers and thunderstorms. From July onwards the ITCZ moves south again with its weather. The wind backs through east in September/October, then to the northeast of winter.
Tornadoes. These West Africa tornadoes are thunder squalls with heavy precipitation. They move across the region as large scale CB on a north/south line when winds are in the east, i.e. in March/ April and September/October. They originate in the upper Niger valley due to the high moisture content of the air and the large scale convection.

Weather North of 20°N

January (winter). The weather in Morocco and Mauretania is dominated by westerly winds off the sea. These bring cloud and precipitation. Cloud base can be low due to cooling of the air over the Canaries current. Some cold fronts also reach the area giving thundery activity. In north Algeria some cold fronts originate in the Mediterranean. The Atlas mountains prevent their movement further south. There is some orographic instability cloud and precipitation in this mountainous region.

July (summer). This is the dry season with surface winds from the northeast bringing some dust. Visibility can also be reduced by low ST and fog along coasts.

Upper Winds and Freezing Levels

There are the expected easterly upper winds around the ITCZ with light westerlies beyond. In winter the westerly subtropical jet lies over Morocco (30°N). Over Algeria there are westerlies around 40 kn. In the summer light westerly winds in the north, become light easterly from 20°N southwards.

Average freezing levels are 15 000 ft throughout the year. Area details, weather and upper winds are shown at Figures 18.21 and 18.22 for January and July respectively.

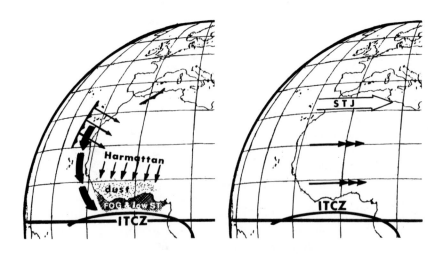

Figure 18.21. North-West Africa – Weather Details in January

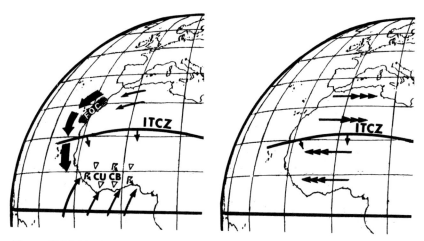

Figure 18.22. North-West Africa – Weather Details in July

Routes East of 25°E

The region includes Egypt, Sudan, Ethiopia, Somalia, Kenya, Uganda, Zaire, Tanzania, Malawi, Zambia, Zimbabwe, Mozambique and South Africa. With any route area crossing the equator, the terms winter and summer can be confusing. Instead, January and July will be used to differentiate the weather. January will infer winter for northerly latitudes and summer for southerly latitudes. For July, vice versa.

January Period Weather

In the extreme north the occasional cold front from the Mediterranean can extend down to some 15°N. These bring thick CU CB and thundery showers. Otherwise dry dusty conditions apply from the Mediterranean sea to about 6°N. The Khamsin blows in this region as a dusty southerly wind from December to April. During this period the ITCZ has moved south to give a wet season to Kenya (November/December). By January the ITCZ is established over Zimbabwe/Mozambique. It then moves north giving CU, CB, NS heavy showers and thunderstorms for all the countries between 20°S and Kenya over the total period November to March. Mozambique can sometimes be effected by tropical cyclones from November to May but are more frequent from January to April. These originate in the Mozambique channel and can sometimes move even further west into Zimbabwe and the north of South Africa. The usual tropical cyclonic weather applies.

This is also the west season in South Africa which is south of the ITCZ line. There is low cloud and fog in the early morning which

Figure 18.23. Africa East of 25E – Weather Details in January

Figure 18.24. Africa East of 25E – Weather Details in July

clears quickly. Later in the day large CU and showers and also some thunderstorms can reach the area from the southwest. Surface winds are generally southerly in the Egypt/Sudan area, becoming east or northeast at the lower latitudes and down to the ITCZ region. They then become southerly. In the extreme south surface winds are westerly throughout the year.

July Period Weather

The ITCZ is around 20°N in July giving CU CB NS, heavy showers, thunderstorms and some more general NS rain. This can apply from the equator to north of Khartoum. Haboobs form in the north Sudan region from May to September. These are severe dust storms associated with CB on the ITCZ. Upcurrents under the CB help to lift dust to 10000 ft or more. These dust storms can be seen approaching as a wall of dust. They form during daylight when convection is high and are often associated with line squalls forming on the ITCZ. From March to May there are the 'long rains' of Kenya but further south it is the dry season. In the extreme south the Guti surface winds can blow. These are moderate to strong southeast winds from the Mozambique channel. They bring very low ST and SC and occur from April to October, usually in one to five-day spells.

Upper Winds and Freezing Levels

In January from 10°N to 20°S upper winds are easterly becoming light westerly further south over South Africa. To the north of 10°N winds are westerly increasing to the westerly subtropical jet over northern Egypt.

In July there are easterlies from 10°S to 20°N and winds can approach jet stream values in the Khartoum region. Further north winds are light westerly. They are also light westerly south of 10°S and become moderate westerly over South Africa.

Average freezing levels are 16000 ft in the equatorial region and 14000 ft at the higher latitudes.

The weather details for January and July are displayed at Figures 18.23 and 18.24 respectively.

North America

The route area includes south Canada, the USA and the Gulf States.

Geographic Considerations

There are vast western highlands which cover a large portion of the land area. These comprise the Pacific coastal ranges of western Canada, California and Oregon. Further inland are the Sierra Nevada ranges which include a large plateau extending south to Mexico: Further east still are the Rocky mountains in Canada and in the USA where they are very broad covering some 10° of longitude. On the opposite side of the continent are the highlands from Labrador into the Appalachian range further south. There is a great central plain between the mountains which is open to warm air from the south and cold air from the north. The great lakes are in this region and can modify the climate. The mountainous areas of the west restrict the passage of air masses to the east and west. There are strong Fohn effects in these areas. They are also noted for strong and frequent mountain waves.

Ocean currents modify the temperatures of passing air. Notable are the warm Gulf stream and Florida current up the east coast. This contrasts with the cold California current of the west coast. The cold Labrador current in the northeast has a significant effect on fog formation. A map showing the geography is at Figure 18.25.

Figure 18.25. North America – Geography

Pressure Systems

The North America high is established in winter with particular centres in northwest Canada and the middle of the central plain. Further south from Mexico pressures gradually reduce. Within Canada and the USA there are many travelling frontal depressions from the Polar and Arctic fronts. The eastward paths of these lows is variable but they are furthest south at this season. In summer the centre of the continent is a low pressure area due to surface heating. High pressure is now over arctic Canada. The Atlantic subtropical high has moved north and has extensions into southwest USA. Polar front lows now have tracks further north at this season and the arctic front is over northern Canada.

Tornadoes occur in the southern central plain together with thermal lows. In the Gulf of Mexico hurricanes occur in the summer season.

Winter Conditions

Polar front lows cross the continent from the west mainly in the 35° to 45° latitude band. North of this there are a few Arctic front lows. The polar front depressions bring heavy snowfalls, large cloud amounts and freezing rain along the east coast of USA and Canada. Often this is in association with slow moving warm fronts. Aircraft tracks north of these lows will experience easterly surface winds and thus bad weather. Aircraft tracks to the south of lows can experience southerly winds bringing fog. Fog also occurs in the Newfoundland area with this wind direction.

The central plain can experience cold frontal weather with snow showers and strong winds. On occasions warm Chinook winds can raise temperatures over the middle and northern central plains. High mountains to the west of the plains and the prairie regions have only small amounts of precipitation and cold anticyclonic weather is dominant. There can be frequent radiation fogs in these anticyclonic conditions. In the Great Lakes area thermal lows cause CU CB and heavy snow showers.

The Pacific coast is warmer than the east and is subject to Pacific lows from the west. Often these produce wide warm sectors with much ST with a low base. Alternatively strong winds can apply. Smog can also be a persistent problem around industrial cities. Along the central east coast large CU and heavy snow showers occur as the cold air from the centre reacts with the warmer sea.

The Gulf States region experiences frontal activity with lows forming in the Gulf and the States. These can produce cold frontal thunderstorms. Whilst temperatures are reasonably high through-out the year, at this season there can be cold waves of air from the north. This cold dry air can occasionally reduce temperatures below freezing. There can sometimes be low ST and fog when tropical air from the Gulf moves north. Poor visibility also applies with any warm front precipitation.

Summer Conditions

Polar front lows have now moved further north, the tracks being mainly in the 40° to 55° latitude band. These produce weak cold fronts with thunderstorms over eastern Canada. Fog is a maximum along the entire northeast section of the continent. Along the coast it is particularly consistent due to the Labrador current. Much low cloud also occurs.

The central plains enjoy high summer temperatures but in the north there are cool conditions in the rear of polar front lows. Over the prairies this is the wet season due to convection cloud and frontal rainfalls. Further south surface heating causes much thunderstorm activity and tornadoes in the upper Mississippi/ Missouri region.

Along the Pacific coast there is an anticyclone regime with northerly winds giving generally dry weather. Temperatures are warm, but lower than further inland where thunderstorms can occur. There can be coastal fog but south of 35°N including California, low ST predominates. An occasional hurricane can traverse along the coast from the south to the Gulf of California.

The Gulf States experience convective CU CB thunderstorms and heavy showers. The hurricanes of this season have tracks through the region giving violent weather. These can cause airport closure at coastal sites around the Gulf.

Upper Winds

The main wind direction is westerly. The westerly subtropical jet is around 30°N in winter with speeds around 100 kn. In summer this jet lies around the 40°N parallel and speeds are nearer to 70 kn. Polar Front jets are common in association with individual fronts and have a general westerly direction. Over the Gulf States in summer the upper winds are easterly.

Freezing Levels and Icing

In July freezing levels range from 16000 ft in the south to 10000 ft over Canada. In January they are around 12000 ft in the south quickly becoming at ground level further north. Along the Pacific coast where temperatures are warmer the level is around 5000 ft.

Icing is most severe with freezing rain and clear icing in association with frontal activity along the eastern section north of 35°N. This is especially so in the Baltimore to Boston region. Clear ice can be a problem in the large CU CB clouds of summer for en route flying. Figures 18.26 and 18.27 show the winter and summer conditions.

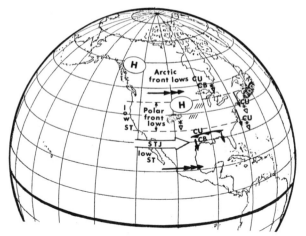

Figure 18.26. North America – Weather Details in January

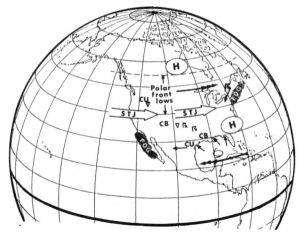

Figure 18.27. North America – Weather Details in July

Atlantic North

This region includes the Atlantic ocean from 15°N to 65°N and the surrounding coastal areas.

Geographic Considerations

The main factors in this almost entirely sea region are the sea currents. These are: the warm Gulf stream from the Gulf of Mexico spreading northeast to the British Isles and Norway and the cold Labrador current which extends from the north to the east coast of Newfoundland and Maine in the USA.

Climate zones include Cold Temperate, Warm Temperate and non-arid subtropical.

Pressure Systems
The main pressure systems are: The Azores subtropical anticyclone, The North American High of winter, Polar Air depressions, depressions on the Polar Front and the summer hurricanes in the extreme southwest. The Iceland low which appears on statistical charts is only of significance because many low pressure systems pass through that region. It is not a low pressure source.

The Azores anticyclone is centred on 30°N in winter with an average central pressure of 1020 mb. There is an extension to the west covering the Bermuda region which is sometimes referred to separately as the Bermuda high. In summer the anticyclone moves north to a centre around 35°N with a central pressure of 1025 mb. It is a major source of southwesterly tropical maritime air.

The North America high is in winter only and is a source of polar continental air affecting the West Atlantic. The same area in summer is a low pressure area. The high pressure effectively moves north in summer into northern arctic Canada.

Polar Air depressions have a source to the north of the Polar Front including Greenland and are mainly a winter feature. Polar Front depressions are the major source of weather. The depressions form on the front off the eastern seaboard of North America and travel east or northeast towards Europe. The polar front line is from Florida to southwest British Isles in winter and Newfoundland to north Scotland and Bergen in summer. Hurricanes form off the west African coast, or in the West Indies. They move east towards the Gulf of Mexico and then usually northeast across Florida into the Atlantic. Here they can occasionally join with a polar front depression to give very active weather.

Winter Conditions
On northern routes the dominant weather feature is depression activity. Polar front depressions are the main cause of weather being disturbed and changeable. The movement of these lows to the northeast from the Florida region is at about 30 kn but speeds can be much greater. Their fronts, warm cold and occluded, bring all cloud types with continuous type precipitation as well as showers.

Polar Air depressions are only in the north of the region. They bring CU CB showers, thunderstorms and secondary cold fronts. They move from the north in a southeasterly direction. A few lows enter the oceans in the north west from the North American polar front. Sometimes these develop secondaries. Between lows, ridges of high occur. When these develop into full anticyclones they can become 'Blocking'. Thereby forcing travelling lows to the northeast.

There is a distinct difference in the weather on the west and east coast of the ocean. Along the American east coast in the New York/ Washington area there can be extensive snow showers, low temperatures and icing. This is due to the proximity of the cold centre of North America and its polar continental air which reacts with the warmer air over the sea. On the west coast of Europe conditions are far less severe. The polar continental air from Siberia is much less common than the North American case. Further, the Gulf Stream has a warming effect in contrast to the cold Labrador current.

Visibility can be poor around the coasts of Newfoundland and northwest USA due to advection fog. The Labrador current helps this to form. To a lesser extent similar fogs form over the British Isles. Radiation fogs occur inland from most northern coasts.

Total cloud amounts average 6/8th. The cloud is also extensive vertically and bases can be close to the surface. For the more southerly routes there is less frontal activity due to proximity of the Azores anticyclone and cloud amounts are less. Surface winds are generally westerly, but changeable with the passage of fronts. Winds are strong and gales common. Easterly winds occur to the north of depressions and also in the southerly part of the area.

Freezing level is often at the surface in the north. The extensive cloud can therefore produce moderate to heavy icing. Rain ice can occur ahead of warm fronts and occlusions. In the south of the area, the freezing level is around 11 000 ft and icing is less of a problem.

Summer Conditions

Despite the disappearance of the North American high and the warmer temperatures, the difference in weather is of degree rather than kind.

The polar front has moved north and the line of the depressions moves with it. There are fewer polar front lows and Polar Air depressions are rare at this season. There are more anticyclones but cloud amounts are little different from winter. This is because of the stability type cloud forming with southwesterly flows from the Azores. Additionally there is cloud formed by hurricanes. The hurricanes in the extreme southwest have a main season from August to October. There are some five to ten storms a year. They give the usual tropical cyclone weather with CB, thunderstorms, torrential rains and winds of 100 kn plus at all levels. They can render terminal airfields unusable in the West Indies and Gulf coastal regions. There is also some Easterly wave activity along the

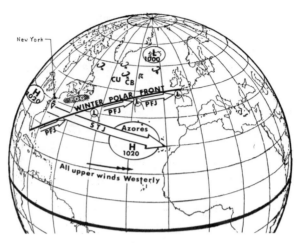

Figure 18.28. Atlantic North – Weather Details in January

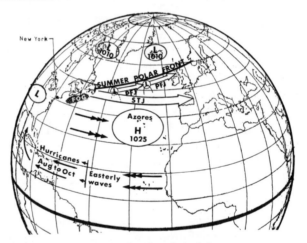

Figure 18.29. Atlantic North – Weather Details in July

southern borders of the area. Visibility around coasts can be reduced by advection fog. Although it can occur in winter, spring and early summer are the seasons of greater frequency over the sea. Surface winds are less strong but the general directions are as for the winter months. Freezing level is around 6000 ft in the north and 16000 ft in the south. Icing can still be a problem, but rain ice is unlikely.

Upper Winds

The upper winds are mainly westerly in accord with the thermal wind. Average speeds are 50 to 100 kn. Despite this there are occasions when other directions can apply due to upper level ridges and troughs. The strongest westerlies are found on the west side of the ocean. This is because of the greater mean temperature difference below high level over the North America continent and the nearby sea. The subtropical westerly jet with speeds of 100 to 200 kn is positioned from New York to Morocco in winter. In summer it moves north to a line from Montreal to Bordeaux. Jet streams in association with fronts are common and have a direction parallel to the fronts. Directions are usually northwesterly ahead of warm fronts and southwest behind cold fronts. Clear air turbulence is usual in association with all these jets.

The weather details are shown at Figures 18.28 and 18.29.

Atlantic South/South America

The region includes the ocean from 15°N to 50°S together with the South American continent to the east of the Andes.

Geographic Considerations

The high Andes mountain chain in the north along the west coast holds back Pacific polar front activity. In this same region, the climate is almost of the arctic type because of the elevation. Further south the mountains are lower and some polar maritime air can reach Argentina. However moisture content is very much reduced by the mountains.

In southern Brazil there are highlands which can produce orographic lifting with easterly airflows. There is tropical rain forest in the Amazon basin region. The Atlantic coast is affected by the warm Brazil current and further to the south by the cold Falklands current.

Pressure Systems

There is the Atlantic subtropical anticyclone at around 30°S with a central pressure of 1020 mb. Pressure is generally low in the centre of the continent although in winter the pressure could be classified as a weak high.

The equatorial trough/ITCZ in January is close to the equator, dipping south from northeast Brazil the line then moves north and west to Columbia. Thereafter northerly movement positions the trough in the extreme north of the continent around 5°N by July. There are polar front depressions forming around 40°S near the east coast. These travel north and can even enter the tropics. Easterly waves can occur but the associated CU CB is hidden somewhat by orographic lifting over the east coast.

Summer and Autumn (January-March/April)

For the north, including the Amazon basin and down to 15°S the ITCZ/equatorial trough can give CU CB, very heavy showers and thunderstorms. There are also frequent convective showers and thunderstorms extending into south Brazil. On shore winds cause orographic cloud along coasts from Rio de Janeiro northwards. Polar air from the south moving into Brazil can occur but invasions are somewhat weaker than in July. Further south in Argentina down to 40°S there is convective instability cloud and precipitation. Autumn rainfall from Atlantic polar front lows over the ocean is a maximum at this season. Further south over Patagonia, the air is warm and dry. Chile is affected by cold frontal weather from the Pacific.

The only fogs at this season are the advection type caused by the Falklands current. These can apply throughout the year. Surface winds in the north are easterly and include the northeast trades. There are southeast trades further south. Southerly winds can occur with Atlantic polar front activity.

Freezing levels are 16 000 ft in the north and centre and 10 000 ft in the south. There can be heavy icing in the extensive CB in the north.

Winter and Spring Conditions (July – Sept/Oct)

The ITCZ/equatorial trough is to the far north and therefore precipitation is relatively light south of the equator. The northeast coastal strip has orographic cloud and precipitation caused by easterly winds and this can extend inland. Atlantic polar front activity with cold polar air can move overland from the south and affect the area north of 40°S. The cold air can even penetrate into central tropical Brazil and cause marked temperature falls.

Some cold frontal type cloud and precipitation occurs. There is some convective cloud and precipitation, but further south into Patagonia there can be dry desert conditions and low temperatures.

Frontal and advection fogs can occur in Brazil. There are no advection fogs off the coast because of the warm Brazil current. Further south the cold Falklands current can cause advection fog off the coast from 40°S towards the southern Cape.

Surface winds are generally easterly with southeast trades in the north. There are southerly winds with Atlantic polar front activity. Further south where the elevation of the Andes is lower some westerly winds can occur.

Freezing levels are 14 000 ft in the north and 8000 ft in the south. Rime and clear icing can occur above these levels.

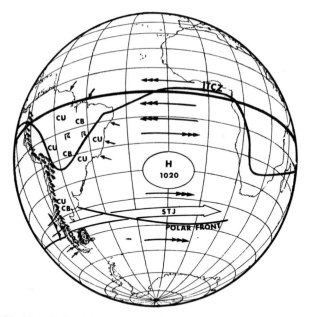

Figure 18.30. Atlantic South/South America – Weather Details in January

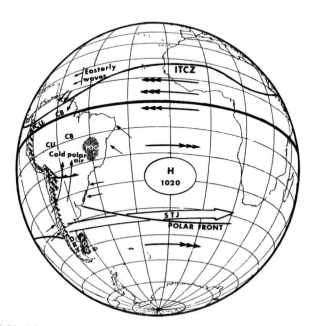

Figure 18.31. Atlantic South/South America – Weather Details in July

235

Upper Winds

The equatorial easterlies are mainly north of the equator in July and to the south in January. Speeds are light but increase across the ocean towards Africa in January. Either side there are westerly winds. Further south the westerlies become moderate to strong.

The subtropical jet lies across southern Argentina throughout the year, but is further south in January. The wind is westerly with speeds up to 100 kn plus. There are also some westerly jets in association with the Atlantic polar front. They travel north and south as the polar air moves. Figures 18.30 and 18.31 show details of the weather for January and July respectively.

Arabian Gulf Region

The region includes the Gulf plus the Arabian sea to the north west of the Indian subcontinent. The land areas include: Bahrain, Baluchistan, Iran, Iraq, Kuwait, Oman, Saudi Arabia and the United Arab Emirates.

Geographic Considerations

The main land areas are arid desert. To the northeast the Zagros mountains hold back much of the cold polar air from Siberia in winter. Day temperatures are warm due to the latitude and the type of surface. This is exemplified by the high summer temperatures in Baluchistan where there is a south-facing bare rock hinterland. This leads to the establishment of a low pressure area. In the east the region comes within the compass of the southwest monsoon. The mountains and valleys of northern Iraq help to control surface wind directions.

Pressure Systems

The Siberian high of winter can produce some cold front lows from the north. There is passage of thermal lows from the Mediterranean sea in winter. The low pressure over Baluchistan is formed in the summer. At the same season, the equatorial trough/ITCZ affects the east of the region.

Winter Conditions

With the exception of Oman and to the east, this is the wet season. There are the thermal lows from the Mediterranean crossing the region to Iran. These bring CU CB heavy showers and thunderstorms. In the north there are cold front lows. These are often dry, but where the cold air passes over the Caspian sea, CU, CB showers and thunderstorms can occur. This weather affects the northern valleys of Iraq and can continue south to the northern Gulf. Temperatures are warm by day, but can fall to below freezing level at night particularly in the north. The whole area can be effected by rising dust which can easily extend to thousands of feet. Early morning radiation fog can form inland from the coast, however this quickly disperses after sunrise. Surface winds are mainly northerly. Ahead of the thermal lows from the west surface winds are southerly becoming westerly and then northwesterly as they traverse the region.

Summer Conditions

At this season it can be very warm with temperatures above 50°C. In the west of the area it is a dry season with much lifted dust affecting visibility. In the east from Oman to Bombay, the Equatorial trough/ITCZ is the main weather feature, bringing the wet season. This can include CU CB heavy continuous showers and poor visibility in the precipitation. Tropical cyclones form in association with the ITCZ and the southwest monsoon from June to September. They bring typical tropical cyclone weather and form over the sea to the east of the Oman peninsula to Bombay. The Baluchistan low is dominant and results in surface winds being northerly in the west. This area is also effected by the Shamal. This is a dust laden northwest wind. It originates in Iraq due to strong convection lifting

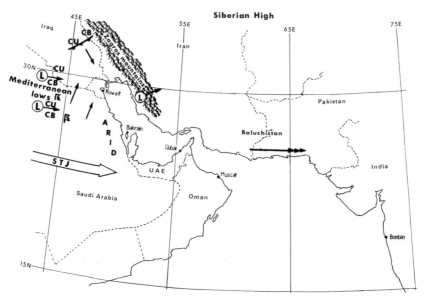

Figure 18.32. Arabian Gulf – Weather Details in January

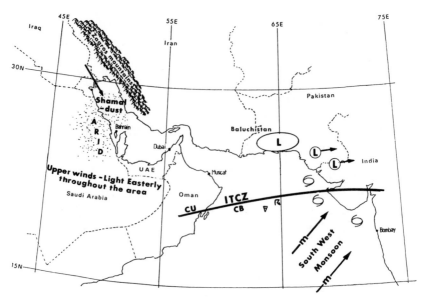

Figure 18.33. Arabian Gulf – Weather Details in July

clouds of persistent dust. It is assisted by the southerly pull of the Baluchistan low and can extend east to Karachi. It decreases at night. To the east the surface wind is the southwest monsoon.

Upper Winds
In winter the subtropical westerly jet covers the area above 30 000 ft with speeds in excess of 100 kn. Speeds reducing below this figure at the lower latitudes around 25°N. In summer the whole region has light easterly winds above 20 000 ft.

Freezing Levels and Icing
In January 9000 ft to 12 000 ft and in July 15 000 ft to 18 000 ft. Icing should not present problems except where descent is through large heap clouds in winter.

Diagrams of the winter and summer conditions are at Figures 18.32 and 18.33 respectively.

Bangladesh/Burma/Malaysia/Thailand
The area includes Bangladesh, Burma, Malaysia, Thailand, the Bay of Bengal, The Andaman Sea, Sumatra, Singapore and the Gulf of Siam. The area is shown at Figure 18.34.

238

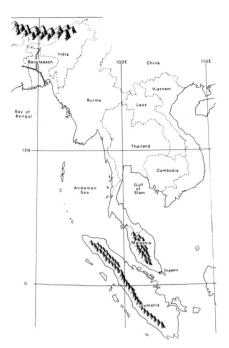

Figure 18.34. South East Asia, Bangladesh, Burma, Malaysia, Singapore, Thailand and the adjoining Sea Areas – Geography

Geographic Considerations

Bangladesh is protected to the north by the Himalayas. The river delta region in the south is low lying and very moist. The geography of Burma is somewhat similar again with a south coast river delta area. Malaysia has a southern central spine of mountains which form a barrier to prevailing winds. Sumatra with its high mountains provides a similar barrier. The straits of Malacca are important for the formation of night CB clouds.

Pressure Systems

The Asian high is dominant in winter. In summer this region becomes low pressure assisting the movement of the equatorial trough/ITCZ to the northeast. Tropical cyclones effect the Bay of Bengal and the Gulf of Siam.

Winter Conditions

In the north, the Northeast monsoon from Asia provides cold clear dry weather. Bangladesh and Burma are largely protected from this cold air, but occasional thunderstorms can develop due to convection. Further south the northeast winds pass over the eastern portion of the south China sea and the Gulf of Siam becoming warmed and picking up moisture. Some CU and CB can occur over Thailand. Over Malaysia these onshore winds can cause lifting over the coast and the central mountains resulting in large scale CU CB thunderstorms and heavy showers along the east coast and further inland. The southern part of Sumatra can be similarly affected. The Bay of Bengal region has little activity until the northeast monsoon is lifted by the east coast of India. Early morning mist or fog occurs in the delta regions of Bangladesh and Burma.

Summer Conditions
The southwest monsoon is the dominant factor with the ITCZ. This is over Sumatra and Singapore in March moving north to be in the Bangladesh region in May/June. The ITCZ is over the same country again in October moving south to be in the Singapore/ Sumatra area in November. The southwest monsoon with the ITCZ brings CU CB heavy showers and thunderstorms. This weather is particularly severe along the western coasts due to orographic lifting. The ITCZ does still apply in the Bay of Bengal, the Gulf of Siam and Thailand with similar weather. The west coast of Malaya is sheltered from the southwest monsoon to some degree of Sumatra. In common with all the land areas, there is much convection cloud at this season. This results in almost daily thunderstorms in all the countries.

The tropical cyclones in the Bay of Bengal are called Cyclones and occur from early May to September. They provide very heavy rainfall with thunderstorms and masses of CB over Bangladesh. They can also cause tidal waves near the coast. The tropical cyclones over the Gulf of Siam can occur at any time from June to December and are called Typhoons. Occasionally they can move over the east coastal regions of Malaya.

There are violent thundery showers which form at night in the Straits of Malacca between Malaya and Sumatra. They occur due to land breezes and katabatic effect from the mountains draining relatively cold air over the warmer sea. The extensive thunderstorms and bright lightning which results are referred to as 'Sumatras'.

Upper Winds
In winter in the north there are strong westerlies with the subtropical jet nearby. Further south the westerly speeds reduce and the winds become easterly from 10°N to Singapore.

In summer all the winds are easterly above 20 000 ft. Speeds are around 40 kn and there is some evidence of winds reaching jet stream speeds.

Freezing Level and Icing

The average freezing levels throughout the year are between 13 000 ft and 17 000 ft. Icing is more of a problem in summer during the descent through heap clouds where clear icing can occur. Weather details are shown diagrammatically at Figures 18.35 and 18.36.

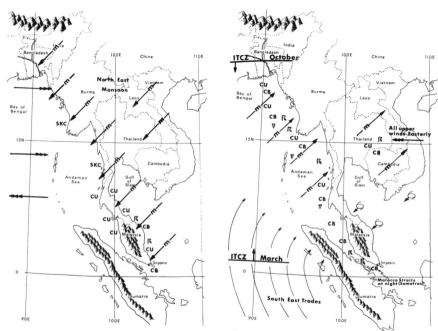

Figure 18.35. South East Asia –
Weather Details in January

Figure 18.36. South East Asia –
Weather Details in July

Northern Europe and the Mediterranean

The region extends from Scandinavia and the British Isles in the north to Spain in the south. From France in the west to Poland, European Russia and Rumania in the east. The Mediterranean includes the sea and the adjacent lands.

Geographic Considerations

Europe has a southern mountainous region forming a barrier with the Mediterranean. In the north there are the mountains of Scandinavia. Between these two mountainous regions there is the central plain of Europe with no barrier to Atlantic winds and weather, nor to winter winds from the east.

The Mediterranean is a warm sea in winter with relatively low pressure and therefore air will move into the region at this season from nearby lands. The mountains to the north will provide only a partial barrier. Similarly the mountains of Spain will prevent much Atlantic air from entering the sea region. In summer the cold temperature of the air over the sea will provide relatively high pressure and there will be a general air movement towards the adjacent lands. The Black Sea together with the Mediterranean can be the breeding ground for thermal lows.

Pressure Systems
WINTER

Polar front depressions affect the whole region from the Atlantic, with the majority crossing north Scandinavia and the British Isles. A number also enter the central European plain. The frequency of depressions decreases with reduction in latitude so that only a few enter the Mediterranean via the straits of Gibraltar. Other depressions include Polar Air depressions, secondaries and warm front lows from the south. In the Mediterranean area there are Mediterranean front lows, thermal lows and orographic depressions. Anticyclones include the Siberian high which provides cold polar continental air to the whole region but more particularly to eastern Europe. There is also the Azores anticyclone which provides tropical maritime air. Temporary highs often follow behind the cold fronts of depressions.

SUMMER

The number of polar front depressions reduces and they do not enter the Mediterranean at this season. Thermal lows form inland over the whole of Europe. The Azores high becomes a dominant feature and extensions cover the Mediterranean and can also provide high pressure over western Europe.

Winter Conditions
NORTHERN EUROPE

Extensive cloud sheets, low cloud base and continuous type rain and snow are caused by the polar front lows. These will be more active in the west. Secondaries can form as trailing cold fronts push up against the Alps. These can move northeast into Poland and Russia bringing active weather. Warm air from the Danube basin area can move north causing ST and drizzle with a very low base particularly over Poland and Germany. In the northwest Polar Air depressions can bring CU CB and thunderstorms with heavy showers.

Frontal thunderstorms can occur with any cold front activity. Along the coastal regions of the North Sea ST and SC can form by Siberian air reacting with the warmer sea. Along the east coast of the UK this can result in CU and heavy snow showers. Thermal lows from the Black Sea area can cause large CU and heavy snowfalls over Czechoslovakia, Hungary and Rumania. The eastern countries experience very low temperatures due to extensions from the Siberian high. Poor visibility in 4 to 10 day spells due to radiation fog is widespread when pressure is high at this season and in the autumn. Visibility can also be reduced by smoke. Longitudinally from west to east the number of depressions decreases; precipitation decreases; temperatures reduce and prevailing surface winds change from westerly to easterly. Precipitation in the Scandinavia region is predominately snow.

MEDITERRANEAN

This is the wet season with CU CB type cloud and precipitation from Mediterranean front depressions, thermal lows and orographic lows. Layer type clouds and more continuous rain is associated with the few polar front lows in the west. The thermal lows develop mostly in the central and eastern Mediterranean and then move east. Orographic lows south of the Alps develop in the northern Adriatic sea and in the Gulf of Genoa. The latter depressions can move south along the west coast of Italy causing poor flying weather. Orographic lows form south of the Atlas Mountains bringing showery type conditions to Algeria. The orographic lows to the south of Turkey are known as Cyprus lows. These can cause instability weather, strong northerly winds and often move east to the Lebanon. In this region thunderstorms can occur at the rate of four a month. The Khamsin in the east and the Sirocco in the west are dust laden southerly winds forming ahead of depressions moving along the sea from west to east. In both cases the dust can be taken to many thousands of feet and cause reduction in visibility over countries to the north. In the case of the Sirocco, additionally, it can cause low ST and drizzle for airfields along the south coast of France. Other local winds include the Mistral of southern France and the Bora in the northern Adriatic. These can bring CU and heavy snow showers into the coastal regions of France and Yugoslavia/northeast Italy respectively. Cloud precipitation and fog are much less than in Europe to the north. However, radiation fog can be a persistent problem in north Italy in the Milan region.

Summer Conditions
NORTHERN EUROPE
The number of polar front lows entering the region is much reduced. Nonetheless they can still provide much low cloud and precipitation mostly in the west. Widespread thermal lows develop causing CU CB and thunderstorms. This is predominately the thunderstorm season. They also occur in southern Germany due to lifting of moist air from the south over the Alps. Mountain waves can also form due to the movement of southerly winds over these mountains. Extensions from the Azores anticyclone can give periods of clear warm weather in the west. Visibility can be reduced by dust from North Africa with southerly winds. In the east continental heating gives high temperatures and convective cloud and showers. The Baltic sea is a particular fog area in spring.

MEDITERRANEAN
High pressure extensions from the Azores anticyclone predominates, giving warm clear weather with a little fair weather CU. Exceptions to this concern orographic lifting over the mountains of Italy, Algeria, Greece, Yugoslavia and Turkey. This can cause occasional CU CB and thunderstorms with heavy showers. Surface winds can be much affected by sea breezes. In the west there is the Levanter wind blowing in the region of Gibraltar. This can cause low cloud over the rock, fog and mountain wave conditions. In the eastern land areas the Simoon hot dry wind forms due to convection. It has whirlwind characteristics and can lift dust to reduce visibility. In the central sea area there are persistent dry summer winds from the north, called Etesians. They can sometimes develop CU to the south and reach the north African coast.

Upper Winds
In winter the winds are westerly with westerly jets in association with polar front lows. In the eastern Mediterranean there is the westerly subtropical jet with speeds of 100 to 200 kn at 40000 ft. In summer the subtropical jet should be in the general latitude of the Alps but the mountain interference reduces speeds to the 30 to 40 kn level from the west. This is the general speed and direction throughout the area except for some jets in association with polar front lows in the northern Europe area.

Freezing Levels and Icing

For central France freezing levels are 4000 ft in January increasing to 12000 ft in July. To the east the levels can be at the surface in winter. Further north they can be on the surface too in Scandinavia in January, increasing to 8000 ft in July. In the northern Europe area icing on descent and on the approach can be a problem in winter with the masses of frontal cloud. All icing types can occur and rain ice can form over eastern France, Germany and Poland. In summer icing (other than carburettor) is an occasional en route problem only.

In the Mediterranean winter freezing levels vary between 3000 ft and 4000 ft in the north, to 9000 ft over North Africa. Icing, clear and freezing rain types occur over north Italy where freezing levels can occasionally be on the surface. Clear ice is the main problem

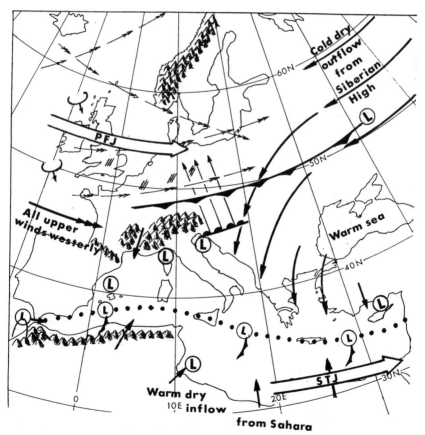

Figure 18.37. European Weather Details in January

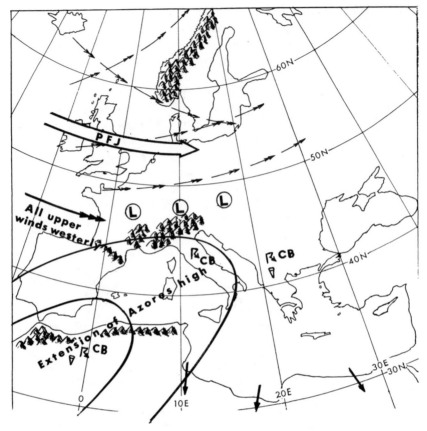

Figure 18.38. European Weather Details in July

elsewhere; this is mainly an en route problem. However in thunderstorm areas the icing can affect descent and approach. In summer freezing levels vary from 13 000 ft in the north to 15 000 ft over north Africa and icing is not a problem. The weather is detailed by diagrams at Figures 18.37 and 18.38.

India/Pakistan

Geographic Considerations

The subcontinent is a large scale peninsula with ample moisture from the surrounding seas. The land is sheltered to a degree in the north from the cold polar air masses, by the Himalayas. There are the Ghat mountains inland from the coastal areas in the southern half of the region. Between these two north and south mountain regions the land is largely flat.

Pressure Systems

The two dominating pressure systems are the Siberian high of winter and the equatorial trough/ITCZ of summer. The latter is assisted in its movements north by the low pressure in central Asia. There are a few eastward moving depressions in the north. Tropical cyclones over the Arabian Sea and the Bay of Bengal can touch on coastal regions.

Winter Conditions

The cold dry North East monsoon can enter the north of the area along minor valleys giving bright clear weather. Small depressions can enter the region from the west giving brief interludes of cloud and rain. This can become heavy from the low lying plains to the east of Delhi through to Bangladesh. Thunderstorms can occur in association with the occasional cold fronts. Elsewhere in the north weather is generally good. However, visibility can be reduced by dust in the west and early morning fog can form near northern coastal areas.

South of 20°N the North East monsoon picks up moisture over the Bay of Bengal and lifting over the east coast causes large CU and CB with heavy showers and thunderstorms. Further inland the CU is not so extensive and showers are relatively light. Visibility is generally good except in precipitation.

Summer Conditions

South of 20°N the south west monsoon produces CU CB and much thick layer cloud along the western coast. There is heavy rainfall but further inland from the Western Ghats, the cloud and rain reduces. Whilst the east is less effected by the monsoon there can still be much rainfall particularly around September/October. There are convective thunderstorms giving heavy rain anywhere in the south. Thunderstorms occur on some 6 to 10 days a month from June to October. Tropical cyclones can occur over the sea area to the west of Bombay and near the east coast in the Bay of Bengal. There are some 10 of these a year bringing heavy thunderstorms to nearby coastal areas. They tend to form at the onset and end of the monsoon season.

North of 20°N Pakistan has its cloudy and wet season. In the south near Karachi the cloud is mainly Stratiform with light to moderate rain. Further north the cloud tends to break up and there can be duststorms. Further north still in the Lahore Peshawar region lifting of the south west monsoon causes heavy CU CB and thunderstorms with heavy rain which can be torrential. Further east into India dust can occur but is less of a problem. This is because of the frequent CU CB together with SC in association with the monsoon. Convection thunderstorms also occur. In the east there can be some 10 thunderstorm occasions a month. In the Ganges/Calcutta area thunderstorms can approach from the north-west with 8/8 CU CB, very heavy showers and varying wind directions. These are called 'Northwesters'. To the north of the region in extreme northeast India, the effect of the monsoon, together with convective and orographic lifting against the Himalayan slopes causes extensive CU and CB. This heavy shower activity results in this region around Shillong having one of the highest annual rainfalls in the world.

Upper Winds
In January the subtropical jet lies across the north of the sub-continent, speeds can be in excess of 150 kn at 40 000 ft. Winds are

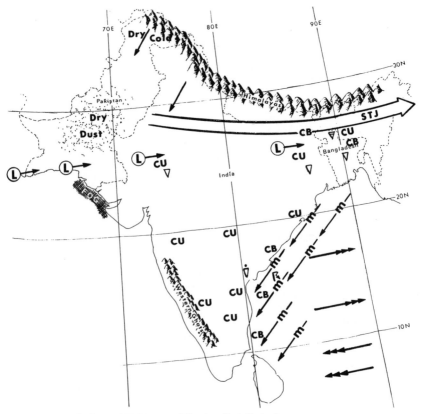

Figure 18.39. India and Pakistan – Weather Details in January

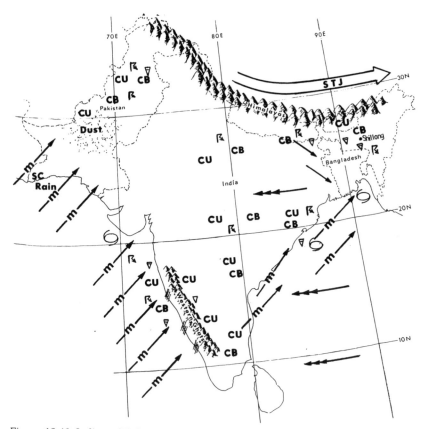

Figure 18.40. India and Pakistan – Weather Details in July

generally westerly down to the southern tip of India where they can become light westerly or easterly.

In July the subtropical jet has moved to the north of the Himalayas and the winds are easterly throughout with speeds averaging 20 to 30 kn.

Freezing Levels

In the north in January 12 000 ft and in July 18 000 ft. South of 20°N the level averages 15 000 ft throughout the year. Icing is no real problem except for en route flying with instability clouds. Figures 18.39 and 18.40 give diagrams of the weather in January and July respectively.

North Polar Area

The area includes land and sea within the Artic Circle, i.e. north of

249

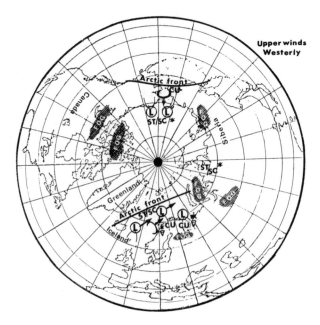

Figure 18.41. The North Polar Area – Weather Details in January

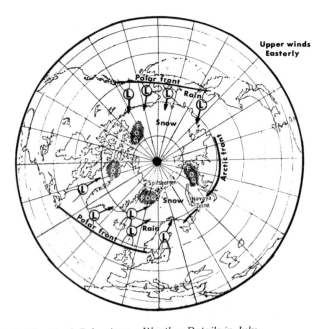

Figure 18.42. The North Polar Area – Weather Details in July

66½°N. This includes Iceland, Spitzbergen, northern Scandinavia, Novaya Zemla, north Siberia, the Canadian north, Greenland and the Arctic seas. The map at Figure 18.41 shows the area.

Geographic Considerations
North of 75°N the area is ice covered throughout the year. This includes pack ice in the seas. Further south pack ice and frozen conditions apply only in the winter months. The winter is a period of total darkness for some five to six months of the year. The summer with continuous daylight is short averaging two to three months. This provides the only time when temperatures are above 0°C in the south. The low temperatures prevent cloud of any depth and CB and thunderstorms cannot occur.

The 'Northern Lights' — Aurora Borealis — are common and particularly visible in the winter months. Serious radio interference affecting communications and navigation aids is associated with this activity.

Pressure Systems
The area is dominated by the polar anticyclone. In winter some arctic front and polar front depressions invade the south of the region. In summer these depressions become more numerous and travel further north into the region.

Winter Conditions
A few polar front lows enter the Arctic Ocean via the seas to the south of Spitzbergen. They move east and tend to fill over Novaya Zemla. Occasionally vigorous Polar Air depressions can occur over the sea areas adjacent to the lands of north Norway, the Barents Sea and the Alaska/Bering Strait. They can produce gales and heavy snow storms. Cloud otherwise is mainly layer type with a low base. This gives continuous light snow type precipitation. Similar conditions apply with a few lows from the arctic front in the area between northern Siberia and Alaska. Apart from the above there can be cloudless skies.

Visibility can be reduced by blowing snow and by fog. Inland radiation fogs occur in all the land areas in both winter and autumn. With saturation occuring with only low levels of absolute humidity, even the water vapour from engine exhausts can cause fog to form.

Summer Conditions
At this season the polar front moves north and the number of

depressions moving into the areas increases. The short summer months are thus the cloudiest of the year. Cloud bases are higher than winter but still low except in the south. Precipitation is sleet and rain with snow further north.

Advection fogs and arctic smoke are frequent over the sea in the south and over the pack ice further north.

Surface winds are mainly easterly over Siberia and Canada. Over the seas of the north Atlantic and north Pacific winds are mainly west or southwest. At all seasons wind strengths are strong over the sea and pack ice.

'White Out'

These conditions refer to particular difficulty in assessing the position of the horizon for flying. Where there is merging of low cloud with ice fog at the surface or blowing snow, a normal visual horizon does not exist. This can cause problems on the descent and during the landing approach.

Upper Winds

There are strong westerlies in winter. In spring these decrease becoming generaly easterly in summer.

Freezing Level

Winter freezing levels are on the surface. In summer 5000 ft in the south rapidly becoming on the surface further north. Only rime and carburettor icing should be expected.

Weather conditions for January and July respectively are shown at Figures 18.41 and 18.42.

North Pacific and the Rim

The area includes the north Pacific ocean together with the Rim countries of Singapore, Vietnam, The Phillipines, China, Korea and Japan.

Geographic Considerations

Important sea currents include the warm Kuroshio in the southwest and the cold Oyashio current further north. To the east there is the cold California current. The Rim countries are positioned on the fringe of Asia and the climate is therefore controlled by continental and maritime air masses.

Pressure Systems

In January the polar front lies across the ocean from the north of the Phillipines to 45°N to 50°N close to the American west coast. It then moves north to be in the 50°N to 60°N latitude band in July. Polar front depressions form in the west and move eastwards to produce a statistical low centre in the Aleutian Islands region in winter. In summer polar front activity is much reduced. The Pacific subtropical high with a central pressure averaging 1025 mb, is positioned between 30°N and 40°N from January to July. It is located somewhat east of the centre of the ocean. The Siberian high of winter together with the Asiatic low of summer influence the Rim. Typhoons begin to form in the central southern ocean region and then move west and northwest. They are fully developed in the sea areas from the Phillipines to Japan. The main season is summer and autumn. The ITCZ/Equatorial trough is in the area in summer.

Winter Conditions

THE OCEAN AREA

In the extreme south there is equatorial low pressure and 'doldrum' conditions with calm or light winds. These become easterlies further east. The subtropical high produces northeast trades. At the higher latitude side the high forms westerly surface winds and further north still there are polar front lows. These form in the west with the reaction with polar air, travelling and developing further east. The usual widespread cloud and precipitation occurs in association with the warm and cold fronts. General movement is towards the Aleutians. There are migratory ridges of high between the lows which can develop into temporary anticyclones. There is much SC present over the seas and convective CU CB over the islands at all season. Some Polar Air depressions form in the polar maritime air to the north bringing CU CB and shower activity.

RIM COUNTRIES

The Siberian high produces the northeast monsoon in the south. It provides cold northerly winds over China and northwesterlies over the Yellow sea and the Sea of Japan to Korea and Japan. In the south convection over Singapore together with orographic lifting of the now moist laden northeast monsoon over eastern Malaya/Vietnam produces CU CB thunderstorms and heavy showers. The west of Vietnam/Laos is relatively dry apart from convection effects. South China inland is relatively dry. Sheltering by the high mountains to the west results in warmer temperatures than at the coast both here and in central China. Elsewhere the weather is cold and dry apart from a few lows in the Yangtze river valley where fog can also form affecting the Shanghai region. In the north cold and dry. Dust from the interior can reduce visibility. Along the coasts from Vietnam to Shanghai Crachin conditions can occur. These produce low ST, fog drizzle and gloomy weather. It is caused by reaction of the warm air from the sea with cold coastal temperatures.

The northwest outflow from Siberia over the Yellow sea is warmed and picks up moisture to give large CU and snow showers over Korea. A similar situation applies with the airflow over the sea to Japan. The warmed air is lifted over the west coast and the mountains giving large CU and heavy snow showers. On the east coast temperatures are warmer because of Fohn heating of the northwest flow over the mountains. There is also warming from the Kuroshio sea current. In the north of Japan temperatures are lower and the cold Oyashio current can cause fog. In the Tokyo area and near other large cities visibility can be reduced to fog limits by industrial smoke. Polar front conditions can apply near the east coast. The weather can be a mixture of CU and ST with drizzle.

Figure 18.43. North Pacific/Rim – Weather Details in January

Summer Conditions
THE OCEAN AREA

In the extreme south the ITCZ is now just north of the equator in the ocean centre. It gives widespread CU and some CB. The southwest monsoon hardly affects the central region and the surface winds are still largely southeasterly. Further north there are northerlies on the east side of the subtropical high and southerlies to the west. Here the southwest monsoon does apply and although weather can be generally fair some CU cloud is likely. Typhoons breed in the central sea area and can traverse the Caroline islands before moving to the west. Island communities such as Guam have their heaviest rainfall at this season. Further north the polar front is relatively inactive. The number of depressions is small and they tend to be shallow.

RIM COUNTRIES
In summer the southwest monsoon with the ITCZ is dominant. ITCZ weather and convective CU CB and thunderstorms occur throughout the countries. Convection effects and rainfall are much heavier in the south. The ITCZ is in the Singapore region in March, over central China in May and South Korea/Japan in July. It brings CU CB and thunderstorms together with some more general rain from NS. The rain over China is referred to as 'The Plum Rains'. Typhoons spread north affecting all the countries except Singapore. The season can extend in the south to December. In the north, Japan can expect one or two typhoons a month from June to November. Coastal fog can be expected along the China coast. Further north extensive sea fogs formed by reaction with the Oyashio current are widespread.

Upper Winds and Freezing Levels
WINTER
Over the whole area the upper winds are light easterly up to 10°N with speeds around 10 kn. Further north the winds are westerly with the subtropical jet around 25°N to 40°N. Speeds can be up to 150 kn and in the Japan area speeds can reach 300 kn. There are also some westerly jets in association with polar front lows further north.

Freezing levels extend from 2000 ft in north Japan to 16000 ft to 18000 ft further south. Icing can be expected at low levels from central China northwards.

SUMMER
Over the whole area the easterly winds extend from the equator to 25°N with speeds in the range from 10 kn to 30 kn. Further north they become light westerly. Subtropical and polar front jets are little in evidence at this season.

Freezing levels are from 12000 ft in north Japan to 18000 ft in the south. Icing is not a problem except en route in CU CB.

The weather is detailed by diagrams for January and July respectively at Figures 18.43 and 18.44.

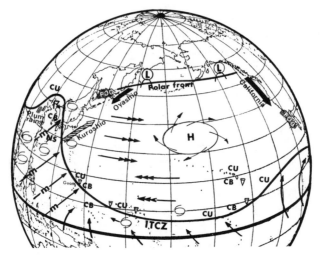

Figure 18.44. North Pacific/Rim – Weather Details in July

South Pacific and the Rim

The area includes the South Pacific ocean and the Rim countries. These include the East Indies, Australia and New Zealand.

Geographic Considerations

The East Indies are disposed around the equator and will therefore experience an equatorial climate. Mountainous regions in Sumatra, Java, Borneo, eastern Australia and the South island of New Zealand can cause orographic cloud and precipitation. The centre of Australia is desert which can cause widespread dust and poor visibility. The Peru current follows the subtropical anticylone wind directions giving a cold easterly flow near the equator and a westerly flow further south.

Pressure Systems

The subtropical anticyclone directs warm air to the south in the west of the ocean and to the north in the east. In January the ITCZ/ Equatorial Trough is around 20°S in the west swinging north to be near the equator in the centre and east of the ocean. In July the position is close to the equator except in the far west where it moves into the northern Pacific. Tropical cyclones occur from

December to March with a main season of January/February. They originate from the Timor Sea down to the north coast of Australia. Additionally from the Coral sea to the east coast as far south as the Brisbane area. The polar front with its depressions is around 45° to 50°S parallels of latitude most of the year. There is a major branch from 30°S 150°W to South America. The polar front lows originate as waves to the east of South Africa, hence further east to Australia and New Zealand, they become largely cold front or occluded troughs.

THE EASTERN OCEAN

In the east the ITCZ is around the 5°N line throughout the year leading to easterly winds around the equator. South of these are the trade winds in association with the subtropical high. These are southwesterly winds in the far east and can cause CU CB and heavy showers along the coasts of Chile, Peru and Ecuador. Further south the westerly winds apply and there is increasing cloudiness in association with polar front activity. There is also much low ST caused by advection over cold sea areas. In summer (February) there are advection fogs south of 45°S associated with quasi-stationary pressure systems and advection.

THE WESTERN OCEAN

In the west the surface winds south of the equatorial easterlies are southeast trade winds. These become westerly further south around the 40°S parallel. The winds here and to the east are called the 'Roaring Forties'. There is very little land at this latitude to interfere with the strong westerly wind flow. The subtropical high is often broken into a series of separate high pressure systems traversing the area from the west. The line is around 30°S in July and 40°S in January. Between the highs there are associated cloud and precipitation. Tropical cyclones occur over the south sea islands and particularly over the New Hebrides and New Caledonia. Whilst the main season is January/February they can sometimes occur at other times of the year.

THE EAST INDIES

These islands are affected by the ITCZ/Equatorial Trough from January to March moving north and again from November/December to January moving south. There is also extensive convection cloud. This is augmented by orographic cloud as the northwest monsoon of January and the southeast trade winds of July are lifted over coasts and the high mountain regions. The overall result is widespread CU CB thunderstorms and heavy showers. This is one of the most active thunderstorm areas in the world. The area is never free of instability cloud and showers. However this activity is much less in July when the ITCZ is in the northern hemisphere and weather is then relatively clear. The only other seasonal change is the northwest surface wind of January becoming the southeast of July.

AUSTRALIA
The centre of Australia is arid desert and the climate throughout the year accords with this. In the summer season (January) the north and northwest are subject to the ITCZ and Tropical Cyclones from the Timor sea. These are sometimes called Willy Willys in the northwest. Tropical Cyclones from the Coral sea reach the east coast and then usually in the Brisbane region move to the east or southeast. In all the coastal hinterland areas there are convective CU CB and showers. In the far south frontal troughs can produce frontal weather. South of Sydney, passage of a frontal trough can give ST and and drizzle followed by CU CB and thunderstorms with the cold front and strong gale force southerly winds. These are called "Southerly Busters" and can cause a significant temperature fall. In winter (July) the subtropical anticyclone as a series of separate highs cross the continent moving east. In between are weak lows and cols. The outflow from the highs brings dusty conditions to all the coastal areas. Along the southeast coast there is orographic cloud and precipitation caused by lifting of the southeast trades. This is a relatively dry season but convection cloud can still occur.

NEW ZEALAND
New Zealand is two islands separated by a narrow strait and located on a roughly north/south axis. In summer (January) travelling high pressure systems are in the 40°S area across the middle of the north island. The frontal troughs between the highs give cold front weather. Weather is warm but temperatures are cool in the mountain regions. This is a wet season in both islands. Tropical Cyclones leaving the Australia coast can curve to cross the North island giving the normal revolving storm weather. These are less frequent than the Australian cyclones. In winter (July) the subtropical separate high systems are further north around 30°S. The frontal troughs are also further north giving much precipitation with the fronts which are now north of the country. The North island is now cool at this season. The South island is cold and

radiation fogs can occur inland. Sea fogs can form off the east coast.

At all seasons the land is open to strong westerly winds. The lifting of these over the mountains which rise to 8000 ft causes large CU CB and heavy showers. The west coast particularly is nearly always windy. Precipitation is much heavier on the west coast and in the centre. The east coasts can be rain shadow areas and precipitation is relatively light. However overall the rain throughout the year can amount to 100 inches in places on the west coasts.

Upper Winds

There are light easterlies in the north with westerlies further south. The westerly subtropical jet is around the latitude Perth to Sydney in January with a speed of 70 to 80 kn. This jet extends across the North island of New Zealand and further east to 170°W. In July the westerly jet is across the centre of Australia with speeds of 100 kn. Again this jet extends to the 160°W to 170°W meridian with speeds of 80 to 90 kn. Further east the wind speed reduces.

Polar front jets with speeds up to 70 kn are in evidence but tend to be localised.

Freezing Levels and Icing

In the north freezing levels are 16 000 ft all year. Further south they vary from 6000 ft over southern Australia in July to 12 000 ft in January. Over New Zealand values are 8000 ft in July in the North island rising to 14 000 ft in January. In the South island the values are 4000 ft in July rising to 10 000 ft in January. Icing is only a problem in the south and the main icing type is clear ice in association with CU and CB.

The weather is detailed by diagrams for January and July respectively at figures 18.45 and 18.46.

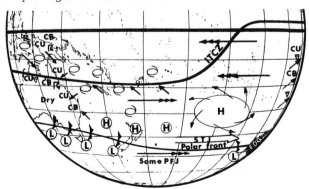

Figure 18.45. South Pacific/Rim – Weather Details in January

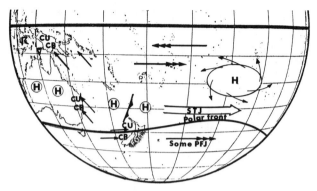

Figure 18.46. South Pacific/Rim – Weather Details in July

Russia and the Adjacent Republics

The area includes part of Europe in the west and virtually the whole of central Asia. The extent is from 24°E to the Pacific Ocean and from 40°N to the Arctic Ocean.

Geographic Considerations

The main land area of the centre is at an elevation of around 1000 ft. There is high ground to the east (Siberia) and northeast. To the west there is the narrow Ural mountain range extending north/south. This impedes the movement of Atlantic polar front activity from the west. The Caucasus mountains in the southwest are between the Caspian and Black seas. In the south the Himalayan range up to some 29 000 ft, provides a formidable barrier to any influx of warm air from the south. The barrier extends to the southeast over China. The central land mass is dry and very cold in winter. In summer the centre heats rapidly. However due to the mountain barriers any influx of moist air will be largely confined to the north and northwest; the moist air originating from the Arctic and northwest Pacific. Again the central region between 45°N and 55°N parallels will be almost arid and spread to the Gobi desert in the east.

The Caspian, Black and Aral seas can provide moisture and winter thermal depressions in the southwest. The geography of the area is displayed at Figure 18.47.

Pressure Systems

In winter, polar front lows from the Atlantic can move through European Russia. These are held back by the Urals and are then sometimes moved north and east. These together with arctic front

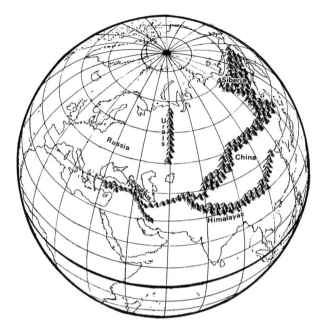

Figure 18.47. Russia and the Adjacent Republics – Geography

lows can affect central and northern Siberia. Otherwise the dominant pressure systems are the cold anticyclones with central pressure values around 1035 mb. In the south the high pressure is interrupted by thermal lows forming over the inland seas. These can passage over nearby land areas and then move north and east.

In summer the heating of the land causes a general low pressure regime. This leads to thermal lows but these tend to be shallow due to the lack of moisture in the central region. Over northern Siberia there are arctic front depressions which are a maximum at this season.

Winter Conditions

In the west including European Russia and the Baltic area, there is polar front activity and moist temperate air. With increasing easterly longitude the air becomes drier and temperatures reduce. It becomes bitterly cold in Siberia particularly around Verkoyansk. The Siberian high is dominant with strong inversion conditions. It is centred around 55°N 100°E. Turbulence cloud can form around the edge of the high. Typically SC with light snow around the northern edges with an easterly flow. Otherwise in the north there are some depressions associated with the arctic front. They can traverse the area on occasions, with the cold air in the rear causing severe blizzards. These are called the 'Buran' or the 'Purga'. Generally between the Urals and the far east, the central region is cold and dry with good flying weather.

South of 45°N, in the southwest, thermal lows from the Mediterranean, Black and Caspian Seas give CU CB, heavy showers and a few thunderstorms. These lows are enhanced by orographic lifting. They can move north and east to affect other areas. In the Caucasus region Fohn winds can be common, occurring on 100 days in a year in some places, with predominance in winter. Visibility can be much reduced by radiation fogs in the west, with autumn the main season. Over Siberia the inversions and light winds cause radiation ice fogs. Some sea fogs occur along the east coast. Winter conditions are shown at Figure 18.48.

Summer Conditions

Polar front activity in the European and northwest region is much reduced at this season. Central Asia becomes a dominantly low pressure area. Whilst thermal lifting occurs due to the high land temperatures, the low humidity results in CU only, with high bases by European standards. Precipitation is only light showers, however these do produce the rainfall for the Steppe region. In the north the arctic front unusually moves south at this season and thus arctic front depressions are more frequent than in winter. There can also be strong northeast winds. These are also called 'Buran' — the same name as the winter northwesterly blizzards.

In the southwest weather can be warm, clear and fine with light winds and sea breezes from the Black Sea. There can also be thunderstorms caused by convection and orographic lifting giving very heavy showers.

This is the main season for advection fogs along the east coast in the Kamchatka region and along the arctic coast. In this latter region the fogs can be very persistent. Summer conditions are displayed at Figure 18.49.

Upper Winds

In winter mean winds are relatively light apart from the jet streams in association with the polar front lows in the west. The winds average 270/30 kn in west Russia becoming northwesterly in the east and north with mean speeds of 30 to 40 kn. In July in the southwest there is some effect from the subtropical jet and mean winds become 270/50 to 60 kn. Elsewhere winds are lighter than in

Figure 18.48. Russia and the Adjacent Republics – Weather Details in January

Figure 18.49. Russia and the Adjacent Republics – Weather Details in July

winter, averaging 270/10 kn to 20 kn in the north and 270/20 kn in eastern Russia.

Freezing Levels and Icing

In winter the freezing level is virtually at the surface over the whole area. In the south some clear type icing can occur. All types are possible in the west with polar front clouds. Elsewhere the small cloud amounts and the very low temperatures restrict icing to the light rime variety.

In summer the level averages 12000 ft in the south, lowering to some 5000 ft in the north. Airframe icing is unlikely to be a hazard except in association with CU, CB in the southwest for en route flying. Carburettor icing can occur almost anywhere.

Chapter 19
Met. Services and Documentation

Introduction

The main meteorological offices provide reporting, forecast and warning services together with the necessary documentation. There are also the reporting responsibilities of aircraft captains. The basis for all the above is contained in publications issued by the International Civil Airways Organization (ICAO). These documents provide recommendations that are closely followed by most countries. There are nevertheless, small variations from the recommendations that national authorities find necessary. In the UK the responsible body is the Civil Aviation Authority. This issues Aeronautical Information Publications. The UK Air Pilot designated CAP 32 MET Section covers the services and documentation applicable to the UK.

The kind permission of the Civil Aviation Authority to publish the main extracts from the June 1990 edition of CAP 32 which follows this introduction, is gratefully acknowledged. The necessity to consult the current edition of CAP 32 and any subsequent NOTAMS is particularly registered here. Further international changes are likely at the triennial ICAO review.

The relevant UK AIP MET Tables are at the Appendix to this Chapter.

Applicable ICAO Documents

The Standards, Recommended Practices and, when applicable, the procedures contained in the following ICAO documents are applied:

Annex 3	–	Meteorological Service for International Air Navigation.
Doc 7754	–	Air Navigation Plan — EUM Region.
Doc 8755	–	Air Navigation Plan — NAT Region.
Doc 8896	–	Manual of Aeronautical Meteorological Practice.
Doc 8400	–	PANS — ICAO Abbreviations and Codes.
Doc 9328	–	Manual of Runway Visual Range Observing and Reporting Practices.

Differences from ICAO Regulatory Material

The unit millibar will continue to be used for the measuring and reporting of atmospheric pressure in the UK.

Meteorological satellite photographs or mosiacs and/or nephanalyses are not routinely displayed in most Flight Briefing Units.

Ground-based weather radar information is not routinely displayed in most Flight Briefing Units. Air Reports, including pictorial cross-sections in completed AIREP forms, are not routinely displayed in Flight Briefing Units.

Types of Service Provided

Pre-flight Briefing

The primary method of meteorological briefing for aircrew in the UK is by self-briefing, using facilities, information and documentation routinely available or displayed in aerodrome briefing areas; briefing for flights below 15 000 ft amsl is also available from the AIRMET telephone recording service, English is the language used for all UK documentation and verbal briefing. The primary method of briefing does not require prior notification.

Where this primary method is not available, or is inadequate for the intended flight, Special Forecasts may be provided.

When necessary the personal advice of a forecaster, or other meteorological information, can be obtained from the designated Forecast Office for the departure aerodrome. Forecaster advice or other information for safety related clarification/amplification will only be given from a Forecast Office on the understanding that full use has already been made of all meteorological briefing material available at the departure aerodrome or, where appropriate, by telephone recording. The Designated Forecast Office for North Atlantic flights departing from any UK aerodrome is Bracknell CFO.

Broadcast Text Meteorological Information

Aerodrome Meteorological Reports (METAR), Aerodrome Forecasts (TAF) and warnings of weather significant to flight safety (SIGMET) and Volcanic Activity Reports are broadcast by teleprinter throughout the UK and internationally in text form. This information is distributed within the UK through dedicated communication channels (OPMET 1, 2 and 3), by AFTN and by autotelex. Details of the OPMET networks and their contents are shown at MET 2-4 Table E.

Short-term Landing Forecasts valid for two hours (TREND), may be added to METARs.

Information on runway state is added to the METAR when weather conditions so require and continues until these conditions have ceased.

Special Aerodrome Meteorological Reports are issued when conditions change through limits specified at MET 3-9 Table K. Selected Special Reports (SPECI) are defined as Special Reports disseminated beyond the aerodrome of origin; civil aerodromes in the UK do not normally make Selected Special Reports. Aerodromes reporting only a SYNOP will not normally provide Special Reports to the Air Traffic Service Unit.

TAFs are normally provided only for those aerodromes where official meteorological observations are made. For other aerodromes, Local Area Forecasts can be made on request for international flights inbound to UK aerodromes. Amended TAFs or Local Area Forecasts are issued when forecast conditions change significantly, see MET 3-9 Table K.

The formats and codes used for METAR, SPECI, TREND and TAF are described at MET 3-2 Table 1. Area Forecasts for the AIRMET service are broadcast in text form by teleprinter. Area Forecasts can also be issued routinely by teleprinter for selected offshore areas of the UK FIR. Amended Area Forecasts are issued when forecast conditions change significantly, see MET 3-9 Table K.

AIRMET Service
Three routine Area Forecasts, in plain language, covering the UK and near Continent, with vertical coverage from the surface to 15 000 ft amsl, with winds and temperatures to 18 000 ft amsl, are provided in spoken form at dictation speed via the public telephone network and in text form via AFTN and telex.

The AIRMET telephone service is intended for use by pilots who do not have access to meteorological forecast charts or to the AIRMET Forecasts disseminated in text form by teleprinter.

Special Forecasts and Specialized Information
For departure from an aerodrome where the standard pre-flight meteorological briefing service is not available or is inadequate for the intended flight, a special Forecast may be issued on request to the appropriate Forecast Office for a specific period for a designated route, or area which includes the route. Special Forecasts can include Aerodrome Forecasts for the departure aerodrome and

the destination aerodrome plus a maximum of three alternates. Normally, this Forecast is only issued for the flight to the next transit aerodrome that provides the necessary meteorological service. A through Forecast may be provided by prior arrangement.

Forecast Offices normally require prior notification for Special Forecasts as follows:

i) For flights up to 500 nm, at least two hours before the time of collection;
ii) For flights of over 500 nm, at least four hours before the time of collection.

It is in the interest of all concerned that the maximum possible period of notice is given. The Forecast Office will give priority to emergencies, in-flight forecast and to forecast requirements which have been properly notified. Other requests could be delayed at busy periods and might not comprise full forecasts. A forecast collected a long time in advance of departure will be less specific and might be less accurate than one prepared nearer departure time.

Take-off Forecasts, containing information on expected conditions over the runway complex in respect of surface wind, temperature and pressure, can be made available from Forecast Offices. Prior notification is not normally required.

Meteorological information for specialized aviation use, as defined below, is not included in the AIRMET service or given as Special Forecasts but arrangements can be made for its provision on prior request:

i)   To enable glider, hang glider, microlight and balloon organisations to obtain low level wind, lee-wave, QNH, temperature and thermal activity forecasts;
ii) to provide meteorological information for special aviation events for which routine forecasts are not adequate;
iii) to provide helicopter operators in off-shore areas with forecast winds and temperatures at 1000 ft amsl, information on airframe icing, and sea state and temperature.

Appropriate forecasts for (i) and (ii) above will be made available up to twice in any 24 hour period. The initial request should be made at least two hours for (i) and to the authority for approval six weeks for (ii) and (iii), in advance of forecast(s) being required, specifying the nature of the aviation activity, the location(s) involved, meteorological information required and time periods. If appropriate an AFTN, telex or DOCFAX address should also be specified. Applicants will be advised of the time at which the information will be available and the means of collection.

In-flight Procedures

Information to aircraft in flight is usually supplied in accordance with area Meteorological Watch procedure, supplemented when necessary by an En-route Forecast service. Information is also available from the appropriate ATS unit at the commander's request, or from meteorological broadcasts. MWOs are responsible for the preparation and dissemination of SIGMETs to appropriate ACC/FIC within its own and agreed adjacent FIRs. Aircraft in flight should be warned by the ACC/FIC of the occurrence or expected occurrence of one or more of the following SIGMET phenomena for the route ahead for up to 500 nm or two hours' flying time:

i) At subsonic cruising levels (SIGMET);
    − active thunderstorms[1]
    − tropical cyclone
    − severe line squall (passage of cold front in which squalls at the surface are expected to reach 50 kn or more. Normally accompanied by one or more other SIGMET phenomena)
    − heavy hail
    − severe turbulence
    − severe icing
    − marked mountain wave (vertical air current exceeding 500 FPM)
    − widespread sand storm/dust storm
    − volcanic ash cloud
ii) At transonic and supersonic cruising levels[2] (SIGMET SST);
    − moderate or severe turbulence
    − cumulonimbus cloud
    − hail
    − volcanic ash cloud.

---

[1] This refers to an area of widespread cumulonimbus cloud, cumulonimbus along a line with little or no space between individual clouds, or to cumulonimbus embedded in cloud layers or concealed by haze. It does not refer to isolated or scattered cumulonimbus not embedded in cloud layers nor concealed by haze.
[2] FL 250 – FL 600 London to Scottish UIRs, FL 400 – FL 600 Shanwick OCA.

SIGMETs are not normally valid for more than four hours (except for volcanic ash cloud where the period may be up to 12 hours) and are re-issued if they are to remain valid after the original period expires. They can be cancelled or amended within the period of validity. Active thunderstorms, tropical cyclones and severe line squalls each imply moderate or severe turbulence, moderate or severe icing and hail. SIGMETs are numbered sequentially from 0001 UTC.

An in-flight En-route Forecast service is available in exceptional circumstances by prior arrangement between the operator and the meteorological Forecast Office serving the departure aerodrome. A meteorological office is designated to provide the aircraft in flight with the winds and temperatures for a specific route sector. Applications for this service should be made in advance, stating:

    i) The flight level(s) and the route sector required;
    ii) the period of validity necessary;
    iii) the approximate time and position in flight at which the request will be made;
    iv) the ATS unit with whom the aircraft is expected to be in contact.

Aircraft can obtain aerodrome weather information from any of the following:

    i) VOLMET broadcasts;
    ii) Automatic Terminal Information Service (ATIS);
    iii) by request to an ATS unit but whenever possible only if the information required is not available from a broadcast.

When an aircraft diverts, or proposes to divert, to an aerodrome along a route for which no forecast has been provided, the commander may request the relevant information from the ATS unit serving the aircraft at the time, and the necessary forecasts will be provided by the associated Forecast Office.

Marked Temperature Inversion

At certain aerodromes a Warning of Marked Temperature Inversion is issued whenever a temperature difference of 10°C or more exists between the surface and any point up to 1000 ft above the aerodrome. This warning is broadcast on departure and arrival ATIS at aerodromes so equipped, or in the absence of ATIS passed by radio to departing aircraft before take-off, and to arriving aircraft as part of the report of aerodrome meteorological conditions.

Aerodrome Warnings

Aerodrome Warnings are issued as appropriate when one or more of the following phenomena occurs or is expected to occur:

i) Gales (when the mean surface wind is expected to exceed 33 kn, or if gusts are expected to exceed 42 kn) or strong winds according to locally-agreed criteria.

ii) Squalls, hail or thunderstorms.

iii) Snow, including the expected time of beginning, duration and intensity of fall; the expected depth of accumulated snow, and the time of expected thaw. Amendments or cancellations are issued as necessary.

iv) Frost warnings are issued when any of the following conditions are expected:

a) A ground frost with air temperature not below freezing point;

b) the air temperature above the surface is below freezing point (air frost);

c) freezing precipitation;

d) hoar frost, rime or glaze deposited on parked aircraft.

v) Fog (normally when the visibility is expected to fall below 600 m).

Windshear Alerting Service — LONDON/Heathrow and BELFAST/Aldergrove Airports

Forecasters for LONDON/Heathrow and BELFAST/Aldergrove airports review the weather conditions at Heathrow and Aldergrove airports respectively on an hourly basis and monitor any aircraft reports of windshear experienced on the approach or climb out. Where a potential low level windshear condition exists an Alert is issued, based on one or more of the following criteria:

i) Mean surface wind speed at least 20 kn;

ii) The magnitude of the vector difference between the mean surface wind and the gradient wind (an estimate of the 2000 ft wind) at least 40 kn;

iii) Thunderstorm(s) or heavy shower(s) within approximately 5 nm of the airport.

Note: Alerts are also issued based on recent pilot reports of windshear on the approach or climb-out.

The Alert message is given in the arrival and departure ATIS broadcasts at Heathrow and by R/T to arriving and departing aircraft at Aldergrove in one of three formats:

  i) 'WINDSHEAR FORECAST' – when the meteorological conditions indicate that low level windshear on the approach or climb-out (below 2000 ft) might be encountered;

 ii) 'WINDSHEAR FORECAST AND REPORTED' – as above, supported by a report from at least one aircraft of windshear on the approach or climb-out within the last hour;

iii) 'WINDSHEAR REPORTED' – when an aircraft has reported windshear on the approach or climb-out within the last hour, but insufficient meteorological evidence exists for the issue of a forecast of windshear.

Pilot reports of windshear on approach or climb-out can greatly enhance the operational efficiency of this Service. In addition, they also serve in the continuous evaluation of the criteria upon which Alerts are forecast. Thus pilots who experience windshear on the approach or climb-out are requested to report the occurrence to ATC, as soon as it is operationally possible to do so, even if an Alert has been issued. Windshear reporting criteria are shown at MET 2-5 Table F. Pilots who experience windshear at any UK aerodrome are requested to report it in the same way.

Observing Systems and Operating Procedures

Surface wind is normally measured by a three cup anemometer and vane system referenced to a height of 10 metres above the runway(s). Surface wind reported by an ATS unit for take-off and landing is usually an instantaneous wind measurement with direction referenced to Magnetic North. At those aerodromes where the wind measurements can be electronically processed, the wind reports for take-off and landing are averaged over the previous 2 minutes. Variations in the wind direction are given when the total variation is 60° or more and the mean speed is above 5 kn. In reports for take-off, surface winds of 5 kn or less include a range of wind directions whenever possible. Variations from the mean wind speed (gusts/lulls) during the previous 10 minutes are reported only if the variation has exceeded 10 kn; such variations are expressed as the maximum and minimum speeds attained. Surface wind measurements contained in METAR and SPECI reports are averaged over the previous 10 minutes and are referenced to True North. If there has been a change of 10 kn or more in wind speed and/or a 30° or more change in direction during the 10 minute period, and this has been maintained for a period of at least 3 minutes immediately prior to the time of observation, the new speed and/or direction is reported. METAR and SPECI reports do not give variations in wind direction or minimum wind speeds; maximum wind speed is only given if it exceeds mean speed by 10 kn or more. At aerodromes with two or more anemometer/vane systems, METAR (and SPECI) surface wind reports are always obtained from one designated 'aerodrome' system irrespective of the system currently in use by the ATS unit for take off and landing reports.

Information on cloud height is obtained by the use of ceilometers (nodding beam or laser), cloud searchlights and alidades, balloons, pilot reports and observer estimation. At some aerodromes an additional, remote, cloud ceilometer is installed.

The cloud heights reported from a remote ceilometer are:

i) The most frequently occurring value during the past 10 minutes if this value is 1000 ft or less.

ii) If cloud is being indicated at heights 100 ft or more below that indicated at i) above then the height of the lowest cloud is also reported, prefaced by 'OCNL'.

iii) If the most frequently occurring value is above 1000 ft but the lowest value is 1000 ft or below then only the lowest is reported; for example: most frequent 1200 ft, lowest 900 ft 'CBR 24 OCNL 900 FEET' (24 refers to the nearest runway).

Temperature is reported in whole degrees from liquid-in-glass or electrical resistance thermometers located in a ventilated screen.

Horizontal surface visibility is assessed by human observer. Visibility is reported in increments of 100 metres up to 5000 metres and in units of kilometres above 5000 metres. In METARS, SPECI and TAFs, the maximum value is '10 km or more'. When the visibility varies in different directions the lowest visibility is reported. When the lowest visibility is less than 1500 metres and visibility in another direction is more than 5000 metres, the maximum visibility and the direction in which it occurs may be reported as supplementary information.

Pilots are reminded that surface visibility forecast in a TAF, TREND or Area Forecast might be subject to marked deterioration caused by smoke from the burning of agricultural residues in fields. This burning takes place during the Summer and Autumn without notification. Such deteriorations in surface visibility will be reported as they occur in Routine or Special Aerodrome Meteorological Reports, and forecasts might consequently be amended. It is not possible to forecast the onset or cessation of the smoke, or the precise amount of the visibility deterioration. Turbulence and breathing difficulty might also be encountered.

Runway Visual Range (RVR)

RVR assessment is made by either a Human Observer or an Instrumented RVR system (IRVR). Most IRVR systems have an upper limit of 1500 metres; the upper limit of the Human Observer system is normally less than this.

The UK standard RVR reporting incremental scale is 25 metres between 0 and 200 metres, 50 metres between 200 and 800 metres, and 100 metres above 800 metres. Some IRVR systems and most Human Observer systems are unable to report every incremental point in the scale.

The assessment and reporting of RVR begins whenever the horizontal visibility or the runway visual range is observed to be less than 1500 metres. At those aerodromes where IRVR is available, RVR is also reported when the observed value is at or below the maximum reportable value or when shallow fog is forecast or reported. RVR is passed to aircraft before take-off and during the approach to landing. Changes in the RVR are passed to aircraft throughout the approach. Additionally, information from pilot reports or ATC observation that the visibility on the runway is worse than that indicated by the RVR report, for example patches of thick fog, are passed.

At some aerodromes the RVR systems suppress mid-point and/or stop-end values when:

    i) They are equal to or higher than the touchdown zone value unless they are less than 400 metres,

or

    ii) they are 800 metres or more.

At other aerodromes the RVR systems suppress mid-point and/or stop-end values unless they are 550 metres or less.

At those aerodromes having multi-site IRVR the standard UK procedure is that the touchdown zone RVR is always given first, followed by any values for the mid-point RVR and/or stop-end RVR which have not been suppressed. With the above in mind, the co-operation of the pilots is sought in avoiding unnecessary radio requests for mid-point and/or stop-end values when they have not been given. When all three values are given they are passed as a series of numbers; for example, 'RVR 600, 500, 550' relates to touchdown zone, mid-point and stop-end respectively. When touchdown zone and only one other value is given, the latter is prefixed with its appropriate position, for example, 'RVR 700, stop-end 650'.

If a single transmissometer fails, and the remainder of the IRVR system is still serviceable, RVR readings are not suppressed for the remaining sites and these values are passed to pilots. For example, if the touchdown zone transmissometer is unserviceable, 'RVR: touchdown missing, mid-point 600, stop-end 400'. If two trans-missometers fail in a three-site IRVR system, the remaining value is passed and identified provided that it is not the stop-end value, in which event the system is considered unserviceable for that runway direction. In a two-site IRVR system, giving touchdown zone and stop-end values, if the touchdown zone transmissometer fails, the system is considered unserviceable for that runway direction. Exceptionally, if the Civil Aviation Authority determines in a particular case that the distance between the two trans-missometers is sufficiently small, the system may be considered serviceable for that runway direction.

When RVR information is not available, or when the RVR element of Aerodrome Operating Minima falls outside the range of reportable RVR, pilots are advised to use meteorological visibility in the manner specified in their operations manuals, or in the advice for non-public transport flights (recommended Aerodrome Operating Minima).

Information on specific types and locations of observation systems at particular aerodromes is available on request from the Meteorological Authority or the aerodrome operator.

Aircraft Meteorological Observations and Reports

Routine Aircraft Observations

Routine Aircraft Observations are not required in the London or Scottish FIR/UIR or the Shanwick FIR, but in the Shanwick OCA, aircraft are to conform with the requirements for meteorological observations.

Special Aircraft Observations

Special Aircraft Observations are required in any UK FIR/UIR/OCA whenever:

    i) Severe turbulence or severe icing is encountered;

or

    ii) moderate turbulence, hail or cumulonimbus clouds are encountered during transonic or supersonic flight;

or

    iii) other meteorological conditions are encountered which, in the opinion of the pilot in command, might affect the safety or markedly affect the efficiency of other aircraft operations, for example, other en-route weather phenomena specified for SIGMET messages, or adverse conditions during the climb-out or approach not previously forecast or reported to the pilot in command. Observations are required if volcanic ash cloud is observed or encountered, or if pre-eruption volcanic activity or a volcanic eruption is observed;

or

    iv) exceptionally, they are requested by the meteorological office providing meteorological service for the flight; in which event the observation should be specifically addressed to that meteorological office;

or

    v) exceptionally, there is an agreement to do so between the Meteorological Authority and the aircraft operator.

Turbulence, icing and windshear reporting criteria are given at MET 2-5 Table F.

Meteorological Units of Measurement

The following meteorological units of measurement are in use in the United Kingdom:

Speed	— Knots
Height and Altitude	— Feet and Flight Levels
Visibility 5000 metres and below	— Metres
Visibility Above 5000 metres	— Kilometres
RVR	— Metres
Temperature	— Degrees Celsius
Barometric Pressure	— Millibars
Distance (except visibility)	— Nautical Miles
Time	— 24 hour clock UTC

Additional Note

Details of forecast charts including symbology and abbreviations in use are shown at MET 2-2 and MET 2-3.

A list of meteorological abbreviations used in sigmets, special forecasts etc. is at MET 3-8.

Annexes to Chapter 19: UK AIP (28 June 90) MET 2-2, 2-3, 2-4, 2-5, 2-6, 3-2, 3-3, 3-4, 3-8, 3-9, 3-10.

TABLE D
METEOROLOGICAL CHARTS – SYMBOLOGY

1   SYMBOLS FOR SIGNIFICANT WEATHER, TROPOPAUSE AND PRESSURE SYSTEMS

Symbol	Meaning	Symbol	Meaning
⟂	Thunderstorm	,	Drizzle
ϩ	Tropical cyclone	⦀ ⦀	Rain
⌐ᴧᴧ	Severe line squall	✳	Snow
▲	Hail	▽	Shower
⌒	Moderate turbulence	S	Severe sand or dust haze
⌇	Severe turbulence	⌇	Widespread sandstorm or duststorm
CAT	Clear air turbulence	∞	Widespread haze
◔	Marked mountain waves	=	Widespread mist
⋃	Light aircraft icing	≡	Widespread fog
⋓	Moderate aircraft icing	≢	Freezing fog
⋓	Severe aircraft icing	⌁	Widespread smoke
⌒⌣	Freezing precipitation		

NOTES: Altitudes between which phenomena are expected are indicated by flight levels, top over base. 'XXX' means the phenomenon is expected to continue above and/or below the vertical coverage of the chart. Phenomena of relatively lesser significance, for example light aircraft icing or drizzle, are not usually shown on charts even when the phenomenon is expected. The thunderstorm symbol implies hail, moderate or severe icing and/or turbulence.

440	Tropopause altitude (FL440)	～～ Boundary of area of significant weather.

 'High' centre and tropopause altitude (FL400)

— — — Boundary of area of clear air turbulence. The CAT area may be marked by a numeral inside a square and a legend describing the numbered CAT area may be entered in a margin.

 'Low' centre and tropopause altitude (FL340)

– – – – – Altitude of the 0°C isotherm in flight levels.

2   FRONTS AND CONVERGENCE ZONES

▲▲ Cold front at the surface		⌒⌒ Occluded front above the surface	
△△ Cold front above the surface		●▼● Quasi-stationary front at the surface	
●● Warm front at the surface		⌒▽ Quasi-stationary front above the surface	
⌒⌒ Warm front above the surface		→→ Convergence line	
●▲● Occluded front at the surface		⫼⫼ Inter-tropical convergence zone	

NOTE: An arrow with associated figures indicates the direction and the speed of the movement of the front (knots).

3   CLOUD ABBREVIATIONS

3.1   Type

CI = Cirrus   NS = Nimbostratus   CB = Cumulonimbus (CAUTION: CB
CC= Cirrocumulus   SC = Stratocumulus   implies hail, moderate or severe icing
CS = Cirrostratus   ST = Stratus   and/or turbulence.)
AC= Altocumulus   CU= Cumulus   LYR = Layer or layered (instead of the
AS = Altostratus   cloud type.)

3.2   Amount

Clouds except CB   CB only
SKC = clear (0 okta)   ISOL   = individual CB's (isolated)
SCT = scattered (1/8 to 4/8)   OCNL = well separated CB's (occasional)
BKN = broken (5/8 to 7/8)   FRQ   = CB's with little or no separation (frequent)
OVC = overcast (8/8)   EMBD = thunderstorm clouds contained in layers of
                                         other clouds (embedded)

3.3   Altitude

Altitudes are indicated in flight levels, top over base.

4   WEATHER ABBREVIATIONS

DZ   = drizzle   COT   = at the coast   SH = showers
LOC = locally   WDSPR = widespread   FZ = freezing
TS   = thunderstorm

5   WIND SYMBOLS

5.1   Wind/Temperature Chart

Wind 300°(T) 30 kn, temperature −36°C at arrow head

Wind 090°(T) 60 kn, temperature −56°C at arrow head

Wind 240°(T) 15 kn, temperature +2°C at arrow head

5.2   Significant Weather/ Tropopause/Maximum Wind Chart

Maximum wind 270°(T), 110 kn at FL380

6   UK LOW LEVEL WEATHER CHART

6.1   The chart covers flight conditions from the surface to 15 000 ft and comprises three sections: a forecast chart, a tabular forecast, and relevant warnings and/ or remarks. The forecast chart and tabular sections relate to the fixed time shown in the chart heading.

6.2   Forecast chart

6.2.1   The surface position of pressure centres is shown by 'X' for a low centre and 'O' for a high centre, together with the letter L or H respectively, and the central pressure in millibars. The direction and speed of movement (in knots) of centres and fronts is given. Movement of less than 5 knots is shown as 'SLOW'.

6.2.2   Weather areas are enclosed by continuous scalloped lines. Each area is allotted a distinguishing letter that refers to an entry in the tabular section.

6.3   **Tabular section**

6.3.1   The top line for each area gives the main expected conditions under the headings VIS (visibility), WEATHER, CLOUD, TURBULENCE, ICING and 0°C. If significant differences from the main conditions are likely within that area at the Fixed Time, these are given on subsequent lines after an explanatory remark in the VARIANT column.

6.3.2   Surface visibility is expressed in metres using four figures up to 5000 M, and in whole kilometres using one or two figures for 6 km or more.

6.3.3   Weather if any is given in plain language or by using a combination of abbreviations.

6.3.4   Cloud amount and type, with altitude of base and top is given. All altitudes are expressed in hundreds of feet AMSL. 'XXX' is normally used for tops in excess of 15000 ft but an altitude is always specified for CB tops. The expected occurrence of turbulence is indicated using the standard symbols alongside the associated cloud type, icing, where applicable, will be indicated using the standard symbols alongside the associated cloud data and will normally cover the altitude from the main level of the 0°C isotherm to the cloud top. When additional layers with sub zero temperatures occur below the main 0°C level the altitude of the bottom and top layer will be shown in the 0°C section with any amplifying information in the remarks section. The words 'HILL FOG' imply cloud covering hills, with a consequent visibility of 200 metres or less. 'TS' and 'CB' each imply hail, moderate or severe icing and/or turbulence.

6.3.5   The main level (highest altitude) in hundreds of feet AMSL of the zero degree Celsius isotherm over the area given. The altitude of any layers where the temperature is lower than 0°C which occur below the main level will also be given. Any amplifying details may be given in the warning and/or remarks section.

6.3.6   Single numerical values given for any element represent the most probable mean in a range of values covering approximately ±25%.

6.4   **Warnings and/or remarks**

6.4.1   Significant changes with time (for example CB developing, fog dispersing) expected during the period stated in the top right hand corner of the chart are given.

6.4.2   Warnings are given to supplement the forecast information given in the tabular section (for example surface gales, low level turbulence).

6.4.3   Additional information is given on sub-freezing layers.

7   **UK LOW LEVEL SPOT WIND CHART**

7.1   Each box refers to the spot winds and temperatures at the latitude/longitude position shown at the top of the box.

8   **NORTH SEA SIGNIFICANT WEATHER AND SPOT WIND/TEMPERATURE CHARTS**

8.1   These two charts follow the formats of the UK low level weather and spot wind charts.

TABLE E

Contents of OPMET 1 Teleprinter Broadcast

METARs, TAFs and SIGMETs for the following areas, plus QFA Alps:

United Kingdom including Channel Islands and Isle of Man

Belgium	Spain, Portugal, Canaries etc.
Switzerland	Iceland
Germany	Italy
Netherlands	Scandinavia
France	Finland
Irish Republic	

Contents of OPMET 2 Teleprinter Broadcast

METARs, TAFs and SIGMETs for the following areas:

Austria	Israel
Greece	Tunisia
Central Mediterranean (Malta, Libya)	Turkey
Yugoslavia	Near East (Iraq, Iran, Jordan etc)
Eastern Europe	Egypt
(Poland, USSR, Czechoslovakia, East Germany)	Algeria*
Middle Europe (Hungary, Rumania, Bulgaria)	Morocco
Eastern Mediterranean (Lebanon, Syria)	Spain, Portugal, Canaries etc*
Cyprus	Middle East (Gulf States, Karachi)

* 18/24 hour TAFs only

Contents of OPMET 3 Teleprinter Broadcast

METARs, TAFs and SIGMETs for the following areas, plus QFA Alps:

United Kingdom including Channel Islands and Isle of Man

Belgium	Central Mediterranean (Malta, Libya)
Switzerland	Iceland
Germany	Irish Republic
Netherlands	Morocco
France	Middle Europe (Hungary, Rumania, Bulgaria)
Spain, Portugal, Canaries etc	Austria
Algeria	Italy
Greece	Scandinavia
Yugoslavia	Finland
Tunisia	

Further details of the OPMET networks, including the reporting aerodromes in each area, are available from the Meteorological Authority.

Note 1: METARs are broadcast as routine at half-hourly (exceptionally hourly) intervals during aerodrome opening hours.

Note 2: TAFs valid for periods of less than 12 hours, usually for 9 hours, (FC) and QFA Alps are broadcast every three hours and TAFs valid for periods of 12 to 24 hours (FT) every six hours. Amendments are broadcast between routine times as required.

Note 3: SIGMETs available only for areas within 1000 nm of the UK.

TABLE F
TURBULENCE, ICING AND WINDSHEAR REPORTING CRITERIA

Clear Air Turbulence (CAT)

CAT remains an important operational factor at all levels but particularly above FL 150. The best information on CAT is obtained from pilots' Special Aircraft Observations; all pilots encountering CAT are requested to report time, location, level, intensity and aircraft type to the ATS unit with whom they are in radio contact. High level turbulence (normally above FL 150 not associated with cumuliform cloud, including thunderstorms) should be reported as CAT, preceded by the appropriate intensity or preceded by Light or Moderate Chop.

CAT and other Turbulence Criteria Table

Incidence: OCCASIONAL – less than ⅓ of the time
INTERMITTENT – ⅓ to ⅔
CONTINUOUS – more than ⅔

Intensity	Aircraft Reaction (transport size aircraft)	Reaction Inside Aircraft
LIGHT	Turbulence that momentarily causes slight, erratic changes in altitude and/or attitude (pitch, roll, yaw). IAS fluctuates 5–15 kn. Report as 'Light Turbulence'. or turbulence that causes slight, rapid and somewhat rhythmic bumpiness without appreciable changes in altitude or attitude. No IAS fluctuations. Report as 'Light Chop'.	Occupants may feel a slight strain against seat belts or shoulder straps. Unsecured objects may be displaced slightly. Food service may conducted and little or no difficulty is encountered in walking.
MODERATE	Turbulence that is similar to Light Turbulence but of greater intensity. Changes in altitude and/or attitude occur but the aircraft remains in positive control at all times. IAS fluctuates 15–25 kn. Report as 'Moderate Turbulence'. or turbulence that is similar to Light Chop but of greater intensity. It causes rapid bumps or jolts without appreciable changes in altitude or attitude. IAS may fluctuate slightly. Report as 'Moderate Chop'.	Occupants feel definite strains against seat belts or shoulder straps. Unsecured objects are dislodged. Food service and walking are difficult.
SEVERE	Turbulence that causes large, abrupt changes in altitude and/or attitude. Aircraft may be momentarily out of control. IAS fluctuates more than 25 kn. Report as 'Severe Turbulence'.	Occupants are forced violently against seat belts or shoulder straps. Unsecured objects are tossed about. Food service and walking impossible.

Note 1: Pilots should report location(s), time(s) (UTC), incidence, itensity, whether in or near clouds, altitude(s) and type of aircraft. All locations should be readily identifiable.
Example:

      (a)   Over Pole Hill 1230 intermittent Severe Turbulence in cloud, FL 310, B747.

      (b)   From 50 miles NORTH of GLASGOW to 30 miles WEST OF HEATHROW 1210 to 1250, occasional Moderate Chop CAT, FL 330, MD80.

Note 2: The UK does not use the term 'Extreme' in relation to turbulence.

Airframe Icing

All pilots encountering unforecast icing are requested to report time, location, level, intensity, icing type* and aircraft type to the ATS unit with whom they are in radio contact. It should be noted that the following icing intensity criteria are **reporting** definitions; they are not necessarily the same as forecasting definitions because reporting definitions are related to aircraft type and to the ice protection equipment installed, and do not involve cloud characteristics. For similar reasons, aircraft icing certification criteria might differ from reporting and/or forecasting criteria.

Intensity	Ice Accumulation
Trace	Ice becomes perceptible. Rate of accumulation slightly greater than rate of sublimation. It is not hazardous even though de-icing/anti-icing equipment is not utilized, unless encountered for more than one hour.
Light	The rate of accumulation might create a problem if flight in this environment exceeds one hour. Occasional use of de-icing/anti-icing equipment removes/prevents accumulation. It does not present a problem if de-icing/anti-icing equipment is used.
Moderate	The rate of accumulation is such that even short encounters become potentially hazardous and use of de-icing/anti-icing equipment, or diversion, is necessary.
Severe	The rate of accumulation is such that de-icing/anti-icing equipment fails to reduce or control the hazard. Immediate diversion is necessary.

* Rime Ice: Rough, milky, opaque ice formed by the instantaneous freezing of small supercooled water droplets.
* Clear Ice: A glossy, clear, or translucent ice formed by the relatively slow freezing of large supercooled water droplets.

Windshear

Pilots using navigation systems providing direct wind velocity readout should report the wind and altitude/height above and below the shear layer, and its location. Other pilots should report the loss or gain of airspeed and/or the presence of up-or-down draughts or a significant change in crosswind effect, the altitude/height and location, their phase of flight and aircraft type. Pilots not able to report windshear in these specific terms should do so in terms of its effect on the aircraft, the altitude/height and location and aircraft type, for example, 'Abrupt windshear at 500 feet QFE on finals, maximum thrust required, B747'. Pilots encountering windshear are requested to make a report even if windshear has previously been forecast or reported.

TABLE I
ACTUAL AND FORECAST WEATHER DECODE

Actuals

Report Type	Location Identifier	Time	Wind	Visibility	RVR	Weather	Cloud	Cloud	Temp Dewpoint	QNH	Trend
METAR	EGKK	0420	12005KT	0800	R1400	44FG	4ST001	8SC015	00 M01	1002	NOSIG

Report Type
METAR   Aviation routine weather report.
SPECI   Aviation selected special weather report.
COR   Correction; sometimes CCA, CCB etc.
RTD   Retard (late entry); sometimes RRA, RRB etc.
AMD   Amendment; sometimes AAA, AAB etc.

Location Identifier
ICAO four-letter code.

Time
UTC
The report type and time of observation do not always appear in the places shown. In the bulletin heading the METAR form is indicated by SA and the SPECI form by SP, followed by two letters to represent the country, for example SAUK, followed by the bulletin number and time of observation.

Wind
Wind direction in degrees True (three digits), followed by the windspeed in knots (two digits, exceptionally three). Calm winds are indicated by 00000, variable wind directions by the abbreviation VRB followed by the speed. A further two or three digits preceded by a diagonal gives the maximum gust speed in knots when it exceeds the mean speed by 10 kn or more. Overseas METARs may be in kilometres per hour ('KMH' instead of 'KT'), or metres per second ('MPS').

Visibility
Horizontal surface visibility in metres. 9999 indicates a visibility of 10 km or more; 0000 a visibility of less than 100 metres.

RVR
Preceded by R, then the RVR in metres. When the RVR is greater then the maximum reportable value, the RVR is reported as 'P' followed by the maximum reportable value. When the RVR is less than the minimum reportable value, the RVR is reported as 'MM' followed by the minimum reportable value. RVR is only reported when the surface visibility is 1500 metres or less except when IRVR is available and the indicated value is equal to or less than the maximum reportable value. For multi-site RVR/IRVR systems, the value given is that for the Touchdown Zone (TDZ). If RVR is assessed on two or more runways simultaneously, the RVR for each runway is given, each value being followed by a diagonal and the runway designator.

Weather
A two digit number precedes these weather code letters to define the weather more precisely for meteorological purposes:

FU	smoke	FC	funnel cloud (tornado or
HZ	dust haze		waterspout)
SA	duststorm, sandstorm, rising	DZ	drizzle
	dust or sand	RA	rain
PO	dust devils	SN	snow
BR	mist	GR	hail
FG	fog	SG	snow grains
TS	thunderstorms	PE	ice pellets
SQ	squall	SH	showers

Additionally:

MI shallow	DR low drifting
RE recent (within the last hour but now ceased)	BL blowing
	BC patches
XX heavy	FZ freezing

Cloud

A single digit showing oktas (eighths) of cloud cover, followed by:

CI cirrus	NS nimbostratus
CC cirrocumulus	SC stratocumulus
CS cirrostratus	ST stratus
AS altostratus	CU cumulus
AC altocumulus	CB cumulonimbus

followed by height of cloud above aerodrome in hundreds of feet. A height of '000' means less than 100 feet or cloud on the surface.

Reporting of layers or masses of cloud is made as follows:

First group; lowest cloud of any amount (1 okta or more)
Second group; the next higher cloud of 3 oktas or more
Third group; the next higher cloud of 5 oktas or more
Fourth group; cumulonimbus cloud if not already reported in the first three groups.

Sky obscured is coded '9//' followed by the vertical visibility in hundreds of feet. A further three diagonals in place of the vertical visibility means it is indeterminate.

CAVOK

The visibility, RVR, weather and cloud groups are replaced by CAVOK when the following exist:

(a) visibility is 10 km or more
(b) no cloud below 5000 ft or below the highest Minimum Sector Altitude, whichever is greater, and no cumulonimbus
(c) no precipitation, thunderstorm, shallow fog or low drifting snow.

Air Temperature/Dewpoint

Degrees Celsius, M indicates a negative value.

QNH

Rounded down to next whole millibar.

Trend

Landing forecast of conditions during the two hours after the observation time.

NOSIG no significant change

GRADU gradual change at approximately constant rate throughout the period or during specified part thereof

TEMPO temporary variation lasting less than one hour or, if recurring, lasting in total less than half the TREND (or TAF, see MET 3-4) period; that is, changes take place sufficiently infrequently for the prevailing conditions to remain those forecast for the period.

INTER intermittent variations, more frequent than TEMPO; conditions fluctuate almost constantly

RAPID changing over less than half an hour

TEND changing, but none of the other change groups applies

Followed (except for NOSIG) by the forecast weather changes in the METAR code. The weather change can be preceded by the time of the significant change or of the beginning of the period during which the change is expected to take place, expressed as four digits and the letters HR. SKC means sky clear, WX NIL means the end of thunderstorms or freezing precipitation, regardless of any other weather phenomenon that might be expected.

Runway State
An additional eight-figure Runway State Group will be added to the end of the METAR (or SPECI) when there is snow or other runway contamination. The decode of this group is shown at the end of this decode section.

Notes
1. Plain language supplementary information can be added to the end of the METAR (or SPECI).
2. Information that is missing is replaced by diagonals.

Forecasts

Many of the METAR groups are also used in Aerodrome Forecasts, significant differences being shown below:

Report Type	Location Identifier	Validity Times	Wind	Visibility	Cloud	Probability	Variant	Validity Times	Visibility	Weather	Good
TAF	EGLL	1322	13010KT	9999	5CU025	PROB20	INTER	1619	4000	81XXSH	7CB012

Forecast Type

TAF   Aerodrome Forecast

The report does not always appear in the place shown. In the bulletin heading, the TAF form is indicated by FC or FT, followed by two letters to indicate the country, and the bulletin number. FC forecasts are valid for periods of less than 12 hours, FT forecasts for periods of 12 to 24 hours. The validity times can also appear in the heading instead of the place shown.

Validity Times

First two digits are whole hours of time of commencement of forecast, the second two digits are the time of the ending of the forecast in whole hours.

Probability

Probability of occurence as a percentage (never more than 50%).

Variant Validity times

Two pairs of digits denoting the hours of validity of the sub-period.

Cloud

NSC means no cloud below 5000 ft or below the highest Minimum Sector Altitude, whichever is the greater, and no cumulonimbus, that is, no significant cloud. Cloud (other than cumulonimbus) above 5000 ft/MSA is not forecast in a TAF.

The abbreviation SKC may be used if there are no clouds and the term CAVOK is not appropriate.

Weather

WX NIL means the cessation of weather conditions forecast in the main part of the TAF.

Non-UK Groups

Three further TAF groups are not used in the UK but are shown here to assist in decoding overseas TAFs:

Forecast Temperature   O G_F G_F T_F T_F

O   Group indicator

$G_F G_F$ Time in whole hours to which temperature refers

$T_F T_F$ Forecast Temperature (M indicates minus)

Airframe Ice Accretion   6 l_c h_j h_j h_j t_l

6   Group Indicator

l_c Type of airframe ice accretion: 0 none
1 light
2 light in cloud
3 light in precipitation
4 moderate
5 moderate in cloud
6 moderate in precipitation
7 severe
8 severe in cloud
9 severe in precipitation.

$h_j h_j h_j$ height above ground level of lowest icing level (hundreds of feet).

t_l thickness of icing layer:
0 up to top of clouds
1-9 thickness in thousands of feet.

Turbulence   5   B h_B h_B h_B t_1

5   Group indicator

B   Turbulence: 0 none
                                                    1 light
                                                    2 moderate in clear air, infrequent
                                                    3 moderate in clear air, frequent
                                                    4 moderate in cloud, infrequent
                                                    5 moderate in cloud, frequent
                                                    6 severe in clear air, infrequent
                                                    7 severe in clear air, frequent
                                                    8 severe in cloud, infrequent
                                                    9 severe in cloud, frequent

$h_b h_b h_b$ height above ground level of lowest level of turbulence
               (hundreds of feet).

t_1 thickness of turbulent layer: 0 up to top of clouds
                                                       1-9 thickness in thousands of feet.

TABLE J
METEOROLOGICAL ABBREVIATIONS USED IN SIGMETS, SPECIAL FORECASTS ETC

Note: The following abbreviations are those that have not already been described.

AAL	above aerodrome level		LAN	inland or overland
ACT	active		LSQ	line squall
ADJ	adjacent		LTD	limited
AGL	above ground level		LV	light and variable (wind)
AIREP	Air Report			
AMSL	above mean sea level		M	metres
			MAR	at or over sea
BLO	below clouds		MAX	maximum
BLW	below (other than layers)		MB	millibars
BTL	between layers		MNM	minimum
BTN	between (other than layers)		MOD	moderate
			MON	above or over mountains
C	degrees Celsius		MOV	move or moving or movement
CBR	cloud base recorder (ceilometer)		MPS	metres per second
CC	counter clockwise		MS	minus
CIT	near or over large towns		MSL	mean sea level
CLA	clear ice		MT	mountain
CLD	cloud		MTW	moutain waves
CNS	continuous (for cloud, vertically)		MX	mixed clear and rime ice
CUF	cumuliform			
CW	clockwise		NC	no change or not changing
			NM	nautical miles
DECR	decrease		NSC	no significant cloud
DEG	degrees			
DENEB	fog dispersal operations		OBS	observed or observation
DIF	diffuse		OBSC	obscure or obscured or obscuring
DP	dewpoint		OPA	rime ice
DTRT	deteriorate or deteriorating		OTP	on top
DUC	dense upper cloud			
			PS	plus
EXP	expect or expected or expecting		PSN	position
EXTD	extend or extenting		PROV	provisional
FA	area forecast (ARFOR)		QFA	meteorological forecast
FBL	light (ice etc)			
FCST	forecast		RAG	ragged
FLUC	fluctuating or fluctuation or fluctuated		RWY	runway
			SEV	severe
FM	from		SFC	surface
FOQNH	forecast Region QNH		SFLOC	synoptic report of the location of sources of atmospherics
FPM	feet per minute			
FR	route forecast (ROFOR)		SIGWX	significant weather
FT	feet		SLW	slow
FU	upper wind and temperature forecast (WINTEM)		SPOT	spot wind
			STF	stratiform
			STNR	stationary
GND	ground		T	temperature
			TC	tropical cyclone
HGT	height or height above		TCU	towering cumulus
HPA	hectopascals		TDO	tornado
HURCN	hurricane		TIL	until (time)
			TIP	until past (place)
IAO	in and out of clouds		TURB	turbulence
ICE	icing		TYPH	typhoon
IMPR	improve or improving			
IMT	immediate or immediately		UA	Air Report (AIREP)
INC	in cloud		VAL	in valleys
INCR	increase		VER	vertical
INTSF	intensify or intensifying		VERVIS	vertical visibility
INTST	intensity		VIS	visibility
IR	ice on runway		VSP	vertical speed
			WKN	weaken or weakening
JTST	jetstream		WRNG	warning
			WS	SIGMET or windshear
KM(H)	kilometres (per hour)		WTSPT	waterspout
KT	knots		WX	weather
			XS	atmospherics

TABLE K – CRITERIA FOR SPECIAL AERODROME METEOROLOGICAL REPORTS, TRENDS, TAF VARIANTS, TAF AMENDMENTS, AND AMENDED ROUTE/AREA FORECASTS

Element	Special Report	Trend	TAF variant and TAF AMD	Amended Route/Area Forecast (advisory criteria)
Surface Visibility	Change through 200*, 400*, 600*, 800, 1500, 5000 metres, 10 km. * Only if RVR not available	Change through 200, 400, 600, 800, 1500, 3000, 5000 metres.	Change from one of the following ranges to another: 200 metres or less; 800 metres or less but more than 200 metres; 1500 metres or less but more than 800 metres; 5000 metres or less but more than 1500 metres; Less than 10 km but more than 5000 metres; 10 km or more.	Changes liable to have an appreciable effect on aircraft operations. AIRMET and low level forecasts: Changing through 10 km, 5000 metres, 1500 metres, 800 metres, 200 metres.
Weather	1 Onset (at any intensity, including XX) or cessation of: FZRA, FZDZ, SN, SNSH, RASN, RASN showers, BLSN, DRSN, SQ, TS, TSGR, GR, FC, SA. 2 Changes in the intensity of elements as follows: FZRA <-> XXFZRA FZDZ <-> XXFZDZ SN <-> XXSN SNSH <-> XXSNSH RASN <-> XXRASN RASN showers <-> XXRASN showers GR <-> XXGR SA <-> XXSA TS <-> XXTS TSGR <-> XXTSGR	1 Onset of the following if causing visibility to fall below 1500 metres and/or cloudbase to fall below 1000 ft: RA, RASH, RASN, RASN showers, SN, SNSH, DZ. 2 Onset or cessation of TS or freezing precipitation (or continuation of these, except in the case of NOSIG).	1 Onset or cessation of: TS, FC, SA, GR, SQ, XXRA (including SH), XXDZ, moderate or heavy SN (including SH), moderate or heavy RASN (including showers), freezing precipitation, FZFG, drifting snow. 2 If a TAF variant group is being used for indicating changes in visibility and/or cloud conditions the onset or ending of any of the following elements, if associated with visibility 1500 metres or less and/or cloud ceiling 1000 ft or less, should also be mentioned: slight/moderate RA (including SH) slight/moderate DZ, slight SN (including SH), slight RASN (including showers).	*(see sub-table below)*

Amended Route/Area Forecast (advisory criteria) — detail:

Element	Original Forecast	Revised Opinion
1 TS, SQ, GR, SA, freezing precipitation	Not included	Now expected
	Included	Not now expected
2 Turbulence	NIL or FBL	MOD or SEV
	SEV	FBL or NIL
	MOD	NIL
3 Airframe icing	NIL	Any intensity
	FBL or MOD	A higher intensity
	SEV	FBL or NIL
	MOD	NIL
4 Fronts, Tropical disturbances	Significant front or disturbance not included	Now expected
	Significant front or disturbance included	Not now expected or position materially different from forecast

Definitions:
1 'Change through' — having been greater than, decreases to a value equal to or less than, or having been less than, increases to a value equal to or greater than.
2 'Cloud ceiling' — height of cloud covering more than 4 oktas.
3 <-> — change in either direction left hand value and right hand value.

TABLE K – CRITERIA FOR SPECIAL AERODROME METEOROLOGICAL REPORTS, TRENDS, TAF VARIANTS, TAF AMENDMENTS, AND AMENDED ROUTE/AREA FORECASTS

Element	Special Report	Trend	TAF variant and TAF AMD	Amended Route/Area Forecast (advisory criteria)
Wind direction	None if wind indicators in ATC; otherwise 30° or more, mean speed before and/or after the change being at least 20 kn.	30° or more, mean speed before and/or after the change being at least 20 kn.	30° or more, mean speed before and/or after the change being at least 20 kn.	30° or more, speed before and/or after the change being at least 30 kn.
Wind speed	None if wind indicators in ATC; otherwise 10 kn or more, mean speed before and/or after the change being at least 30 kn or when speed variation (gusts/lulls) has increased by 10 kn or more, the mean speed being at least 15 kn.	10 kn or more, mean speed before and/or after the change being at least 30 kn.	1 10 kn or more, mean speed before and/or after the change being at least 30 kn. 2 Increase/decrease of 10 kn or more in maximum speed, mean speed before and/or after the change being at least 15 kn.	20 kn or more.
Cloud Amount	Amount of lowest cloud at 2000 ft or below changed from 4 oktas or less to more than 4 oktas, or from more than 4 oktas to 4 oktas or less (also applies to any layer where there are multi-layers with base 1000 ft or below)	When the height of cloud ceiling is reported/forecast below 1500 ft, 4 oktas or less to more than 4 oktas, or more than 4 oktas to 4 oktas or less (lowest layer only if more than one layer reported/forecast at 1000 ft or below).	When the base is 1500 ft or below, 4 oktas or less to more than 4 oktas, or more than 4 oktas to 4 oktas or less.	Changes liable to have an appreciable effect on aircraft operations. AIRMET and low level forecasts: changes in the lowest layer from NIL or SCT or BKN or OVC to SCT or NIL.
Cloud Height/ Altitude	Height of cloud ceiling changed through 100, 200, 300, 400, 500, 600, 800, 1000, 1500, 2000 ft. For Remote CBR: when the height of the most frequently occurring cloud base and/or the height of the lowest layer (as defined in para 7.2) changed as to require a reported value changing through 100, 200, 300, 500, 700 ft.	When the height of cloud ceiling is reported/forecast below 1500 ft, changing through 100, 200, 300, 500, 1000 and 1500 ft (all layers) if more than one layer reported/forecast at 1000 ft or below).	Heigh of cloud ceiling changing from one of the following ranges to another: 200 ft or below Not above 500 ft but above 200 ft. Not above 1000 ft but above 500 ft. Not above 1500 ft but above 1000 ft. Above 1500 ft.	Changes liable to have an appreciable effect on aircraft operations. AIRMET and low level forecasts: changes of any layer of ± 25% or 2000 ft, whichever is the smaller.
Temp/ Dewpoint	—	—	—	5°C or more.
QNH/QFE	1.0 mb or more	—	—	—

Chapter 20
Satellite Weather Picture Interpretation and Uses of Airborne Weather Radar

Weather Satellite

Introduction

There are two types of satellite in use, these are 'Polar Orbiting' and 'Geostationary'. The Polar Orbiting vehicles are fixed in position relative to the sun and provide a series of pictures as earth discs. These discs give complete earth coverage but there is overlapping of the discs at high latitudes.

The Geostationary satellites are earth sychronous and are thus essentially stationary above the same point on the equator. They also provide a series of pictures as earth discs with complete longitudinal coverage every 30 minutes. Due to distortion with increase of latitude the useful pictures are limited to about 55° of latitude north and south. The sampling rate for pictures is higher than for polar orbiting. These vehicles can be used to continuously view a particular part of the earth's surface. Typically a quarter of the globe between 55°N and 55°S. Early satellites were named TIROS (Television and Infra-Red Observation Satellite). The cameras employed varied their angle of look, but those in present day use provide pictures only when cameras are looking vertically downwards. Present systems employ scanning radio-meters and give both visual and infra-red returns. An example is METEOSAT. This satellite is in use for Europe and covers up to 60°N for the region and down to N. Africa South to 20°N every 30 minutes. It covers the rest of Africa and Eastern South America every three hours.

The Visual Imagery

The visual images are only available in daylight. The brightness extending from a white image through to dark grey will depend on the albedo. This is controlled by the angle of the sun, the reflectivity of the cloud and radiometer sensitivity. Clearly the brightness will reduce from a maximum at local noon for the area being surveyed, to zero after local sunset. The cloud albedo will vary from some 30 per cent for cirrostratus increasing through the lower cloud layers to 70 per cent for CU and SC and up to 90 per cent for CB. Mixtures of clouds can confuse these percentage values. The cloud basic droplet size, ice/water variables and the droplet concentration can cause variations too. When the sun is low visual imagery has the advantage that cloud shadows can provide contrast and the texture of cloud tops can be apparent.

Grey shade images can be produced by:
a) Globular type clouds CC, AC and fair weather CU. The globules are too small to show individually but add to the background albedo.
b) Moisture in the air.
c) The edges of fog.
d) ST or SC developing or dissipating.
e) Haze or sea spray areas.
f) A thin veil of CI or CS.

Visual images where there are grey shades can be compared with the infra-red picture for better interpretation purposes.

Infra-red Images (IR)
The scanning high resolution radiometer can give images in the IR radiation spectrum around 10 to 15 microns. The output can be related to received temperature. The difference in temperature of a cloud top and the underlying surface can be used to display cloud images. Thin cloud at low levels may give no show as the temperature disparity is too small. Similarly, globular low level cloud such as fair weather CU may be too small to be resolved by the radiometer 'look'. In mid latitudes the general rule is: With increasing height of cloud tops, temperatures are lower and thus a whiter response — e.g. cirrus type: Light grey indicates medium level clouds: Darker grey indicates cloud tops at low level.

IR is not affected by night, so a 24 hour cloud response can be obtained. The system is better at resolving a multi-cloud situation when the sun is high. IR can be better than visual over a sand surface but in common with visual, cloud show over an ice or snow covered surface is likely to be nil or confusing. The white to dark grey images are transposed to representative colour schemes on visual displays to more readily indicate contrast.

Cloud Images over Sea Surfaces

The visual and IR images of clouds over a sea surface are usually much clearer as the background is relatively even. However strong surface winds over a sea surface can cause high waves and rough seas. These can produce additional reflective surfaces particularly when the sun is low. Hence visual images can be misleading. This effect is sometimes referred to as 'Glint'. This does not affect IR.

Weather Images

Warm fronts will show by the long axis of the cloud pictures adjacent to the contrasting warm sector higher temperature area. This direction will also give the bearing of the upper winds and the jet stream. The associated CI has a smooth even texture but a transverse pattern (cross-banding) can appear on the cold side. Where this is visible it confirms the jet and the closer the cross-banding is to the normal the greater the expected clear air turbulence.

Cold fronts will normally show better on IR with the lower cloud top temperatures together with larger droplet size and concentration.

Occlusions can be indicated by the jet stream crossing at the occlusion point, the change in cloud sequence and heights. With visual imagery shadow lines can also be of assistance. Polar Air Depressions, being relatively small and forming over the sea, can stand out readily on both image systems. Tropical cyclones can be discerned by CI streams diverging from the perimeter of a cloud mass indicating vorticity. A no show 'eye' area is a clear indication. If this eye reduces in diameter it can indicate that the storm is becoming more intense.

Other Data

With modern systems temperature profiles from the surface can be found and water vapour content of the air can be measured. Upper winds can be measured by reference to a sequence of cloud pictures. This involves the selection of a sensible cloud target and assumptions being made on height for the wind based on cloud temperatures. More sophisticated systems are available to provide winds at all levels in the same time scale.

An example of a visual image Meteostat picture centred on Africa is at Figure 20.1. An Infra-red image is at Figure 20.2 this shows frontal positions and an associated westerly jet can also be discerned. Figure 20.3 displays the relevant MSL Synoptic chart for reference purposes.

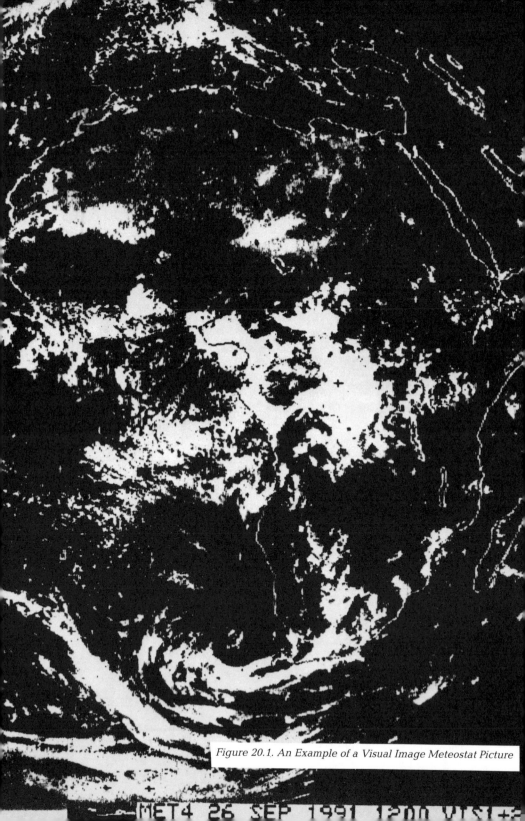

Figure 20.1. An Example of a Visual Image Meteostat Picture

MET4 26 SEP 1991 12nn VIS

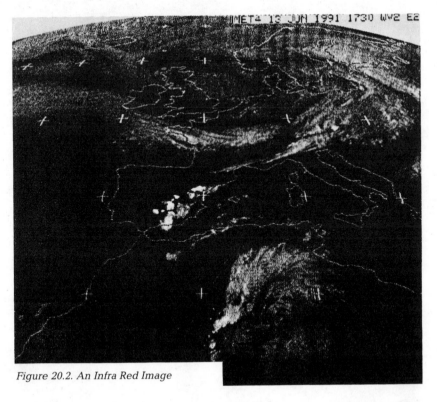

Figure 20.2. An Infra Red Image

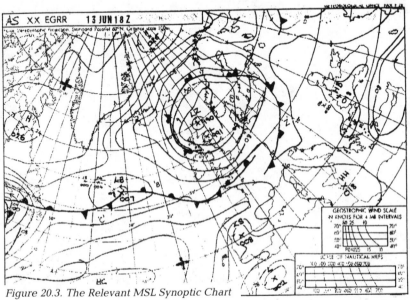

Figure 20.3. The Relevant MSL Synoptic Chart

Airborne Weather Radar

Introduction

These devices use the radar reflective properties of large water droplets, wet hail or snow to paint a visual display of CB and thunderstorms. They are used to provide avoidance from CB and their associated in-flight hazards.

Equipment

Most weather radars operate in the Super High Frequency band with wavelengths around 3 centimetres. This provides good resolution pictures. Additionally these wavelengths allow the relatively small dish, or flat plate aerials involved to be easily accommodated in the nose of aircraft. A circular cone shaped radar beam with a diameter of some 3° is transmitted. This can be disposed anywhere within a typical overall coverage of 90° to 120° either side of the aircraft fore and aft axis and some 15° above and below the horizontal. Scanning and tilt controls are used to register the portion of coverage required to be visually displayed by the radar returns.

The visual display is a plan position indicator on which range and bearing lines are etched. Available range for weather purposes is usually up to 100 nm and different maximum range values can be selected. (Ranges can be up to 300 nm when the equipment is used in the ground mapping mode.)

The Display System

The strength of radar return is basically controlled by the size of water droplets making up the structures of the cloud. Clouds, or parts of clouds where droplets are very small will not provide a radar echo even at short range. The larger droplets including hail and wet snow can provide strong returns. The strongest returns from these reflectors will be received from the parts of clouds where the concentration of large droplets is greatest. The cloud region where droplets are large and heavily concentrated must be where upcurrents and downcurrents are strongest and hence the region where there is greatest turbulence. Clearly such a cloud area should be avoided. The radar thus has the basic capability of differentiating between strong returns and the cloud region of the strongest returns. The PPI display would thus paint bright up areas in white or green dependent on the PPI type, with brighter white or green for the high droplet concentration regions. This would not provide sufficient contrast for sensible interpretation. Therefore a system is usually employed whereby the brightest echo regions can be shown as 'no return' areas, i.e. areas of black within the area of strong white returns. This selection of the black hole type return is sometimes referred to as a 'Contour facility'.

Display Interpretation

The radar can be used to identify the growth stage of a thunderstorm. When echoes first appear and grow in size it indicates the development stage when large CU are forming cells. The mature stage is shown when returns appear clear cut with well defined edges. Use of the contour facility at this stage will show black holes in the echoes. The dissipating stage is indicated by the return edges becoming ill defined and gradually fading. Any original black holes will contract. Sharp edged echoes and large black holes define heavy storm activity and severe turbulence areas.

Hail can show as sharp protuberances from a white return area. These can take up the pattern of a pointing finger, a hooked finger, or a scalloped edge. These patterns can change radically in shape and intensity over short time periods of less than a minute.

Instead of a basic black and white or green screen, some displays use red, yellow and green to show the varying intensity of returns. In these cases the black hole system for strongest returns is replaced by a red pulsating area.

Some modern systems can provide a vertical profile of storm clouds. Whilst this can provide pictures of interest, the important avoidance use for the radar is adequately supplied by the horizontal picture system.

It is again stressed that interpretation should lead to avoidance and not as a means of 'skirting around' a thunderstorm or through a thunderstorm area. The recommended avoidance ranges quoted in Chapter 16 are repeated here:

FL 0 to 250	–	10 nm
FL 250 – 300	–	15 nm
Above FL 300	–	20 nm

Appendix A

STATION CIRCLE DECODE OF FIGURES AND SYMBOLS

The SYNOP telex message carries weather report information. This is displayed around the Station Circle on a Synoptic Chart. (There is an example of a Synoptic Chart at Figure 17.1.) The circle is centred on the geographic position of the reporting station.

The initial five-figure group in the SYNOP message refers to the origin of the report. For example 03962: The 03 refers to the area of origin, in this case the British Isles: 962 is the international reporting station number, which refers to Shannon airport in this case. The five figures are shown on Synoptic charts with the reporting station number alongside the station circle. The subsequent five-figure groups in the SYNOP message contain all aspects of the weather report. The weather information is displayed in coded form by figures and symbols around the station circle. The purpose of this Appendix is to provide a decode of the figures and symbols. The decode is shown below on a 'clock face' basis starting at the 1 o'clock position around the clock.

Pressure
1 o'clock

QFF is shown by 3 figures giving tens, units and tenths of a millibar, e.g. 721 = 72.1 mb. The expected QFF range is from 950 to 1050 mb. The reader is required to prefix the 3 figures by either a 9 or a 10 to conform with the range. Hence in the above example, the full QFF must be 972.1 mb. If for example the 3 figures had been 157 = 15.7 mb. The prefix would have to be 10, giving a QFF value of 1015.7 mb.

3 o'clock

Pressure Tendency, the pressure change in the past 3 hours is shown by a symbol and two figures. The symbols show the type of change:

Overall rise

∕ – A rise followed by a small fall

⌐ – A rise and then steady

∕ – A steady rise

√ – A small fall followed by a rise

Overall fall

∖ – A fall followed by a rise

∖_ – A fall and then steady

∖ – A steady fall

∧ – A small rise followed by a fall

The two figures show the amount of the pressure change in tenths of a mb.

Example 36/

= In the past 3 hours there has been a steady rise of 3.6 mb.

Past Weather
5 o'clock

All weather is shown by symbols only. Weather in this context refers to precipitation; mist haze and fog; thunderstorms and snowstorms. Certain symbols are common to both 'Past Weather' and Present Weather (9 o'clock position):

≡   – Fog or ice fog

,   – Drizzle

●   – Rain

✱   – Snow

▽   – Showers

ℝ   – Thunderstorms

△   – Hail. The symbol is sometimes shown black instead of open.

The arrangement of the common symbols and their combinations have different meanings for Past and Present Weather.
Past weather refers to the past 6 hours for the Major Synoptic hours: 0600; 1200; 1800 and 0000. It refers to the past 3 hours for the Minor Synoptic hours: 0300; 0900; 1500 and 2100. (For hourly produced charts, past weather is in the past hour.)

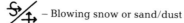 – Blowing snow or sand/dust

⊽ (with dot above) – Rain showers in the past 3 or 6 hours

▽● – Rain showers for most of the past 3 or 6 hours

● ● – Rain for most of the past 3 or 6 hours

● , – Rain in the past 3 or 6 hours followed by drizzle

✱● – Snow in the past 3 or 6 hours followed by rain

Other combinations apply similarly.

Low Cloud
(plus vertical visibility)
6 o'clock

The cloud type is shown by symbol. The amount of sky cover in eighths and the cloud base in hundreds of feet are shown by figures, positioned below the symbol. The figures for cloud amount and base are separated by a slash.

◠ – Small Cumulus

🅰 – Large Cumulus

🅰 – Cumulonimbus without anvil

⌀ – Stratocumulus formed by Spreading Cumulus

‿ᴗ‾ – Stratocumulus

— – Stratus

- - - – Fractus Stratus

‿ᴗ‾
◠ – Cumulus and Stratocumulus with bases at different levels

◻ – Cumulonimbus with anvil

Example —
     3/12 = 3/8th of Stratus base 1200 ft

*Vertical
Visibility*
9/01

These figures are used to indicate that the sky is obscured −9. The two figures after the slash show the vertical visibility in hundreds of feet with /00 meaning vertical visibility less than 100 ft.

Dewpoint
7 o'clock

This is shown by two figures for units and tens of degrees Celsius.
Thermometers are read to the nearest .1 of a degree and then rounded up or down to the nearest whole figure with .5 always allocated to the nearest whole odd number. Values are positive unless prefixed by a minus sign.

Visibility
9 o'clock
(outer position)

Two figures are used to show visibility in metres or kilometres by use of the following range system:

00 to 50 – metres
56 to 80 – subtract 50 giving an answer in kilometres
81 to 89 – subtract 80: multiply the result by 5: then add 30. This gives an answer in kilometres.

Present Weather
9 o'clock
(inner position)

Weather at the time of observation is shown by symbols only.
Weather which has occurred during the past hour but not at the time of observation is also shown at this position.

≡ – Mist

∞ – Haze

〰 – Smoke

⁼⁼ – Patchy fog

≡ – Fog, sky visible, no change in the last hour

≡| – As above but thinned in the last hour

|≡ – As above but thickened in the last hour

≡ – Fog, sky obscured, no change in the last hour

≡| – As above but thinned in the last hour

|≡ – As above but thickened in the last hour

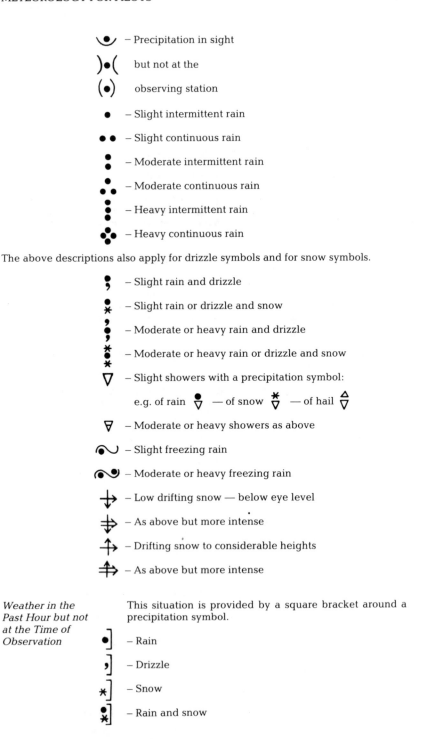

– Precipitation in sight

but not at the

observing station

– Slight intermittent rain

– Slight continuous rain

– Moderate intermittent rain

– Moderate continuous rain

– Heavy intermittent rain

– Heavy continuous rain

The above descriptions also apply for drizzle symbols and for snow symbols.

– Slight rain and drizzle

– Slight rain or drizzle and snow

– Moderate or heavy rain and drizzle

– Moderate or heavy rain or drizzle and snow

– Slight showers with a precipitation symbol:

e.g. of rain — of snow — of hail

– Moderate or heavy showers as above

– Slight freezing rain

– Moderate or heavy freezing rain

– Low drifting snow — below eye level

– As above but more intense

– Drifting snow to considerable heights

– As above but more intense

Weather in the Past Hour but not at the Time of Observation

This situation is provided by a square bracket around a precipitation symbol.

– Rain

– Drizzle

– Snow

– Rain and snow

•⁊] – Rain showers: similarly for ⁂⁊] snow and △⁊] hail

∿] – Freezing drizzle or rain

≡] – Fog or ice fog

⟨] – Thunderstorms

⟨]• – As above with slight rain

⟨]⦂ – As above with moderate or heavy rain

Surface Air Temperature
(or Dry Bulb Temperature)

11 o'clock   As for Dewpoint temperature

Medium Level Cloud   The cloud type is shown by symbol
12 o'clock
(lower)   ∠ – Altostratus — thin

⫽ – Altostratus dense or Nimbostratus

ⵡ – Altocumulus, thin at one level

ϛ – Altocumulus probably lenticular and at more than one
level

ⵦ – Altocumulus increasing amounts

⅄ – Altocumulus formed from spreading Cumulus

⛇ – Altostratus and Altocumulus or dense Altocumulus. (The
Altostratus becomes Nimbostratus if reported below
7000 ft).

Ӈ – Altocumulus castellanus

⟋ – Altocumulus at several levels in a chaotic sky

Example ∠   = The cloud amount in eighths is sometimes given below
  4/62   the cloud symbol followed by a slash and then two figures
indicating the height of the cloud base. These two figures
have a range of 56 to 80. The cloud base is then given in
thousands of feet by subtracting 50. In this example there
is 4/8 of thin Altostratus with a base of 12 000 ft.

High Level Cloud   The cloud type is shown by symbol
12 o'clock
(upper)   ⏜ – Cirrus, not increasing in amount

⏜ᴈ – Cirrus dense, not from CB anvil

� – Cirrus dense from CB anvil

⟋ – Cirrus hooked, increasing amounts

ⵜ – Cirrostratus, increasing amounts

2_c – Cirrostratus, covering the sky

_s – Cirrostratus, not increasing

ƺ – Cirrocumulus

Example ——>
7/82

= Sometimes the cloud amount and cloud base are shown as for medium cloud. Higher cloud bases than the figure 80 (minus 50 = 30 000 ft) are catered for as follows: Range of codes 81 to 89 — subtract 80, multiply the result by 5 and then add 30. This gives the cloud base in thousands of feet. In this example there is 7/8 of cirrus, not increasing in amount with a base of 40 000 ft.

Total Cloud Cover
Shown in the
centre of the circle

Indicated in eighths of the total sky covered by cloud.

○ – Sky clear

◐ – 1/8th

◕ – 2/8ths

◑ – 3/8ths

◑ – 4/8ths

◒ – 5/8ths

◕ – 6/8ths

◑ – 7/8ths

● – 8/8ths

⊗ – Indicates sky obscured — usually by fog, smoke or sand/dust

Surface Wind
Shown by a straight
line from the periphery
of the circle

This line indicates the direction from which the wind is blowing (090 in the examples below). The speed is shown by 'feathers' at the end of the line.

○ – Calm

——— – 1 to 2 kn

——⌐ – 5 kn

——⌐ – 10 kn

——╫ – 15 kn

——╫ – 20 kn, further additions up to 45 kn

——◣ – 50 kn

——◣ – 60 kn

——◣ – 65 kn, further additions as necessary

Note: It should be noted that Meteorological Observers are committed to reporting only those items which can be seen or measured. It is therefore often the case that cloud amounts and bases for medium and high clouds are not given. It can also occur that 8/8 stratus cloud is reported with a base of say 1000 ft, together with moderate continuous rain. This type of precipitation cannot be from stratus. Almost certainly there must be nimbostratus above. However, this will not be reported as it cannot be seen.

Computer Produced Charts

Some small changes to the basic system apply when Synoptic Charts are drawn by computer. The main differences are as follows:

Cloud Information

Details are given horizontally, e.g. 3 ⌢ 5. This is 3/8th of SC with a base of code 5. The cloud base code details are:

0	–	below 100 ft
1	–	150 ft to 300 ft
2	–	300 ft to 600 ft
3	–	600 ft to 1000 ft
4	–	1000 ft to 2000 ft
5	–	2000 ft to 3000 ft
6	–	3000 ft to 5000 ft
7	–	5000 ft to 6500 ft
8	–	6500 ft to 8000 ft
9	–	8000 ft or more (or no cloud)

Hence the full decode of 3 ⌢ 5 is 3/8th of SC, base 2000 ft to 3000 ft.

Ship Reported Visibility

This shown as follows:

90	–	less than 50 metres	95	–	2 km
91	–	50 m	96	–	4 km
92	–	200 m	97	–	10 km
93	–	500 m	98	–	20 km
94	–	1 km	99	–	Greater than 50 km

Underlining

Some items are underlined to indicate that the computer quality control system has been activated. This can simply indicate a change in an item greater than normally expected.

Automatic Reporting

Station circle information produced from an automatic reporting station is indicated by a △ at the reporting position.

Appendix B

DECODE OF SYMBOLS USED IN CLIMATOLOGY AT CHAPTER 18

ITCZ	– Intertropical Convergence Zone
• • • • • • •	– Mediterranean Front
STJ ⟹	– Subtropical Jetstream
PFJ ⟹	– Polar Front Jetstream
▬▬▶▶▶	– Upper Wind
▬▬▬▶	– Surface Wind
▬▬**m**▬▶	– Monsoon
▪ ▸ ▬ ▸ ▬ ▸	– Paths of Polar Front Depressions
➡	– Cold Sea Current
▨▨▨➡	– Warm Sea Current
▨▨▨➡	– Area of Fog
⣿⣿⣿	– Dust
Ⓛ▶	– A Low with Arrow Showing Direction of Movement. These Lows can be Thermal or Orographic.
⅊	– Polar Front Depression
⅊	– Frontal Depression with Cold Front Only
∪	– Polar Air Depression (By Advection)
⊖	– Tropical Cyclone
ʀ	– Thunderstorms
▽	– Showers
////	– Continuous Type Rain

Index